Climate, Weather and Ideology

Climate Change Denial

William McPherson

© 2015

Climate Change Denial

For Barbara

Copyright © William McPherson

Contents

Preface

Weather, climate and ideology have become a volatile mix. As the weather has become more extreme, so has the ideology about climate. What is happening in today's volatile world?

Do you wonder about the extreme weather we have had recently? You are not alone. "Each year we have extreme weather, but it's unusual to have so many extreme events around the world at once," said Omar Baddour, chief of the data management applications division at the World Meteorological Organization, in Geneva. He went on to list a number of events that indicate climate change, including droughts, floods and storms. Such events are increasing in intensity as well as frequency, Mr. Baddour said, an indication that climate change "is not just about rising temperatures, but also about intense, unpleasant, anomalous weather of all kinds." [1] He was communicating a general trend that has been observed by scientists around the world. While each event may have various causes, the number and intensity seems to indicate changes in the climate.

Events such as hurricanes, droughts and floods are occurring around the world and many scientists see them as portents of the future. This assessment of the international scene is confirmed by a report on the United States: "Americans are noticing changes all around them. Summers are longer and hotter, and periods of extreme heat last longer than any living American has ever experienced. Winters are generally shorter and warmer. Rain comes in heavier downpours, though in many regions there are longer dry spells in between." [2] These changes are becoming hard to ignore.

What are the effects of extreme weather? "Residents of some coastal cities see their streets flood more regularly during storms and high tides. Inland cities near large rivers also experience more flooding, especially in the Midwest and Northeast. Hotter and drier weather and earlier snow melt mean that wildfires in the West start earlier in the year, last later into the fall, threaten more homes, cause more evacuations, and burn more acreage. In Alaska, the summer sea ice that once protected the coasts has receded, and fall storms now cause more erosion and damage that is severe enough that some communities are already facing relocation."[3]

Scientists studying climate change confirm that these observations are consistent with Earth's climatic trends. Long-term, independent records from weather stations, satellites, ocean buoys, tide gauges, and many other data sources all confirm the fact that our nation, like the rest of the world, is warming, precipitation patterns are changing, sea level is rising, and some types of extreme weather events are increasing.[4]

Extreme weather is a harbinger of future climate change. While temperatures rise gradually – less than a tenth of a degree each decade in the twentieth century – extreme weather strikes many areas and alerts people to changes in the environment that can be linked to fossil fuel emissions. It is those emissions that are the crux of the debates over climate change and policies to reduce its impacts.

In the time since my books *Ideology Versus Science* and *Tales of a Hot Planet* were published, there have been various responses to extreme weather. Many scientists are becoming more concerned about understanding the link between extreme weather and climate change. Nevertheless, there remains a large group of people who deny human-induced climate change.

After summers of record heat and drought, and superstorms such as Sandy and Haiyan that brought climate change discussion to the fore, one would expect a change of heart among those who deny climate science. Some may have seen the light, but others remain unconvinced of the findings of climate science. Some have become even more vociferous and extreme, as we will see in Chapter 4.

Reasons for this tenacious denial will be explored in this book. Suffice it to say that the increasing evidence of climate change is enough to convince some people but not all. Those who continue to deny climate science can be termed "denial ideologues," a phrase that I will use throughout this book. The term "denial" does not stand for anything except denial of climate science, despite rhetorical attempts to make it seem like a pejorative term based on a Holocaust analogy. [5] Some have extended the term to include those who deny climate policies: "Our definition of denial is anyone who is obstructing, delaying or trying to derail policy steps that are in line with the scientific consensus that says we need to take rapid steps to decarbonize the economy." [6] While no firm distinction between denial of science and denial of policies is useful, most of denial ideology stems from the denial of climate science and that usually extends to denial of the need for climate policies.

Examples of denial ideology abound in the popular press. One author propounded the following canard: "As a result of the focus on manmade greenhouse gases, climate science has not progressed in two decades. Climate scientists are no closer now at being able to discern any fingerprint of human-induced climate change than they were two decades ago." [7] This is patently untrue, as climate science has established a "fingerprint" of human-induced climate change through analysis of Carbon-14, a particular isotope that enables scientists to identify human sources of carbon emissions. Fossil fuels contain no Carbon-14 as they were formed millions of years ago and the half-life of Carbon-14 is 6000 years. Absence of Carbon-14 is a "fingerprint" of human emissions.

While some ideologues continue to deny climate change, it is increasingly likely that people will begin to see the connection between weather trends (not just weather events) and climate change. The Yale Project on Climate Change Communication has shown that a larger number of Americans are now concerned about climate change than earlier reported. [8] The Yale Project reported that:

3

Nearly all Americans (92%) say the president and the Congress should make developing sources of clean energy a "very high" (31%), "high" (38%), or "medium" priority (23%). Very few say it should be a low priority (8%).

• A large majority (77%) say global warming should be a "very high" (18%), "high" (25%), or "medium" priority (34%) for the president and Congress. One in four (23%) say it should be a low priority.

• Six in ten Americans (61%) say the U.S. should reduce its own greenhouse gas emissions regardless of what other countries do.

• A large majority of Americans (88%) say the U.S. should make an effort to reduce global warming, even if it has economic costs.[9]

Whether these sentiments will be translated into action remains to be seen. Other surveys have indicated that climate change has a very low priority. President Obama, for example, won reelection in 2012 but has not made climate change a priority; in fact, he has specifically ruled out a carbon tax for the time being. Most economists who address the subject believe that a carbon tax is the most effective policy, especially when linked to reduction of other taxes such as the payroll tax or elimination of sales taxes on certain energy-efficient items. Even if the president acts, Congress can try to reverse his policies because a large group of members of Congress deny climate change reality.[10] An example: Senator James Inhofe (R-OK) says that climate change is a "hoax." He asserts that EPA (Environmental Protection Agency) "will nationalize the electricity market and force Americans to live out the President's Green Dream."[11] Republican members of the House Appropriations Committee voted to deny EPA funding for power plant rules:

"The legislation also includes provisions to stop various harmful, costly, and potentially job-killing regulations by the EPA," the House Appropriations Committee said in a Tuesday statement. The proposal would stop the EPA from using any of its funds to work on any rule to limit carbon dioxide pollution from power plants. That ban would include the proposal last month to reduce carbon emissions from existing plants, as well as a plan earlier this year to limit emissions from newly built plants.[12]

Members "vote their districts," which may include coal power plants or mines, but many also vote based on denial ideology. Most of them are Republicans, but they do not necessarily represent Republican voters, especially young ones: in a recent poll some Republican voters under 35 said climate deniers are "ignorant," "out of touch," or "crazy." What is the future of Republican Congressmen if their young supporters consider their views "crazy?"[13]

Why would Congress defy public opinion? I examine this topic in greater detail in my book *Ideology versus Science.* One researcher offered an insight into why members of Congress are ignoring or opposing views of their constituents. A researcher asked how they knew what their constituents thought about climate change. "When I ask about the polling they have done that led them to this belief, I have routinely been told that they had not done polling and, instead, base their impressions on phone calls, emails and conversations with and from constituents on the issue. Our findings suggest that the balance of those direct communications from constituents to elected representatives may have created a misimpression of the public's opinions on the issue."[14] When a small minority of constituents becomes highly active on an issue, it can sway opinions against those of the majority of constituents. This is a dynamic exploited by the Tea Party, for example.

Members of the United States Senate and House of Representatives are not the only politicians who have "doubts" about climate change. One local official running for state Senate in Washington State said, "I'm not seeing a hypothesis that has been put forward as to definitively answer the question one way or the other."[15] Aside from being incorrect about hypotheses, which have been put forward and verified, he was waffling about climate science. It was more convenient for him to imply that there is no confirmation of climate change hypotheses than to admit that there is and deal with the implications for public policy.

A few constituents can make a big difference in leaders' opinions – active minorities tend to prevail against less active majorities. Time and again, we see the disproportionate effects of ideology held by a small group of fanatics.[16] This is prominent in the public discussion of climate change: "Consider the particularly combative discourse of denialism, which ... is prominent in the public sphere, especially in Internet forums, and especially in the United States, Canada, and Australia." Unfortunately, this combative approach militates against useful discussion: "Organized denialism cannot provide grist for productive contestation, for at its heart is the construction of opponents not as adversaries to be respected, but as enemies to be defeated ... Anyone who has scrolled through the comments posted on online news articles about climate politics or climate science will be aware that a denialist discourse occupies space entirely disproportionate to its relative weight in society."[17]

One member of Congress, Peter Welch of Vermont, described the unreal nature of denial ideology: "Well, you may have noticed that science does not exist on Capitol Hill. We kind of – we're in a fact-free zone here on some issues. And when it comes to climate change, people kind of make it up as they go along."[18] If Capitol Hill is a "fact-free zone," decisions about climate change will be misinformed and likely to cause more problems than they solve. At the time of this writing, Congress is gridlocked on any issues related to climate change. The Obama Administration is taking executive actions such as regulating coal-fired power plants, based on the Clean Air Act, actions that are sure to be challenged in court.

Some in Congress are trying to overcome the polarization between deniers and climate change activists. Two senators from different parties, Jeanne Shaheen (D-NH) and Rob Portman (R-OH), are sponsoring an energy efficiency bill with bipartisan support. Portman said: "This bill has garnered such widespread support because of a simple fact – it is good for the economy and good for the environment. It's part of an energy plan for America that can help bring the jobs back, help fix our trade deficit, help make our manufacturers more competitive, and actually help to protect the environment."[19]

Energy efficiency is one of those things that many people can agree on. It is one of the "no regrets" policies long advocated by scientists and activists who realize that there is strong opposition to other policies such as cap and trade. The term "no regrets" implies that we will have no regrets about doing things that will save money regardless of our views on climate change. Attaining goals such as energy efficiency doesn't require that political leaders agree on climate science but at least they can agree on the need to address energy issues. Such agreement has become more difficult to achieve with the increase in extreme denial.

In this book you will encounter a number of viewpoints on both the validity of climate science and the need for policies to combat climate change. Please keep in mind that the quotes represent a wide range of opinion, and some of the examples are from rather extreme viewpoints. The quotes are designed to illustrate the range of opinion that applies to issues of climate change, but they do not represent all possible aspects of that broad subject. Few of the quotes represent "typical" views because they are selected to show the more extreme views.

With this caveat in mind, I have designed the book to show how denial ideologues have distorted climate science. Chapter 1 shows how denial claims that the globe is cooling misled many and dulled public knowledge about extreme weather. Chapter 2 describes some examples of extreme weather and reviews the scientific issues about their relationship to climate change. Chapter 3 looks at some of the issues raised by extreme weather, including poverty and economic growth. Chapter 4 provides three examples of extreme denial: "global warming scam," "eco-tyranny" and "totalitaria." Chapter 5 discusses how some denial organizations have capitalized on extreme denial for their own purposes, and how extreme weather becomes problematic for these purposes. Chapter 6 holds a mirror to denial ideology, portraying how scientists look at ideology and ideologues look at science. Chapter 7 reviews some of the issues of science dealing with denial, particularly in the political sphere. Chapter 8 draws some conclusions from all of this *Sturm und Drang.*

Chapter 1:
What Science?

What science are denial ideologues using to rationalize their distortion of climate change? Authentic scientific findings are presented in this chapter show how denial ideology distorts reality in this and subsequent chapters. Denial ideologues have challenged nearly all of these findings, and the false premises they use for these challenges are the basis for denial ideology described throughout this book. A more extensive review will be found in my book *Ideology versus Science: Climate Change Denial.*

We now know that climate change is occurring at a rapid rate. Temperatures have been rising for more than thirty years and effects such as sea level rise, flooding and droughts are increasing. Analysis in the Fourth Assessment Report of the Intergovernmental Panel on Climate Change (IPCC) was rather conservative with regard to some issues such as temperature increases and sea level rise.[20] IPCC has now issued its Fifth Assessment Report[21] and has increased the certainty of its stronger conclusions. Other observers have noted that recent data indicates that temperature increases and extreme weather are accelerating even more than anticipated by the IPCC. *"Global warming may proceed at or even above the upper extreme of the range projected by the Intergovernmental Panel on Climate Change."*[22] NASA (National Aeronautics and Space Administration) has announced that world temperatures are rising faster than foreseen[23] and research indicates that the increases will be higher than most models have projected.[24] These data are not based solely on projections but also on actual measurements, giving the lie to those who say that the globe is cooling.[25] Further discussion of this issue follows in the next section.

Some scientists use the term "global warming" but many prefer "climate change" because it conveys a range of effects, including changes in temperature, sea level rise and extreme weather. Another term that has gained currency is "climate disruption," implying that changes are disrupting the normal stability of the climate. Survey research indicates that "global warming" has a more direct impact on public opinion, since it indicates that temperatures are rising and will impact weather directly.[26]

Is the Globe Cooling?

During the first decade of the 21st Century, the rate of temperature increase slowed but temperatures did continue to rise.[27] Often denial ideologues will conflate this trend by claiming that temperatures are cooling, but in fact they are not. It is only the *rate* of increase that has slowed. With the exception of 1998, the warmest years on record are all in the 21st Century.

Top 10 Warmest Years (1880–2012)

The following table lists the global combined land and ocean annually-averaged temperature rank, and anomalies from the 132-year average, for each of the ten warmest years on record.[28]

RANK 1 = WARMEST PERIOD OF RECORD: 1880–2013	YEAR	ANOMALY °C	ANOMALY °F
1	2010	0.66	1.19
2	2005	0.65	1.17
3	1998	0.63	1.13
4 (tie)*	2013	0.62	1.12
4 (tie)*	2003	0.62	1.12
6	2002	0.61	1.10
7	2006	0.60	1.08
8 (tie)*	2009	0.59	1.07
8 (tie)*	2007	0.59	1.06
10 (tie)	2004	0.57	1.04
10 (tie)	2012	0.57	1.03

*Note: Tie is based on temperature anomalies in °C.

Every one of the record years except 1998 are in the 21st Century, which is on track to be much warmer than the 20th Century. Indications, at the time of this writing, are that 2014 will displace 2010 as the hottest year on record.

Some denial advocates reject these temperature records and consider them flawed.[29] Some go beyond criticizing their validity and accuse scientists of manipulating the data. Many persist in arguing that 1934 is the warmest year on record[30] and that any recent warming is minor, simply part of a cycle that is already in a cooling phase. There are even authors who insist that we are headed for an ice age, regardless of evidence to the contrary. Author John Kehr insists that, from paleoclimatology research, we are now in the cooling phase of an interglacial era.

There are only two possible climate futures.
The natural one is where a full glacial develops over

the next couple thousand years and civilization as we know it today will no longer be possible. The alternative [climate science finding] is that CO2 emissions have altered the climate enough to prevent the natural future from happening... That [CO2] future does not exist.[31]

"That future does not exist" is a rather unequivocal statement about climate science, based on a superficial review of past ice ages and a basic presumption that we are now in a cooling phase. It requires the author to claim that carbon dioxide or other greenhouse gases have little or no effect on climate – that CO2 varies with the ice ages but only as a result of temperature changes, not a cause. [32] Kehr further asserts that "warmists" overstate the effect of CO2: "Warmists generally argue that almost all of the 33°C [above earth's temperature without natural warming] is caused by greenhouse gases." [33] This misreads climate science – climate scientists acknowledge other causes for warming, but concentrate on greenhouse gases because they are responsible for additional warming from human activities.

Kehr's projections from paleoclimatology are qualified by authors such as Peters by noting "we still cannot predict Earth's future climate by calculating our orbital state. What this means – the important point for you – is that scientists cannot say in any precise way when the Holocene will naturally collapse into a renewed deep freeze." [34] This qualification definitely dampens Kehr's heavy-duty claim of cooling through his review of paleoclimatology.

Climate scientists, according to paleoclimatologist Kirsten Peters, are looking at the possibility that "very early agricultural practices changed the concentration of the two most significant greenhouse gases on Earth, carbon dioxide and methane." [35] In other words, humans have long had some influences on climate that would prevent, or reduce the possibility of, the return of the ice ages. Indeed, this trend has accelerated in recent years: "what we have accomplished in the past two hundred years is a sharp departure from anything we may have done earlier." [36] This

12

reorients the discussion of long-term cooling trends toward the short-term changes humans have made in the past 200 years.

Some denial ideologues go so far as to say that because there has been "global cooling" during the past decade, scientists have been deceiving us by altering data. Why would scientists deceive us? Such arguments are premised on an assertion that climate scientists are *alarmists:* "This appears to be very typical of alarmist scientists; to alter the data in order to make it look like global warming is occurring at some catastrophic rate and trying to use this to influence people. It is pure deceit."[37] As will be described in Chapter 6, denial ideology tends to attack scientists for this alleged deceit, and one of their principal lines of attack is based on the false claim of global cooling. Another is the distortion of the role of carbon dioxide in climate change.

The issue of carbon dioxide as a pollutant has surfaced again and again in denial ideology, and has been an issue in political campaigns as well.[38] Perhaps the baldest denial of its role as a pollutant was expressed by the *Cornwall Alliance:*

> Carbon dioxide is a *compound* of carbon and oxygen and not only is non-toxic to humans and other animals but also is essential to life! In fact, humans and other animals exhale it, and plants "inhale"it... No matter the reductions in CO_2, there will be no improvement in air quality. None! Zero! Zilch! Nada![39]

Aside from a misrepresentation of air quality that excludes the role of carbon dioxide as a greenhouse gas, this statement emphasizes the denial ideology view that carbon dioxide is "essential to life." Such a view is frequently expressed in denial publications as a *non-sequitur* response to climate research that relates carbon dioxide to temperature. No climate scientist would assert that carbon dioxide is inessential to life, but that its role in supporting life is separate from its contribution to global warming, particularly the emissions of CO_2 from burning fossil fuels.

Despite evidence to the contrary, denial ideologues will continue to insist that the globe is cooling and that scientific findings to the contrary are a "swindle."

Global warming itself, as many others have noted, is the greatest swindle perpetrated in history. The most rapid warming of the twentieth century happened in the twenty years up to the 1930s. The hottest year in the climate record of the lower forty-eight states remains 1934. Humanity will be blundering completely unsuspectingly into a cold period that will cause widespread crop failures and starvation.[40]

Here the argument asserts that because of natural causes, e.g. the solar cycle, the globe is getting cooler, not warmer. Instead of catastrophic consequences of global warming, there will be catastrophic consequences of global cooling, "widespread crop failures and starvation." The assertions that the highest temperatures were in the 1930's and we are now entering a cooling phase are counterfactual. The hottest decades on record are 1980-2010, not the 1930's. Most recent years were hotter than 1934 (see table, above).[41]

But what about the long run? We are now in the part of the Milankovitch Cycle[42] that would, without taking in account the role of anthropogenic climate change, indicate that Earth is cooling, not warming.

The last time the planet was in a similar situation was about 430,000 years ago, and the interglacial at that time lasted roughly three times longer than average. Ignoring human changes to climate, and going by what happened last time, we would not expect an Ice Age to kick in for another 18,000 years or so.[43]

It would seem that we do have to worry about cooling eventually. However, this is a matter of many millennia, while global warming is taking place on a decadal time scale. Human changes to the climate may in fact overwhelm the natural cycles. "Models suggest that 1,000 billion tons of anthropogenic CO2 would hold off an Ice Age for about 130,000 years. That sounds like a lot of carbon dioxide (well, it is a lot), but we're already about a third of the way there. Sometime, a long, long time from now, a new Ice Age will likely emerge, but we're worried about the next 100 years, not the next 100,000 or more."[44]

Another extension of the denial assertion of a "cooling" trend is that we are already entering a new ice age with glaciers growing and these glaciers are starting to extend over the northern hemisphere. According to this view, growing glaciers will cause food shortages as agriculture begins to fail. "That is the true nightmare scenario. What if half the crops in those regions were lost one year, then two years in a row? ...In 1816 it only took one summer to cause massive disruptions to the food supply. The population is much higher now and more people are dependent on purchasing food instead of growing it themselves."[45] This kind of "ice age" prediction is based on false premises. The claim that glaciers are growing is refuted by many studies.[46] Most glaciers are shrinking.

It is indeed possible that crops will fail, but not due to cooling. Many crops, especially grains, depend on temperate climates and global warming will reduce crop yields. Drought has already caused many crops to fail (see Chapter 2). If temperatures increase by 3 degrees or 4 degrees C, crop failures would be catastrophic: "A three-degree rise causes all crops to experience a precipitous decline in their current growing regions. Overall yields could fall by a third in Africa. By some estimates temperature rises of over four degrees could reduce U.S. production of corn, soybeans, and cotton by 63 to 82 percent."[47]

Denial claims that CO2 increases will improve crop yields is also counterfactual. Research shows the opposite: "But in field conditions, the boon to the crops was not as great as in earlier greenhouse experiments, and probably not enough to offset the heat and other stresses of a warmer planet."[48] Another estimate indicates that "wheat yields drop 10 percent" in the Earth's hotter regions with every degree Centigrade that average temperature increases.[49]

Most often, the claim that the earth is cooling comes in the form, "there has been no warming for the past 15 years." That is sometimes coupled with the observation that carbon emissions have accelerated during this period. It is true that one of the warmest years on record was 1998, and if one starts with that date the *rate* of warming, but not the *trend,* has slowed. However, this is only a rate, not an absolute decline in temperature. Two of the warmest years, 2005 and 2010, came after 1998. With regard to the trends since 1998, researchers have found reasons for the slowing rate. "In fact, global warming has not stopped. The greenhouse gases released by humans are still trapping heat, and the vast bulk of it is being absorbed by the ocean, as has always been the case." [50]

How would scientists know that the ocean is absorbing the vast bulk of global warming? "Researchers have deployed more than 3,000 robotic floats that can measure the temperature in the upper layers of the ocean, and they show continual warming there. This documented ocean warming is hard evidence that scientists have gotten the basic story right when it comes to the effects of human emissions."[51] Despite this research, denial ideologues scoff at scientists who communicate this finding, as if they were somehow creating fictional reasons to explain the slowing rate of global warming.

All valid data shows that the world is warming, not cooling. The World Meteorological Organization in Geneva, which collates data from all over the globe, has said, "Thirteen of the fourteen warmest years on record have all occurred in the 21st century, and each of the last three decades has been warmer than the previous one, culminating with 2001-2010 as the warmest decade on record."[52]

One of the effects of the denial of recent warming is the misinformation spread in the political arena. Politicians continue to repeat the denial canard that the world is cooling. Rejecting the data as a climate science "thesis," Congressman Lenar Whitney (R-LA) said "any 10-year-old can invalidate their thesis with one of the simplest scientific devices known to man: a thermometer." His 10-year-old child's thermometer seems to show cooling during the past decade, unlike most thermometers. He justifies extreme denial on the basis of that canard: "It is perhaps the greatest deception in the history of mankind."[53] As we will see in Chapter 4, the theme of deception, scam, hoax, call it what you will, is a constant theme in denial ideology.

Not all skeptics believe the world is cooling. In fact, one makes the point that even it climate scientists are correct and the globe is warming, that is not a bad thing. "Many of the dire predictions about global warming are simply based on events that have already happened many times in the Earth's past. The problem is that the warmer climate is always better for life on Earth than the colder climate."[54] This analysis, however, leads to a canard often found in denial ideology: "a little warming is not a bad thing." It can mean longer growing seasons in the sub-Alpine regions such as Canada and Siberia. Those who claim that more food can be grown in Canada or Siberia are overlooking a crucial factor: "cheerful assurances that farming would expand poleward, turning northern Canada and Siberia into breadbaskets, failed to consider that acidic, conifer-covered taiga soils would take many millennia to adapt to the loamy demands of grains."[55]

Another claim by denial ideologues is that winters would be milder, so there would be fewer deaths from cold spells.

The chief benefits of global warming include: fewer winter deaths; lower energy costs; better agricultural yields; probably fewer droughts; maybe richer biodiversity. It is a little-known fact that winter deaths exceed summer deaths — not just in countries like Britain but also those with very warm summers, including Greece. Both Britain and Greece see mortality rates rise by 18 per cent each winter. Especially cold winters cause a rise in heart failures far greater than the rise in deaths during heatwaves.

17

Cold, not the heat, is the biggest killer. For the last decade, Brits have been dying from the cold at the average rate of 29,000 excess deaths each winter. Compare this to the heatwave ten years ago, which claimed 15,000 lives in France and just 2,000 in Britain.[56]

Claims in this statement such as lower energy costs, better agricultural yields, fewer droughts and richer biodiversity are dubious at best, and completely counterfactual in most cases. "Fewer winter deaths" is the least tenuous of these claims and it is based on a simple linear extrapolation of temperatures. The problem is that when anthropogenic climate change starts outrunning the natural cycles on which this kind of thinking is based, it can lead to temperatures increasing at an exponential rate. While there would be fewer deaths from cold spells, there would be many more from heat. Climate change today is not entirely natural and it cannot be compared to the natural changes of the past.

One effect of the argument that "climate change is natural" is misleading the public. Polls indicate the effect that it has on the public: "52 percent of Americans agreed with the statement 'the climate change we are currently seeing is a natural phenomenon that happens from time to time.' ...The United States also came in first [among nineteen countries] for disagreement with the statement 'The climate change we are currently seeing is largely the result of human activity.' In the U.S. 32 percent of people disagreed with this."[57] Would 32 percent of any reasonable public disagree with gravity? Maybe they are indeed part of what President Obama called "the Flat Earth Society."

When a third of the public disagrees with climate science, it is difficult to find leaders who are willing to support changes that might arouse voters to oppose them. One of the main tasks of leaders is to educate the public but few are willing to flout a segment of the public that mobilizes against climate science.

Denial ideology instigates opposition from a dedicated minority of voters whose activism can outweigh the majority.

Contrary to denial canards, temperatures and carbon dioxide concentrations have been rising in tandem above the long-run average during the past three decades. This is illustrated with a chart that combines the two trends:

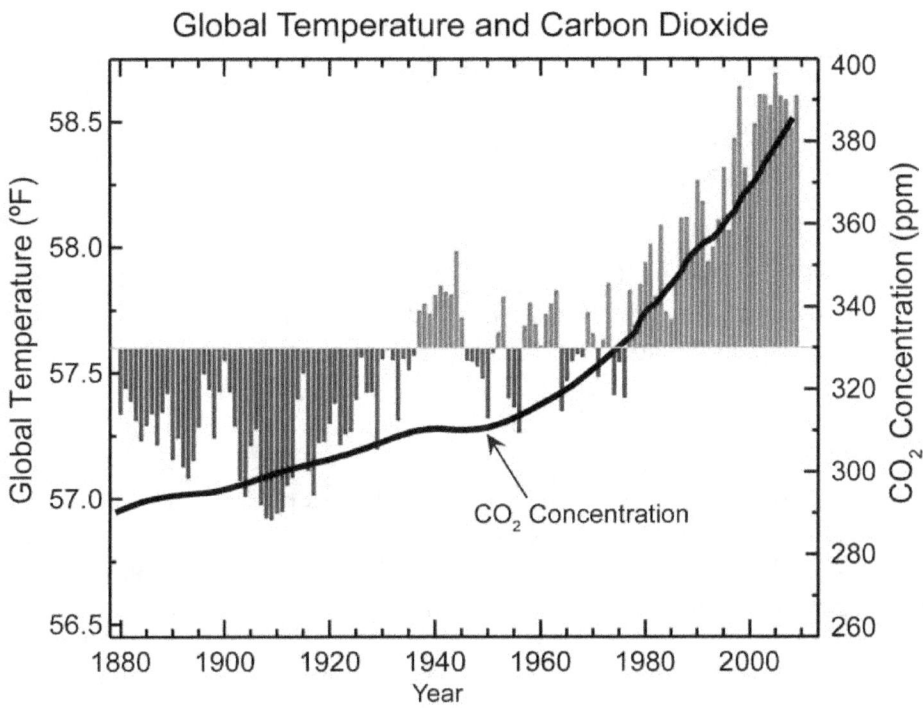

Source: NOAA

In this graph, both temperature (by half degrees below and above the average) and carbon dioxide (by parts per million, or ppm) are charted. As a general rule, concentrations of greenhouse gases determine global warming. If the total emissions from human activities exceed 500 gigatons severe climate disruptions will occur. At present we are at 390 gigatons, about 80% of the total, and emission rates are accelerating. Humans are emitting about 10 gigatons per year, so we do not have many years to reverse the trend. As we approach the limit greenhouse gases will

19

accelerate climate change and severe weather, as the exponential increases in the graph illustrate.[58]

The relationship between carbon dioxide and temperature has been one of the most contentious aspects of climate science in recent years. In Kansas, the legislature debated a resolution that denied the relationship. The text of the resolution read "Substantial amounts and types of real-data evidence clearly indicate a complete disconnect between anthropogenic emissions of CO_2 and the temperature of the earth."[59] Although the resolution did not pass, the fact that it was debated at all indicates that there are politicians willing to consider fictional data in making decisions.

Some may not deny the relationship but instead regard it as miniscule: "Changes in the atmospheric carbon dioxide concentration will have a minuscule effect on climate. Increased atmospheric carbon dioxide is not even a little bit bad. It is, in fact, wholly beneficial. The more carbon dioxide we can put into the atmosphere, the better life on Earth will be for human beings and all other living things."[60] This view of carbon dioxide echoes around denial circles. The state legislature of Montana even debated a bill that would declare that carbon dioxide is beneficial and that humans have nothing to do with climate change. Other denial advocates play down the role of carbon dioxide:

> Carbon dioxide from human activity, and any resulting warming caused, is therefore statistically insignificant and scientifically irrelevant. How could any normal-minded person believe that such a miniscule human contribution to Earth's atmospheric warmth (a small fraction of one percent) poses a problem to the planet? Or are people today simply too stupid, and lacking in common sense, to appreciate this point?[61]

It may be that there are people who are too stupid or lacking in common sense to understand climate, but climate scientists are not among that crowd. Their understanding of the role of carbon dioxide is quite different from denial ideology. "Ample physical evidence shows that carbon dioxide (CO_2) is the single most important climate-relevant greenhouse gas in Earth's atmosphere."[62] The "miniscule human contribution" is in fact a significant one. There are good analogies about how small amounts of change can make major differences, for example, a fever of only two or three percent (two or three degrees above the normal body temperature of 98.6 degrees F) can be an indication of a serious illness. But because the amount of change in temperature seems, at first glance, so small some denial ideologues will use it to obfuscate the issue of climate change.

> One degree Celsius is less than the temperature change you experience between breakfast and lunch, between New York and D.C., between standing at the bottom of a hill and climbing, say, 1,000 feet to the top. So, why are the alarmists urging us to bomb the global economy back to the Dark Ages in order to deal with a menace about ten times less threatening than a weekend's skiing in Vail?[63]

"Alarmists are urging us to bomb the global economy" because of an *insignificant change* in temperature? This reasoning completely ignores the shifts that are inherent in a rise in *average* global temperature, which reflects much more than a "weekend's skiing in Vail." In fact, because of the rise in global average temperature, Vail ski resorts may not have much skiing in the future.

One exasperating aspect of denial ideology is the recognition of the role of carbon dioxide followed by dismissal of its significance in climate change: "I believe that human produced carbon dioxide has the potential to elevate global temperatures, but I think that we currently greatly overestimate its ability to do so. In other words, I believe anthropogenic emissions have marginally contributed to our most recent period of warming. I do not believe that our most recent period of warming is unique or unusual. I believe it is all part of a normal cycle."[64] The argument that we are in a normal cycle is typical of denial ideology. It leads to the false prediction that we are entering a new ice age because we have now completed the warm portion of the cycle and temperatures have begun to decline. As shown earlier in this chapter, that is completely counterfactual.

One of the most difficult things about relating carbon dioxide and temperature is the role of the oceans. When rates of temperature increase slowed down in the 2000-2010 decade, scientists hypothesized that the steadily increasing CO_2 concentrations were partly dissolving in the oceans. This seems to irritate denial ideologues, who contend that climate science is incorrect because CO_2 is not a cause of, but a result of, temperature increases.

CO_2 does not cause temperature change, it simply changes based on the temperature of the ocean. This is why the level of CO_2 changes AFTER the temperature has changed. It does that for both warming and cooling. A cooling Earth removes CO_2 from the atmosphere so the CO_2 level drops. A warming Earth does the opposite and releases CO_2 into the atmosphere which increases the CO_2 level. The real problem is that a theory was proposed before anyone was able to measure global CO_2 levels and link that to the Earth's temperature with any accuracy. Once they looked, they found that CO_2 levels did in fact fluctuate with the Earth's temperature. Since the theory proposed by Arrhenius predicted this, it was considered proof that he was right. Unfortunately there was no way that this wouldn't be the case since the solubility for CO_2 in water will ensure that it will always be true. This is the greatest mix-up of cause and effect to ever happen in science.[65]

As in many other arguments against climate science, this statement conflates the natural processes of the carbon cycle and the human-induced processes. While humans add little in percentage terms to the natural concentrations, this small amount can have a major effect. A good analogy about the small percentage of carbon dioxide involved in global warming is provided by Keating: "A lot of people look at the amount of gases we are adding to the atmosphere and say that it isn't important because it is a very small percentage of the total amount of gas in the atmosphere. Well, it only takes a little bit to change everything." It is difficult to convince some people that a little CO2 can go a long way, but Keating provides an analogy: "A good analogy would be drugs, legal or illegal. Even a very small amount compared to the body mass can have a tremendous effect. The same way, even a small amount of extra energy added to the climate can cause lots of changes."[66]

Ignoring this effect of small changes causing large disruptions is perilous. Nevertheless, denial ideology will often repeat the canard. This kind of extreme denial is examined further in Chapter 4. Suffice it to say that when the fact of a link between carbon dioxide and temperature is denied, a basic premise is established that underpins a completely false ideology of denial.

Some scientists have supported this denial view. Daniel Botkin, professor Emeritus in the Department of Ecology, Evolution, and Marine Biology at University of California Santa Barbara, said "our addition of carbon dioxide to the atmosphere does not appear to be increasing Earth's temperature. Whatever is happening to Earth's climate does not seem to be our fault."[67] *Does not seem to be our fault?* That seems to be a subterfuge by someone who does not acknowledge the role of carbon dioxide emissions from fossil fuels. You might wonder what science he is using to reach his conclusions.

Debates over the role of carbon dioxide have fueled the controversy generated by denial ideology. Some contrarian scientists admit that carbon dioxide has increased in recent decades – it is difficult for them to refute the Keeling curve:[68]

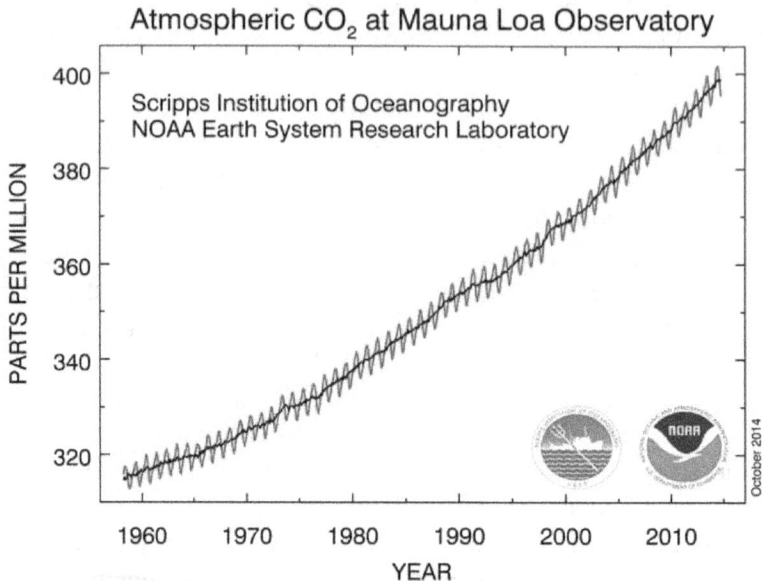

Measurements of carbon dioxide at Mauna Loa, initiated by Charles Keeling of Scripps Institute of Oceanography in 1958, have been maintained on a continuous basis since. Mauna Loa was chosen for its remoteness from human sources of carbon dioxide, so it is measuring a global average not a local one. The curve has a "sawtooth" shape because of seasonal variations – plants absorb carbon dioxide in the spring and summer in the Northern Hemisphere and return it in the fall and winter – but the overall trend is clear.

But is this small amount of carbon dioxide enough to cause climate change? While admitting that carbon dioxide is increasing, some denial ideologues will claim that it will have little effect on temperatures regardless of how much is emitted. Using paleoclimatology (study of ancient climates), one author noted that CO2 levels were lower in the distant past when the earth was warmer:

Why was the Eemian so much warmer than the Earth is today, especially considering that the

CO2 levels [at 280 ppm] were so much lower then, than they are now? That is only the first of two major problems that the Eemian gives to the theory that CO2 is a driving factor in global temperature. The Earth was much warmer 128,000 years ago, but CO2 levels were nothing special. Perhaps something other than CO2 levels caused the Earth to be much warmer during the Eemian besides CO2 levels.[69]

In other words, in past eras 100,000 or more years ago CO2 and temperature were unrelated. Over a 5000-year period the temperature dropped four degrees (C) but CO2 remained steady. That sort of analysis tends to equate past climate and present climate, overlooking the much faster rate of change in recent years. Human activities have increased CO2 much faster than natural rates. "Natural carbon dioxide levels generally take about ten thousand years to change by 100 ppm. We've seen that much increase in the past century or so. Our activity is disrupting the natural carbon cycle."[70] So it is not just the amount of CO2 emitted in the atmosphere, it is the pace of change, which is about 100 times the natural rate. Nevertheless, denial ideologues will tend to cherry-pick and conflate time scales to try to disprove climate science.

John Coleman, a retired meteorologist and co-founder of the Weather Channel, uses a denial argument on CO2 to "prove" there is no global warming. "Efforts to prove the theory that carbon dioxide is a significant 'greenhouse' gas and pollutant causing significant warming or weather effects have failed. There has been no warming over 18 years."[71] He is ignoring the temperature records reported by NOAA and the WMO to assert that a "theory" has failed. As we have seen, it is his argument that failed.

These arguments persist in denial ideology. One peculiar argument takes the form that CO2 has some effect but it is negligible. For example, some assert that increasing carbon dioxide increases temperature on an inverse logarithmic scale, that is, considerably less with each doubling of CO2.

Thankfully, the relationship between atmospheric carbon dioxide and temperature is logarithmic, not arithmetic. The first 20 parts per million of carbon dioxide in the atmosphere provides 1.6 ° C of warming, after which the effect drops away rapidly. From the current level of 400 parts per million, each addition of 100 parts per million adds only 0.1 ° C of warming.[72]

According to this logarithmic scale, if carbon dioxide doubles from a pre-industrial level of 400 ppm to 800 ppm, it will increase global temperature by one-tenth degree centigrade; if it doubles again to 1600 ppm, it will increase temperature by only two-hundredths of a degree. This can be represented graphically, where the vertical axis represents warming by degrees centigrade and the horizontal axis represents progressive doubling of carbon dioxide:[73]

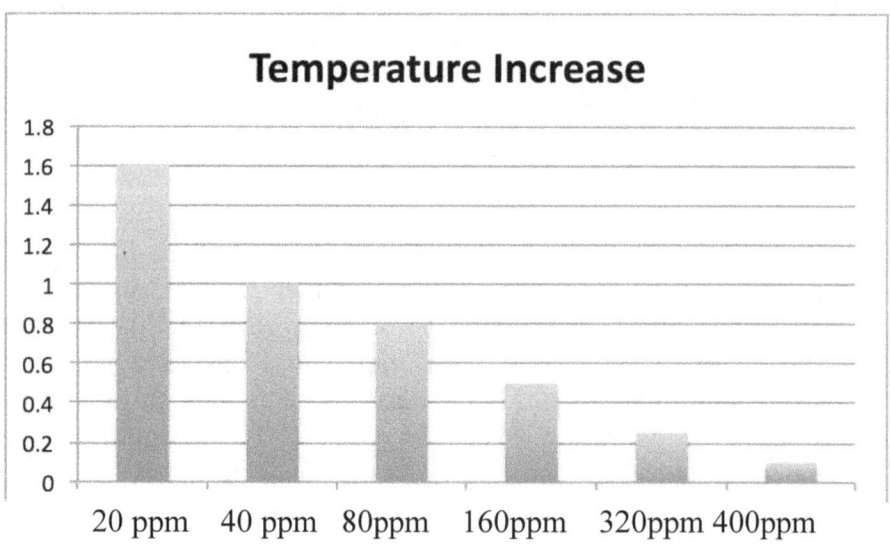

The chart seems to indicate that each CO2 doubling has a significantly smaller effect on temperature. This does not correspond to scientific findings, however. The National Research Council estimated that doubling carbon dioxide concentrations from current levels would increase temperatures by 2 degrees and

26

tripling concentrations would increase temperatures by 3 degrees. This is represented graphically:

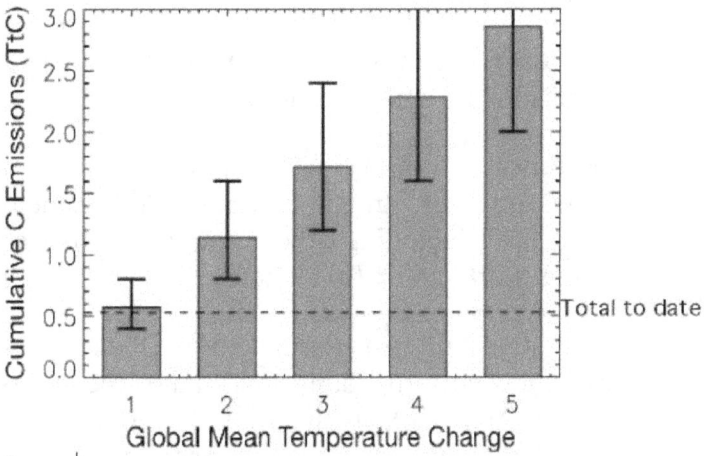

In this graph, TtC refers to teratons (trillions of metric tons) of carbon dioxide. The bars represent cumulative emissions that produce 1-5 degrees warming and the "I" beams represent ranges of probability. As can be seen by comparing the two graphs, the NRC projections are completely opposite from the logarithmic projections. We will return to this issue of carbon dioxide in subsequent chapters, because it crops up everywhere in denial ideology.

Some of the same deniers who use the "logarithmic scale" argument also cite discussions in the 1970's about a "new ice age." Indeed, a *Newsweek* cover article asked, "Are we entering another ice age?" Denial ideologues point to articles in science periodicals that show that scientists were predicting global cooling, and now they are predicting global warming, so how can we believe them? Congressman Bill Posey (R-FL) even raised the specter of another ice age based on misinformation: "When you think back twenty years ago, the worry was global freezing. We're going to freeze again. We're going to have another ice age."[74] In fact, scientific literature never made a decisive declaration of a coming ice age: "Global warming trumped global cooling in the peer-reviewed literature from 1965 and 1979, with 2,043 citations for former and just 325 for the latter."[75] Even back then, most scientists were skeptical of the global cooling hypothesis, and nearly all scientists reject it now. Science progresses by reviewing and revising findings, so we can say that in the past 40 years science has improved its analysis of climate change. Scientific articles now have findings of human-caused global warming in 97% of articles today, compared to 62% in the 1970's.

The mistaken notion that the atmosphere is not warming has real consequences. In an editorial on President Obama's climate policies, including the restriction on coal power emissions, the *Washington Times* states:

> On Aug. 26, though, Mr. Obama crossed a bridge too far, proposing a "Climate Accord" (really, a treaty) that will, in the well-chosen words of The New York Times, "compel nations to cut their planet-warming fossil fuel emissions." Never mind that we are now in the 18th consecutive year of not warming the planet, according to two separate and independent measures of surface and near-surface temperatures. Do, however, mind that word "compel."...How on God's getting-greener earth can the president think the nation can be "compelled," absent the two-thirds vote of the Senate explicitly required by the Constitution?[76]

The *Washington Times* expands on the misstatement that "we are now in the 18th consecutive year of not warming the planet" to criticize the president's climate policy of negotiating an agreement, conveniently overlooking the fact that the U.S. has signed and ratified just such a treaty, the UN Framework Convention on Climate Change (UNFCCC). Just as denial ideologues like to ignore the Clean Air Act's compulsion to reduce carbon emissions, they also would prefer to disregard the UNFCCC.

A reputed pause in temperature increases continues to feed the denial narrative. "The unpredicted pause in the rise in global temperature since the late 1990s is so embarrassing to climate activists, who are filled with a fiery certitude about the 'science,' that it goes unmentioned (the climate marchers could have chanted, 'Hey, hey! Ho, ho! Where did climate change go?'). In their fevered urgency, they give off the sense that they are desperate to save the planet before it might become evident that it doesn't need saving." [77] *It doesn't need saving?* That judgment is at odds with all of the evidence from temperature records and extreme weather incidents.

Scientific Views of Extreme Weather

What is the scientific view of extreme weather and climate change? In general scientists do not associate any one weather event with climate change but look for trends and probabilities. The Intergovernmental Panel on Climate Change (IPCC) recently published a report that indicated that extreme weather is more likely with climate change:

> It is likely that anthropogenic influences have led to warming of extreme daily minimum and maximum temperatures at the global scale. There is medium confidence that anthropogenic influences have contributed to intensification of extreme precipitation at the global scale. It is likely that there has been an anthropogenic influence on increasing extreme coastal high water due to an increase in mean sea level. [78]

In its usual cautionary language, IPCC uses the term "likely" to indicate high probabilities of anthropogenic (human-induced) extreme warming, extreme cold weather and sea level rise. It uses "medium confidence" to indicate the moderate probability of anthropogenic influence on extreme precipitation. All of these are factors in extreme weather, which can be associated with a number of different causes. Climate change is reinforcing the severity of extreme weather.

Despite its cautious language, the IPCC is accused of exaggerating findings of climate change by denial ideologues.

29

Recently, the IPCC released another report claiming "climate change" will melt polar ice, cause the oceans to rise dramatically, generate extreme weather conditions, et cetera. There have always been extreme weather conditions somewhere and the rest of the IPCC claims are just great big lies that have been around for decades.[79]

This statement is typical of the treatment of IPCC in denial literature. In subsequent chapters, we will see how denial ideology has attacked climate science for its "great big lies" and other sins.

Many indicators of climate change, such as heat waves, unexpected freezes, droughts, melting ice in the Arctic and Greenland, and other forms of extreme weather, are likely to occur more frequently and severely in the 21st Century. An example of the one-two punch of extreme weather was the warm spring weather in March 2012 followed by a freeze in April that decimated the apple crop in Michigan. Most germane to this discussion is the accelerating pace of climate change that will cause rapid changes in weather trends and unpleasant surprises in the near future. The National Academy of Sciences has described the nature of these changes:

Given the available scientific knowledge of the climate system, it is prudent for security analysts to expect climate surprises in the coming decade, including unexpected and potentially disruptive single events as well as conjunctions of events occurring simultaneously or in sequence, and for them to become progressively more serious and more frequent thereafter, most likely at an accelerating rate.[80]

Hurricanes such as Superstorm Sandy and Typhoon Haiyan (see chapter 2) are among the more extreme forms of weather events. According to some scientists, they may be related to climate change. This is still a contentious topic of discussion, but it appears that hurricanes will be stronger with climate change. "One the expected effects of global warming will be an increase in hurricane intensity... Higher ocean temperatures lead to an exponentially higher evaporation rate in the atmosphere, which increases the intensity of cyclones and precipitation."[81]

There is some controversy about these findings, but there is a growing consensus that the severity of hurricanes is strengthened by warmer seawater. This is the basis of many analyses of the strength of superstorm Sandy (see Chapter 2). The effects of hurricanes and other superstorms (such as the "derecho" that hit mid-Atlantic states in 2012) are also exacerbated by the tendency of people to build in vulnerable areas such as shorelines. Costs of rebuilding increase with higher density of population and/or more expensive buildings.[82] With these caveats in mind, we need to examine recent extreme weather events in the context of climate change.

Chapter 2:
Extreme Weather

In general, extreme weather is related to climate change while specific events may not be identified with it. In its latest report, the IPCC has described the relationship with "very high confidence:"

> **Impacts from recent climate-related extremes, such as heat waves, droughts, floods, cyclones, and wildfires, reveal significant vulnerability and exposure of some ecosystems and many human systems to current climate variability (*very high confidence*).** Impacts of such climate-related extremes include alteration of ecosystems, disruption of food production and water supply, damage to infrastructure and settlements, morbidity and mortality, and consequences for mental health and human well-being. For countries at all levels of development, these impacts are consistent with a significant lack of preparedness for current climate variability in some sectors.[83]

Using the term "climate variability" allows the IPCC to avoid the controversy over the term "global warming." It includes the concepts of shifts in weather patterns that can change precipitation and storm tracks even when temperature levels are fairly steady.

Climate change does indeed affect a variation in weather, and its effects can be felt anywhere. The U.S. has recently suffered two major droughts, tornadoes and a "superstorm," while the Philippines has felt the impact of a major typhoon. These events illustrate the type of extreme weather that we can expect in the future.

Midwest Drought

On May 3, 2012, the last significant rains of the 2012 growing season fell in most of the Midwest states. In Minnesota, Iowa, Missouri, Arkansas, Texas, North and South Dakota, Nebraska, Kansas, Colorado, Wyoming and Montana farmers had planted crops – corn, wheat and soybeans primarily. Many watched them wither as the summer progressed. In many states, the drought persisted to the end of October.

According to the weekly U.S. Drought Monitor, about 60.2 percent of the contiguous U.S. (about 50.4 percent of the U.S. including Alaska, Hawaii, and Puerto Rico) was classified as experiencing moderate to exceptional (D1-D4) drought at the end of October.[84]

Cattle ranchers in Colorado and other states were forced to sell their herds for lack of feed. Many retired. Some turned their ranches into "dude ranches," trying to attract hunting and fishing tours. Farmers throughout the Midwest retired, or left the farm to find jobs in cities.

American farmers used to produce enough grain to build up large surpluses and export sizeable quantities. In 2011, world surpluses were reduced by droughts in Russia and China, and by 2012 the amounts produced in the U.S. dropped by more than 12 percent. Corn production dropped 27 percent and prices doubled in two years, responding to declines in supply from the 2011 and 2012 droughts and increases in demand.[85] State governments asked the Environmental Protection Agency to lift the regulation on ethanol, produced from corn, because it was driving up corn prices. The drought increasingly threatens U.S. and world food security, leading to unrest in many countries.

Many people have asked if this was due to climate change. One of the most important trends in climate change is disruption of precipitation patterns. This has become obvious in the U.S. Midwest in recent years, particularly 2012.

In mid-August 2012, the extent of the drought conditions was significant: over 70% of the land area of the United States (including Alaska and Hawaii) was affected by abnormally dry and drought conditions. The intensity of the drought varied across the country, but the regions of extreme and exceptional drought were clustered across the Midwest, Great Plains, Southwest, and in the Southeast, particularly Georgia. The widespread nature of drought conditions in the Midwest and Great Plains in the summer of 2012 has led to the deterioration of U.S. crop conditions. Forty-five percent of the corn crop and 35% of the soybean crop were listed in poor to very poor conditions for the week ending on July 23, 2012, and conditions for both commodities had deteriorated for seven straight weeks leading up to July 23. These ratings for corn and soybeans represented the worst conditions for any time.[86]

Drought is a complex weather pattern, with many causes. Not all droughts can be linked to climate change, but like superstorms they show many of the fingerprints of climate change. Climate scientists are asking, "What causes drought?" There are a whole range of answers, some of which are affected by higher global temperatures: "The physical conditions causing drought in the United States are increasingly understood to be linked to sea surface temperatures (SSTs) in the tropical Pacific Ocean. Studies indicate that cooler-than-average SSTs have been connected to the severe western drought in the first decade of the 21st century, severe droughts of the late 19th century, and precolonial North American 'megadroughts.'" La Niña conditions in the Pacific Ocean may be a cause of the 2011 severe drought in Texas.[87]

Other droughts throughout the world have been linked to climate change. The Secretary-General of the World Meteorological Organization, Michel Jarraud, has associated the 2010 drought in Russia with climate change:

> Meteorologists have been at pains to make clear that no major weather event was the result of a single cause, but research into climate change was establishing clear links, Mr. Jarraud said, citing the results of research into the extreme heat wave in Russia in 2010. "Without climate change, this episode would have been very unlikely," he said.[88]

Whether or not the specific events are linked to climate change, it is likely that there will be increasing droughts in the next decades. "The prospect of extended droughts and more arid baseline conditions in parts of the United States could suggest new challenges to federal programs and water projects, which were conceived or constructed largely on the basis of 20th century climate conditions."[89]

Water projects in Western states are threatened as reservoirs dry up. Already Las Vegas' water supply is reduced by decline in the water level of Lake Mead. "Some studies suggest a transitioning of the American West to a more arid climate, possibly resulting from the buildup of greenhouse gases in the atmosphere, raising concerns that the region may become more prone to extreme drought than it was in the 20th century. Some models of future climate conditions also predict greater fluctuations in wet and dry years."[90] These fluctuations will make it difficult for water managers to plan maintenance of water systems.

Climate change will change patterns in a way that will undermine further economic growth and development. "Some studies have suggested that human influences on climate, caused by emissions of greenhouse gases, may be responsible for a drying trend."[91] The "drying trend" suggests that drought is an increasing problem for agriculture, which will become an increasing problem for economic growth particularly in developing countries.

Mechanisms of drought are self-reinforcing. "Evapotranspiration" is a mechanism by which plants and soils evaporate moisture. It accelerates with heat and wind, which will increase with climate change. The moisture has to go somewhere; some of it will go to areas with too much precipitation already. Some increases water vapor, a greenhouse gas, in the atmosphere. The irony of climate change is that it makes some areas too wet as it makes others too dry. The predominant effect in the U.S. west is desiccation.

A likely consequence of higher temperatures in the West would be higher evapotranspiration, reduced precipitation, and decreased spring runoff. These impacts would result from an "acceleration" of the hydrologic cycle, due to increased warming of the atmosphere, which in turn increases the amount of water held in the atmosphere. A possible consequence is more frequent, and perhaps more severe, droughts and floods. However, these changes are likely not to occur evenly across the United States. Observations of water-related changes over the last century suggest that runoff and streamflow in the Colorado and Columbia River basins has been decreasing, along with the amount of ice in mountain glaciers in the West, and the amount of annual precipitation in the Southwest.[92]

The Midwest drought of 2012 reminded some of the Dust Bowl of the 1930's. When Ken Burns created the "Dust Bowl" documentary, reviewers made a connection to 2012:

The giant dust clouds started in 1932, the result of normal heavy winds hitting enormous tracts of plowed-up land with no grasses to hold the soil. A severe, years-long drought worsened the problem. Today, with global temperatures rising, record-setting heat waves, droughts and wildfires sweeping the West and powerful storms afflicting the East, it's apparent that we're doing it again. In the 1920s, desire for profits trumped environmental stewardship, and the economic losses that resulted made the short-term gains from over-farming the Plains states look like chickenfeed. The lesson: Ravaging the environment on such a wide scale has hidden costs that nature will inevitably collect. That's worth keeping in mind today as the federal government continues its irresponsible inaction on climate change.[93]

The 21st Century is not like the 1930's in most respects, but some of the same dynamics are at play. The 1930's had unusually high temperatures – a fact that denial ideologues are quick to point out – but farming practices now are quite different and another dust bowl is unlikely. Other effects of climate change are more likely to occur, especially if the drought persists for years as many scientists expect. U.S. food security and agricultural economics will suffer; grain prices will rise considerably, reverberating through the food chain; and many farmers will leave the sector.

Agriculture is not the only thing affected by the drought. The Mississippi and Missouri rivers, used for bulk transportation of many goods, will be less navigable.

The drought of 2012 has already caused restrictions on barge traffic up and down the Mississippi River. But things are about to get a lot worse.... If water levels fall low enough, the transport of $7 billion in agricultural products, chemicals, coal and petroleum products in

December and January alone could be stalled altogether.[94]

Railroads do not have enough capacity to replace the barges. The Corps of Engineers must maintain minimum water levels for other purposes, and the economic impacts of delayed shipments will be worse than the effects of the drought on crops alone.

Another river affected by drought is the Colorado River. It has a number of reservoirs that feed cities and hydroelectric generators, but these "man-made reservoirs from the Rockies to southern Arizona are being sapped by 14 years of drought nearly unrivaled in 1,250 years."[95] As the reservoirs diminish, water supply to cities such as Las Vegas is threatened. Research indicates that the situation will become worse with climate change. "A brace of global-warming studies concludes that rising temperatures will reduce the Colorado's average flow after 2050 by five to 35 percent, even if rainfall remains the same — and most of those studies predict that rains will diminish."[96]

Regarding the claim that the 1930's had the highest temperatures since thermometers were invented, this has been repeatedly debunked[97] as the data in Chapter 1 indicate. That does not stop the denial ideologues from repeating the misinformation, however. They regard the scientists who measure the recent data as frauds. Sussman and Bell continue to repeat the "hot 1930's" canard (see Chapter 4) but will have increasing difficulty in maintaining their positions as data about the present trends accumulate. Reality has a way of deposing the misinformation of denial ideologues.

Western Drought

In California, the drought began in 2012 and increased in severity during 2013. By January 2014, the wildfire season that normally began in the spring became a year-around phenomenon as more than 100 fires were reported during the month. Governor

Jerry Brown declared a drought emergency and requested that residents reduce water use by 20%. The California Department of Water Resources cut off water supplies to local agencies serving 25 million residents and about 750,000 acres of farmland.[98]

> It is the first time in the 54-year history of the State Water Project that water allocations to all of the public water agencies it serves have been cut to zero. That decision will force 29 local agencies to look elsewhere for water. Most have other sources they can draw from, such as groundwater and local reservoirs.[99]

Conditions in California are monitored on a periodic basis, and maps are produced, by the U.S. Department of Agriculture. As of February 2014, the conditions were mapped as shown:

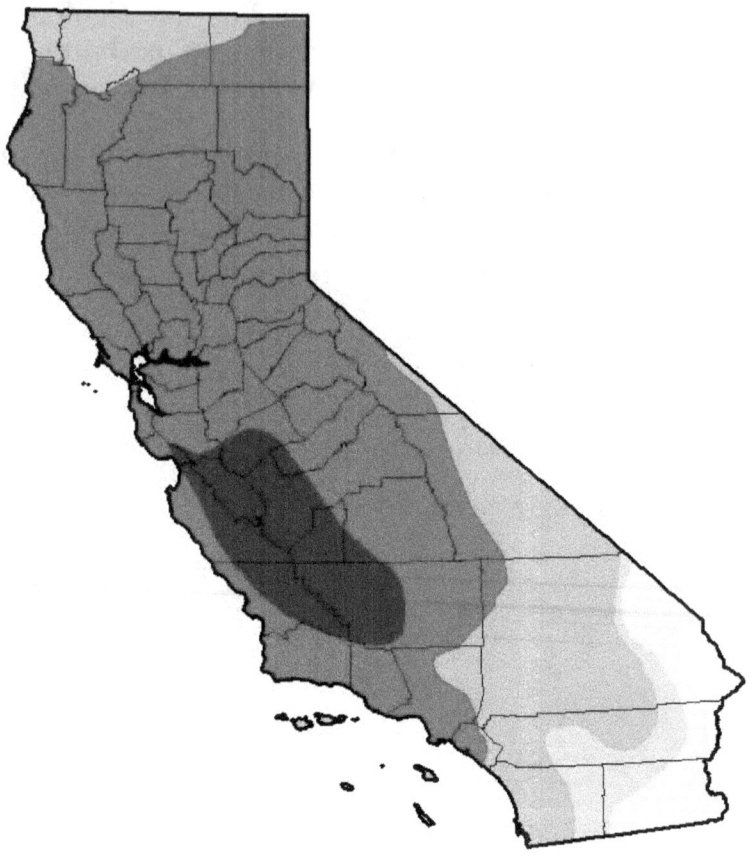

The darker colors on the map show the most severe drought conditions. These extended throughout the agricultural areas and mountains.

Snowpack, the accumulation of snow in the mountains of western states, was at the lowest level it has been for decades. In the Sierra Nevada range of California, snow levels were 12% of normal. In the 2013-2014 season, the snowpack was down by about 20% to 40%. Low snow levels affect not only the California's water supply but also reduce the generation of hydroelectric power.

As in the Midwest, the effects of drought were already affecting Western agriculture. "Many ranchers, forced to buy hay to feed their cows, have sold off much of their herds, while farmers in a number of Western states have been mulling whether to let their fields lie fallow this year [2014]."[100]

Again, as in the Midwest drought, the question arose, is this climate change? US Agriculture Secretary Tom Vilsack thought it was related:

> Mr. Vilsack called the drought in California a "deep concern," and a warning sign of trouble ahead for much of the West. "That's why it's important for us to take climate change seriously," he said. "If we don't do the research, if we don't have the financial assistance, if we don't have the conservation resources, there's very little we can do to help these farmers."[101]

California officials had no doubt about the relationship between the drought and climate change.

> "It's clear that climate change is playing a role," said John Laird, the state's secretary for natural resources. "We are the middle of the three driest consecutive years since records were kept. We're in extreme drought in 100 percent of the state. There is no part of the state that is not vulnerable."[102]

Wildfires are becoming costly to California. The state expects to spend $500 million in 2014 fighting fires. Many homes have been reduced to ashes and cities are becoming desperate to preserve dwindling supplies of water as they fight the fires.

Ironically, the drought has had a deleterious impact on one of California's iconic sites: the Hearst Castle near San Simeon. Springs feeding the castle grounds, including the marble-lined swimming pool, have flow rates at one-sixth of normal and most of the fountains and the pool are now drained of water.[103] William Randolph Hearst, who built the castle, was a leading American

41

conservative in the early Twentieth Century. Would he have denied climate change? We cannot be sure, but his legacy continues in the form of some leading conservative newspapers and media outlets.

There are many suggestions about how to adapt to the drought conditions, but none of them address the real issue: California may well revert to a desert with climate change. One official noted:

> "This is a real idling of land, and there is nothing positive about it," said Daniel A. Sumner, an agriculture economist and the director of the Agricultural Issues Center at the University of California, Davis. "It's not fallowing — that implies a choice. This is not like North Dakota, where we know it's going to get better. We're talking either spending huge sums on bringing water in or thousands of acres lost."[104]

California's farmlands were originally desert, but snowpack in the Sierras as the source of irrigation water transformed them into lush farmland. As the snowpack diminishes, these farmlands may return to desert conditions.

Farming has been one of the mainstays of the California economy, but it will not be sustainable in the future.

> Less than a month ago, Mr. Sumner and other experts estimated that 300,000 acres of rich farmland in the region would go unplanted. Now, he has nearly doubled that estimate. "I haven't learned anything yet that tells me it is less severe than we might have hoped," he said. The drought could translate into an $11 billion loss in annual state revenue from agriculture, according to the California Farm Water Coalition, an industry advocacy group. And in the Central Valley, where farming and food processing provide nearly 40 percent of all jobs, the most acute

pain is most likely to be felt among low-level employees, who scrape by with seasonal work.[105]

While agricultural production might shift to other parts of the country, food prices may well rise because of the decrease in farming and food processing in California. The Central Valley produces about one-third of the fruits and vegetables in the U.S.

Governor Jerry Brown of California has linked the drought to climate change.

> As we send billions and billions of tons of heat-trapping gases, we get heat and we get fires and we get what we are seeing. So we've got to gear up. We're going to deal with nature as best we can, but humanity is on a collision course with nature and we're just going to have to adapt to it in the best way we can. We have more structures, more activity, more sparks, more combustible activity and we've got to gear up for it, and as the climate changes, this is going to be a radically different future than was our historic past.[106]

A sector of the economy that is almost as sensitive to weather as agriculture is the restaurant sector. Its resource base, after all, is agriculture and when the agricultural sector suffers, restaurants suffer as well. One restaurant chain, Chipotles, reflected this sensitivity:

> "Increasing weather volatility or other long-term changes in global weather patterns, including any changes associated with global climate change, could have a significant impact on the price or availability of some of our ingredients," Chipotle said in the filing last month. If the cost of ingredients jumps, the company said it "may choose to temporarily suspend" serving items such as guacamole or some salsas.[107]

Businesses get it, even if the denial ideologues do not. In addition to the major insurance companies such as Munich Re, corporations such as Apple, Microsoft, Cisco, EBay, General Motors, Starbucks, and Unilever are pushing for more aggressive climate policies. Their declaration includes the sentence "We cannot risk our kids' futures on the false hope that the vast majority of scientists are wrong."[108] This "false hope" is inherent in denial ideology.

Ironically, one of the criticisms of climate policies by denial ideologues is conversion of food crops to biofuels, increasing food prices. While this is a valid criticism of ethanol and other biofuels derived from grain and soybeans, it is a rather narrow view of the problem. The broader problem is that food production as a whole, worldwide, is likely to suffer from drought and other effects of climate change to a much larger extent than the effects of biofuel production. A canard of denial ideology is that increased concentration of CO_2 in the atmosphere is enhancing food production. In reality, it decreases agricultural productivity, particularly as temperatures rise and droughts spread.[109]

One of the effects of climate change that has many scientists and policymakers concerned is environmental migration. Refugees from Mexico are part of the illegal immigration problem.[110] Paradoxically, many of these refugees are immigrating to the U.S. West, where drought conditions may make refugees of everyone living there. California will be particularly hard hit by climate change, as it is naturally a desert, becoming the nation's breadbasket by virtue of widespread irrigation of crops. Large cities in California such as Los Angeles and San Diego are heavily dependent on the Colorado River system, which is having drought problems of its own.

Where will they go? People in California and neighboring states will probably head north to Oregon, Idaho, Montana and Washington, and if those states become drier, they may head for Canada.[111] These areas may find that an influx of climate refugees will lead to overcrowding and stresses on their infrastructure, so it is doubtful that the refugees will be welcome.

Climate change is likely to create refugees throughout the world. While the U.S. and Canada can accommodate refugees relatively well, other parts of the world such as South Asia are not as wealthy or robust to handle large migrations.[112] It has become increasingly obvious to policy makers, for example military leaders planning for climate disruptions, that climate change will have increasingly severe effects on international relations: "none of the world's armed forces are wasting time doubting global warming, and all the Arctic nations, plus others, including China, are ramping up their focus on the far north."[113]

Droughts and Climate Change

Droughts are pervasive in history and geography. They are found throughout historical records, and they can occur in nearly every part of the world. While the Midwest drought has ended, the Western drought persists. What makes these recent droughts – in the Midwest and the West – examples of climate change?

On one side of the issue is John Holdren, science advisor to President Barack Obama, who says:

> Scientifically, no single episode of extreme weather, no storm, no flood, no drought can be said to have been caused by global climate change. But the global climate has now been so extensively impacted by the human-caused buildup of greenhouse gases that weather practically everywhere is being influenced by climate change.[114]

On the other side of the issue are some scientists whose research indicates that the 2014 California drought may not be related to climate change.

> Many of those studies have found a likelihood that climate change will indeed cause the American West to dry out, but by an entirely different mechanism — the arrival of more dry air from the tropics. And the most recent batch of studies predicts

that effect will not really apply to the western slope of the Sierra. Climate projections show that the area should get somewhat more moisture in the winter, not less.[115]

Droughts are part of a trend, in which the number of days of dry weather, the length of the hot spells, and the changes in precipitation patterns, are all indicators of climate change. As noted by scholars, these factors make it more likely that as temperatures rise, the severity of droughts and their spread will increase. Why have people ignored the trends?

> Although recent droughts have been disastrous for ranchers and farmers in the United States, Americans still remain somewhat insulated from the full force of climate change and the projected food shortages. But not for long: Agricultural areas throughout the Midwest and especially in California are threatened by the growing water insecurity that accompanies a warming world. We're not doing nearly enough to avert disaster.[116]

It is unlikely that we can ignore the trends much longer. Even though there is caution about linking specific weather to climate change, drought is becoming more pervasive: "areas such as the U.S. Southwest are witnessing more droughts, and these too are consistent with global climate change patterns projected by climate models as a consequence of rising CO2 levels."[117] Certainly the farmers of Western states, not known as radical environmentalists, are becoming aware of the effects of climate change:

> While farmers here tend to be politically conservative – a spot of red surrounded by a sea of blue in [some] of the nation's most liberal states – you'd be hard-pressed to find global warming skeptics, because most of them have seen the effects of a change in the weather firsthand. And they're

afraid – of floods from heavier rainfall, of the disappearing snowmelt from the rugged western slopes of the Cascade Mountains and the Sierra Nevada that provides the estuary's storehouse of fresh water.[118]

As is so often the case, the people whose business depends on the weather are often the first to move away from denial of climate change. Their fears of the future are the indicators that reality now reigns, rather than ideology that previously guided their thinking.

The National Climate Assessment (NCA) noted that the droughts are related to warming, along with fires and insect infestations that also affect the Western U.S. "Increased warming, drought and insect outbreaks, all caused by our linked to climate change have increased wildfires and impacts to people and ecosystems in the Southwest."[119]

While some areas can adapt, much of California and adjacent states may become unlivable. Certainly the urban landscape will change as outlying housing developments such as those near San Diego become vulnerable to wildfires. It is odd to think about climate change in such broad terms, but both our eating habits and our homes are going to be altered by effects of climate change. These changes will happen regardless of what we think of the causes of climate changes that are already underway.

Superstorm Sandy

Superstorm Sandy began as a tropical depression in the Caribbean in mid-October 2012. It intensified to a Category 2 hurricane (winds over 110 miles per hour) when it crossed Jamaica, Haiti and Cuba. Reported deaths included 52 in Haiti and 22 in Cuba. It widened to a storm system with a diameter of 1100 miles (1800 kilometers) as it approached the East Coast of the U.S. on October 27. Winds slowed and Sandy was labeled a "post-tropical cyclone" when it made landfall near Atlantic City, New Jersey. Following landfall on October 29, 2012, Sandy caused more than $100 billion in damage and killed more than 150 people in New Jersey, New York and other East Coast states. Much of the damage was caused by storm surge, with high tides well above normal.

The effect on New York City has been described as follows:

> A record 14-foot storm surge devoured the southern tip of Manhattan and entire waterfront neighborhoods in Brooklyn, Staten Island and Queens. Manhattan's glittering skyline went dark below 34th Street after the salty waters claimed an electrical substation. Nearly 100 million gallons of water rushed into the Brooklyn-Battery Tunnel, a toll road beneath the East River.[120]

A colorful description of the aftermath is painted by Diane Ackerman in *The Human Age:*

> Only a day before Halloween, the scene was beyond macabre, as if a Chagall painting had suddenly come to life in a 90 mph whirlwind of whizzing trees, animals, and objects. People unlucky enough to be caught outside were pulled sideways down the streets. It was as if a monster were wrestling electrical lines to the ground, clawing up roads, turning neighborhoods into sandboxes. Piers and boardwalks crumpled like cardboard as the superstorm slapped them into the sea.[121]

Many asked, was Sandy caused by climate change? Then the debate began. *Bloomberg Businessweek* on November 1, 2012, headlined its cover story "It's the Climate, Stupid." In the text it demurred somewhat from attributing Sandy directly to climate change:

> Yes, yes, it's unsophisticated to blame any given storm on climate change. Men and women in white lab coats tell us – and they're right – that

many factors contribute to each severe weather episode. Climate deniers exploit scientific complexity to avoid any discussion at all. Clarity, however, is not beyond reach. Hurricane Sandy demands it: At least 40 U.S. deaths. Economic losses expected to climb as high as $50 billion. Eight million homes without power. Hundreds of thousands of people evacuated. More than 15,000 flights grounded. Factories, stores, and hospitals shut. Lower Manhattan dark, silent, and underwater.[122]

Although some journalists did see a connection between Sandy and climate change, others scorned this analysis. "Hurricane Sandy is a prime example of the mania of attributing every weather event to humans. The Bloomberg Businessweek cover in Sandy's wake included a grim photograph of a flooded New York street with the headline 'It's Global Warming, Stupid'."[123] "Mania" seems to be a rather pejorative term for an article that suggested the possibility of a connection.

Scientists do hedge their statements with qualifiers about complexity and probability. Superstorm Sandy was not the first hurricane to hit so far north – many have damaged New Jersey, New York and New England during the 20th Century. Hurricane Irene caused major flooding in Vermont in 2011. But Sandy was by far the worst.

One of the most deleterious effects of Sandy, which it shares with other superstorms such as the 2012 derecho that hit the mid-Atlantic, is the effect on the electrical grid. Many power lines were down and some substations in lower Manhattan were flooded. Modern society has become highly dependent on the grid, and superstorms will increase the damage not only to the physical infrastructure but also to business and social life dependent on electricity.

It would be overly simplistic to attribute Sandy only to climate change, but some of the damage can be linked directly to sea level rise and other effects of climate change. Most of the damage was in coastal areas.

> Across the nation, tens of billions of tax dollars have been spent on subsidizing coastal reconstruction in the aftermath of storms, usually with little consideration of whether it actually makes sense to keep rebuilding in disaster-prone areas. If history is any guide, a large fraction of the federal money allotted to New York, New Jersey and other states recovering from Hurricane Sandy — an amount that could exceed $30 billion — will be used the same way. Tax money will go toward putting things back as they were, essentially duplicating the vulnerability that existed before the hurricane. ...Lately, scientists, budget-conscious lawmakers and advocacy groups across the political spectrum have argued that these subsidies waste money, put lives at risk and make no sense in an era of changing climate and rising seas.[124]

Costs for rebuilding and restoring property from the effects of Sandy are estimated at $250 per person for everyone in the United States.[125] That is $1000 for a family of four and it is not something that we will have to worry about in the future – it is already incurred.

Sea-level rise has been a contentious area of climate science. One skeptic notes that sea-level rise in the past has been much more dramatic than the present.

> Today the rate of sea level change is so small that it takes satellites to accurately detect it. There are several places that provide the data for anyone to review. During the early Holocene the sea level was rising so quickly that in a single lifetime the ocean would engulf most coastal communities on the Earth today. That is climate change. That is also part of a very natural cycle that has been repeating for

> hundreds of thousands of years on the Earth. When I
> hear a dire projection about the sea levels changing,
> I have to laugh.[126]

This analyst may laugh because he conflates natural and human causes of climate change. Scientists are well aware of natural causes of sea-level rise and do not ignore them while analyzing the human causes. The statement typifies the denial logic that presumes climate science is not about natural causes of climate change, only human causes, so therefore it must be invalid. This argument is applied most vociferously to the use of models which presumably do not take natural causes into account:

> Climate science is now bogged down, stagnating, unable to free itself of an astronomically high percentage of peer-reviewed climate science studies, which blame, without evidence, manmade greenhouse gases for climate change, without meaningfully taking into account the natural factors that actually cause multidecadal variations in temperatures and precipitation.[127]

Climate scientists are well aware of the difference between the "noise" – natural causes – and the signal – human causes separated out from the natural causes.

While any individual storm has its own characteristics and affects coastal areas differently from other storms, the trend toward increasingly intense storms and the increasing cost of reconstruction will likely force more consideration of the effects of climate change.

Sandy did have a major effect on the climate change debate: it raised the profile of discussion and made many more people pay attention. New York Mayor Bloomberg and New York Governor Cuomo both mentioned climate change in their reports on damage. The question became: what these and other leaders plan to do about rising seas and warm waters that seem to strengthen tropical storms. There may be some reservations about using superstorms as justification for climate policies. One of the leading climate scientists, Kerry Emanuel, observed:

> Conventional wisdom about climate change may have begun to gel in the aftermath of Sandy, but did global warming really cause the vicious hybrid storm that devastated much of the eastern seaboard last week? The short answer is no. Attributing Sandy or any other single event to long-term climate trends is rather like blaming El Niño for a car accident on the Santa Monica Freeway. But that's hardly an excuse for policymakers to keep kicking the climate can down the road. Science actually doesn't tell us much about that kind of causality, so it's time to stop acting like it does.[128]

Individual storms – no – but the cumulative effect will raise questions about adaptation to climate change. It is not a given that politicians or the public will have long enough memories to act in response to cumulative effects from superstorms like Sandy. Other events and problems intervene, and attention shifts to taxes, deficits, health care and a myriad of other issues. Will it take another superstorm to elevate climate change to the level of political decision and action? "For example, we can now begin to estimate how global warming changes the probability of destructive hurricane landfalls. But in the case of hybrid storms like Sandy, which combine hurricane and winter storm characteristics, science hasn't even progressed to the point of assessing probabilities."[129]

Probabilities are not comfortable for many non-scientists. They want to know, is it or isn't it caused by climate change? Because scientists are unwilling to answer this question directly, misunderstandings arise. But there does seem to be an understanding of the confluence of events that are influenced by climate change.

In the case of Superstorm Sandy, there was a double whammy: the tropical storm from the south collided with a cold front from the north and produced a "hybrid" storm, combining intensities from both sides. Some speculated that the cold front from the north had been strengthened by a shift in the jet stream due to warmer Arctic temperatures. The Arctic Sea reached a record low in summer ice in September 2012 and could have provided a reservoir for heat that later impacted the jet stream. "Although this point may seem straightforward, it is routinely spun and misinterpreted. My colleagues and I try to make concise statements such as "Science has not established a link between hybrid events and climate change." But often, such statements are spun by climate skeptics into "Science has established that there is no link between Sandy and climate change."[130]

It would be unfortunate if the denial ideologues take advantage of this mode of thinking. The greatest danger is that skepticism about the origins of a storm turns into denial of climate change. A common argument among denial ideologues is that "climate science is uncertain" and therefore that we need not worry. All science has some uncertainty but climate science is one of the most definitive fields of science today. That does not protect it from being attacked by denial ideologues, however. For example, U.S. Rep. Lamar Smith (R-TX), chairman of the House's Science, Space and Technology Committee, said, "Contrary to the claims of those who want to strictly regulate carbon dioxide emissions and increase the cost of energy for all Americans, there is a great amount of uncertainty associated with climate science."[131]

"Uncertainty" has been exploited by denial ideologues to try to refute climate science. "The communication effort held by the "deniers" is precisely to make it appear that the "scientific uncertainty" constitutes doubt, thus creating or extending a sense of skepticism about the science of global warming. Consequently, the "uncertainty" surrounding global warming science is used against science itself." [132] Uncertainty is an excused to avoid some of the implications of climate science: "It's always easy to find some aspect of the science that is uncertain, or confusing, and focus on that to the exclusion of the larger picture."[133] As an ideologue, the denial advocate does not worry about probabilities and qualifications. Such advocates can state their positions flatly, without reservation, while accusing climate scientists of vagueness because of caveats in the findings.

Unfortunately, uncertainty is a factor in the media treatment of climate science. One author put it succinctly: "There's been plenty of noise in the popular press emphasizing the uncertainty in the climate science, but that's virtually all fossil-fuel-industry-funded nonsense."[134]

Uncertainty is not an excuse for the U.S. military when it comes to climate change. "**While scientists are converging toward consensus on future climate projections, uncertainty remains. But this cannot be an excuse for delaying action. Every day, our military deals with global uncertainty. Our planners know that, as military strategist Carl von Clausewitz wrote, "all action must, to a certain extent, be planned in a mere twilight."** The U.S. military, like insurance companies, must assess risk and prepare for high-risk events, and indeed that is what they have done with *The 2014 Climate Change Adaptation Roadmap,* an annual publication from which the above quote was taken. They have made this preparation explicit: "A changing climate will have real impacts on our military and the way it executes its missions. The military could be called upon more often to support civil authorities, and provide humanitarian assistance and disaster relief in the face of more frequent and more intense natural disasters."

Denial ideology not only precludes understanding of the causes of extreme weather. It also hinders the adaptation of society to the effects: "Unfortunately, adaptation policy also faces some specific problems when it is undermined or even precluded by ideologically driven austerity or anti-science policy makers."[135]

In the following chapters, I review some of the more egregious attacks as illustrations of how far denial ideology is willing to go.

Tornadoes and Climate Change

Late in the afternoon on May 22, 2011, an EF-5 tornado (winds up to 200 miles per hour) struck Joplin, Missouri. It reached a maximum width of one mile through the city. The tornado killed 158 people, injured 1150 others and became the costliest single tornado in U.S. history. The insurance payout was over $2 billion.

On the afternoon of April 20, 2013, another EF-5 tornado struck Moore, Oklahoma with winds estimated at 210 miles per hour. It killed 24 people and injured 377 others. It had a 1.3-mile wide path that crossed through a heavily populated section of Moore and tracked 7 miles long. Estimated costs of repair were $3 billion; the insurance payout was over $2 billion.

Some of the same problems of identifying hurricanes and typhoons with climate change apply to tornadoes. Since tornadoes occur over land rather than the ocean, the dynamics of ocean heat and sea-level rise do not transfer to tornado dynamics. Further, there are multiple causes of tornadoes, including the position of the jet stream and the movement of weather fronts, just as there are multiple causes of hurricanes. Some of these causes may be related to climate change.

Scientists have been looking at the problem. Some scientists have identified trends that may point to climate change effects on tornadoes. A September 2013 study from Stanford University, "Robust increases in severe thunderstorm environments in response to greenhouse forcing," points to "a possible increase in the number of days supportive of tornadic storms."[136] Again, this is not definitive identification of tornadoes with climate change, but an indication of a trend. Kenneth Trenberth, climatologist with the National Center for Atmospheric Research in Boulder CO, has described the relationship as follows:

> The main climate change connection is via the basic instability of the low level air that creates

the convection and thunderstorms in the first place. Warmer and moister conditions are the key for unstable air. The climate change effect is probably only a 5 to 10% effect in terms of the instability and subsequent rainfall, but it translates into up to a 32% effect in terms of damage. (It is highly nonlinear). So there is a chain of events and climate change mainly affects the first link: the basic buoyancy of the air is increased. Whether that translates into a super-cell storm and one with a tornado is largely chance weather.[137]

Extreme weather is not always traceable to climate change, but when climate change increases the chances by 32%, it plays an important role. As with hurricanes and other forms of extreme weather, the links are probabilistic.

A good explanation of this relationship was made by Bill Nye, the Science Guy: "you can't say from any one storm that 'this is the result of, let's say, climate change,' but if there's more heat driving the storm, then there's going to be more tornadoes."[138]

Research continues to examine the link between tornadoes and climate change. The *National Climate Assessment (NCA)* describes some of this research: "Recent research has yielded insights into the connections between global warming and the factors that cause tornadoes and severe thunderstorms (such as atmospheric instability and increases in wind speed with altitude). Although these relationships are still being explored, a recent study suggests a projected increase in the frequency of conditions favorable for severe thunderstorms."[139]

While these statements from the NCA are cautious and founded on scientific research, some politicians have reacted negatively to the very idea that the research would be publicized.

Rep. Ed Whitfield, R-1st District [Kentucky], and two of his colleagues on the House Energy and

Commerce Committee issued a joint statement denouncing the report as "short on details" and part of "an agenda against affordable and reliable energy." The American Coalition for Clean Coal Electricity, an industry group headed by former Republican National Committee Chairman Mike Duncan of Inez, Ky., blistered the White House for "unsubstantiated scare tactics and hyperbole."[140]

Representative Lamar Smith of Texas (R-TX) dismissed the report's analysis of extreme weather as follows: "This is a political document, intended to frighten Americans into believing that any abnormal weather we experience is the direct result of human CO2 emissions."[141]

These reactions seem to be a case of blaming the messenger. To call a report like this "an agenda against affordable and reliable energy" suggests that causes of climate change are not human use of energy but something else unrelated to energy. Unfortunately for Rep. Whitfield, laws of physics do not yield to laws of Congress. To further characterize the report as "unsubstantiated scare tactics and hyperbole" denies clearly identifiable consequences of climate change that already have caused problems. To call it a "political document" is to do a disservice to the scientists who worked on it.

Other politicians simply waffle on the question of causation: "I believe the climate is changing, but I disagree to the extend that's been in the news that man is changing [it]."[142] One used the term "necessarily" to qualify a weak answer in a senatorial debate: "I don't necessarily think the climate's changing, no."[143] One politician who cites his science credentials, Representative Dr. Dan Benishek (R-MI), denies climate science while claiming he knows "peer-reviewed" science: "Well, I am a scientist. You know, I believe in peer-reviewed science. But, I don't see any peer-reviewed science that proves there is man-made catastrophic climate change." Apparently he has not been reading reports of the IPCC, the National Climate Assessment

(NCA), NOAA or WMO research. What science is he reading? Perhaps Heartland "science."[144]

James Taylor, senior fellow with the Heartland Institute, used the occasion of the release of the NCA report to refute any connection between climate change and extreme weather: "The report falsely asserts that global warming is causing more extreme weather events, more droughts, more record high temperatures, more wildfires, warmer winters, etc., when each and every one of these false assertions is contradicted by objective, verifiable evidence."[145] He did not provide this evidence, although the Heartland Institute does hold conferences each year to promote their "evidence" against climate science.

Along with tornadoes, extreme weather sometimes includes severe flooding in some areas. When a major storm flooded the Florida panhandle in April and May 2014, widespread damage was reported and part of the state was declared a disaster area. Senator Mark Rubio (R-FL), a presidential candidate, was quick to adopt the line of denial ideology: "I do not believe that human activity is causing these dramatic changes to our climate the way these scientists are portraying it. And I do not believe that the laws that they propose we pass will do anything about it, except it will destroy our economy."[146] Senator Rubio may not want laws to control emissions, but he will be unable to do anything about the laws of nature that control weather.

Later Rubio backtracked and excused himself by saying "I'm not a scientist." This excuse was cited by President Barack Obama as the reason that many politicians try to avoid taking positions on climate change: "They say, 'Hey, look, I'm not a scientist.' And I'll translate that for you: what that really means is, 'I know that manmade climate change really is happening but if I admit it, I'll be run out of town by a radical fringe that thinks climate science is a liberal plot.'"[147] They have to practice hypocrisy to separate their public and private views on climate science, an expedient strategy that impedes government action on climate change.

Typhoon Haiyan

On November 8, 2013, Typhoon Haiyan struck Leyte Island in the Philippines. The principal city, Tacloban, was almost wiped off the map. Winds of 150 miles per hour toppled most the buildings in the city that were built wood and thatch. The few substantial homes were flooded to the second floor by the storm surge, estimated at more than 12 feet. More than 6000 people were killed, mostly by the storm surge. More than 4 million people were displaced. Damage to buildings and infrastructure amounted to more than $13 billion.

Ironically, one of the largest geothermal plants in the world, near Ormoc on Leyte Island, was heavily damaged. This plant had provided all the electricity for Leyte and several nearby islands. With no greenhouse gas emissions, Leyte Island was contributing to the control of worldwide greenhouse gas emissions just as it suffered from the typhoon.

Climate scientists do not attribute Haiyan directly to climate change, but the cumulative effect of warming and sea level rise can strengthen the storms and increase the height of storm surges. Many observers of Typhoon Haiyan, while aware of other possible causes, did consider its enhanced strength a result of climate change. The Philippine delegate to the 2013 meeting of the UN Framework Convention on Climate Change, Naderev Sano, made an impassioned speech about the typhoon's impact on his country and started a fast. He vowed to continue fasting during the meeting until the UNFCCC agreed on solutions.

What is the scientific view of storms such as Haiyan? "Typhoon Haiyan in 2013 was likely so huge and powerful because of the roughly 1 degree C global temperature rise since industrialization made the western Pacific warmer, and warmer oceans make storms more intense."[148] Scientists largely agree that it appears that storms will become more powerful as the climate changes. Dr. Kerry Emanuel, an atmospheric scientist at M.I.T., helped write a 2010 study that forecast that the average intensity of hurricanes and typhoons — different names for the same phenomenon — would increase by up to 11 percent by the end of the century. Typhoon Haiyan, with winds of at least 150 miles an hour, was one of the strongest storms to make landfall on record. "The data suggests that things like this will be more frequent with global warming," said James P. Kossin, an atmospheric scientist at the National Climate Data Center.[149]

Beyond the controversy about causes, there is a consensus on the effect of global warming on extreme weather. "While warming's effect on tropical storms is hotly debated, a general consensus is emerging: Whether or not it increases their frequency, it very likely increases their strength. Cyclones and hurricanes are fueled by ocean temperatures; more heat means more destructive winds."[150] These storms will affect many areas besides the Philippines. In China, a state agency estimated the cost of climate change: "Climate change fuelled storm waves and rising sea levels that cost China 16.3 billion yuan ($2.6 billion) and killed 121 people in 2013, the State Oceanic Administration (SOA) said."[151]

Whether storms are more frequent, or stronger – they will be more destructive. Of course, costs of storms are dependent on many factors, including the tendency of people to build more homes close to shorelines. This tendency is found in both wealthy communities such as New Jersey and New York beach areas, and in poor communities such as Tacloban. Neither wealth nor poverty is protection against effects of climate change.

Chapter 3:
Issues Raised by Extreme Weather

Descriptions of extreme weather raise issues about how climate affects society. Particular concerns about how society will function, with poverty and economic development a major focus, have become intertwined with climate change and extreme weather.

Poverty and Climate Change

Commentators have tried to distinguish efforts to address climate change from efforts to address poverty.[152] Sometimes these efforts reach absurd lengths, and denial ideologues will blame climate actions for exacerbating poverty. "Because slashing carbon emissions limits use of the most readily accessible and inexpensive energy sources, it hampers the ability of developing nations and the poor in general to climb out of poverty."[153]

Even if they agree that climate change needs addressing, some commentators will assert that poverty and disease need to be given priority.[154] "There are causes to which the climate marchers could devote themselves that would have an immediate positive effect on human welfare: from promoting clean water in the Third World to agitating for cures to all manner of diseases.

None of this, though, is as alluring as anti-industrial apocalypticism."[155] Once again, we see the false dichotomy of human welfare versus "anti-industrial apocalypticism," aka climate activism. None of the climate activists that I know are against clean water or finding cures for diseases.

Denial ideologues use pseudo-economics as well as pseudo-science to blame climate policies for poverty.

> In developed countries, the poor spend a higher percentage of their income on energy than others, so rising energy prices, driven by mandated shifts from abundant, affordable, reliable fossil fuels to diffuse, expensive, intermittent "Green" energy, will in effect be regressive taxes – taxing the poor at higher rates than the rich. To demand that people in developing countries forgo the use of inexpensive fossil fuels and depend on expensive wind, solar, and other "Green" fuels to meet that need is to condemn them to more generations of poverty and the high rates of disease and premature death that accompany it.[156]

There are many "leaps of faith" among the evangelists who produced this declaration. First, they equate "green energy" with taxes, a tactic used by many ideologues who change, for example, "cap and trade" to "cap and tax." It is misleading to state that there is a negative relationship between development and installation of green energy; indeed, many proprietors of green energy installations make them supportive of economic growth. Second, the argument that people will forgo use of fossil fuels is a red herring. Certainly there will be efforts to reduce use of fossil fuels worldwide, but many diplomats and policymakers are careful to exempt some less developed countries. Lastly, the statement that use of green energy will "condemn them to more generations of poverty and the high rates of disease and premature death that accompany it" reverses logic. Use of green energy is likely to prevent more generations of poverty and the high rates of disease and premature death that accompany it, not increase these problems. Climate change is the likely cause of more generations of poverty and the high rates of disease and premature death that accompany it. Pollution from fossil fuel use is likely to increase disease and premature death.

Class Warfare

Just when it seems that climate scientists are somehow attacking the poor, they are also accused of attacking the rich: "In a sense, manmade global warming is simply the latest version of class warfare."[157] This is because climate policies might suggest restraints on the wealth of rich people or that climate solutions somehow mean opposition to industrial development.

It is much more likely that denial ideologues are using poverty as an excuse to oppose climate policies. Naomi Klein offers a cynical view of how denial ideologues view poverty: "this is where the intersection between extreme ideology and climate denial gets truly dangerous. It's not simply that these 'cool dudes' deny climate science because it threatens to upend their dominance-based worldview. It is that their dominance-based worldview provides them with the intellectual tools to write off huge swaths of humanity, and indeed, to rationalize profiting from the meltdown."[158] While no denial ideologue would confess to writing off "huge swaths of humanity," many do confess to believing that the free market solves problems such as climate change (while also keeping them or their sponsors wealthy).

Speaking of class warfare, Republicans in the U.S. House of representatives tried to stop the EPA from reducing emissions from coal-fired power plants, a major source of pollution in areas of poverty. They voted, 229 to 183, to weaken EPA regulations. At this stage, that is unrealistic. Nevertheless, it led to some interesting denial arguments. One congressman said that the EPA would harm workers on behalf of rich residents of Beverly Hills:

This [existing EPA] regulation will cause the greatest amount of harm, lost jobs, diminished incomes, and higher electricity bills in areas where incomes are modest, as are the lifestyles of those who live there. It isn't the rich on Fifth Avenue or in Beverly Hills who will be impacted; it is the American working class.[159]

A similar argument has been made by the U.S. Chamber of Commerce, which claims that new EPA regulations on coal-fired power plants would have the following effects on the economy:

EPA's potential new carbon regulations would:

-Lower U.S. Gross Domestic Product (GDP) by $51 billion on average every year through 2030
-Lead to 224,000 fewer U.S. jobs on average every year through 2030
-Force U.S. consumers to pay $289 billion more for electricity through 2030
-Lower total disposable income for U.S. households by $586 billion through 2030[160]

While this sounds impressive on the surface, the costs are actually quite small in terms of the overall economy. "So what the Chamber of Commerce is actually saying is that we can take dramatic steps on climate – steps that would transform international negotiations, setting the stage for global action – while reducing our incomes by only one-fifth of 1 percent."[161] Some have estimated even lower costs – analysts at Goldman Sachs said the direct economic effects of compliance "do not appear to be large," estimating a GDP decline of 0.1 percent or less.[162] In fact, there may be net gains from climate policies. "For all the fears that climate change mitigation would put the brakes on growth, it might actually enhance it."[163] A carbon tax, for example, would reduce China's emissions while stimulating growth in non-polluting sectors if it were coupled with reduction of other taxes. British Columbia, a province in Canada, has instituted a carbon tax of 30 Canadian dollars per ton of CO2 and maintained its rate of growth at the same level of other provinces.[164]

Studies indicate that there may be growth benefits from spending on investments to mitigate climate change: "the first-ever limits on carbon pollution from power plants can save American households and business customers $37.4 billion on their electric bills in 2020 while creating more than 274,000 jobs. ... The federal carbon pollution standard could fuel a surge in energy efficiency investments, creating new jobs filled by electricians, roofers, carpenters, insulation workers, heating/air conditioning installers and heavy equipment operators, among others."[165]

Nevertheless, what Republican congressmen, the Chamber and other groups try to do is impress people with one kind of costs – the expenses for changing energy systems – without mentioning other kinds of costs such as droughts and extreme weather. They also conveniently overlook the benefits of switching to clean energy.

What these groups try to suggest is that costs of climate change are felt only by those who pay extra for energy. That is an effective strategy only as long as one side of the equation of climate costs is recognized. The denial equation has only one measurement, energy price, without including externalized costs. It further distorts cost calculations by ignoring the costs made by those who take advantage of "free" emissions that are not subject to market constraints. "Everyone involved, directly or indirectly, in promoting or engaging in energy-intensive lifestyles is inextricably drawn into playing down or avoiding discussion of the significance of the evidence of their contribution to climate change."[166]

Under current pricing systems, the true cost of energy is concealed by prices that do not include knock-on effects. Those who want to maintain current lifestyles will argue strenuously against true-cost pricing, such as carbon taxes, because they do not want to admit their role in exacerbating effects of climate change. This often leads to an embrace of climate change denial.

Most fossil-fuel companies have finally acknowledged the facts about climate change, but there are holdouts. The owner of Murray Energy Corporation, Robert E. Murray, sued the EPA over its "endangerment" finding that justifies control of carbon emissions. He justified his action by claiming that the globe is cooling.

> EPA's claims that climate change exists violate the federal Data Quality Act, which requires agencies to rely on quality, objective information to inform its decisions. Under the act, they are obligated to tell the truth, and they are not telling the truth about global warming. They are not telling hardly any truth about the science. The earth has actually cooled over the last 17 years, so under the Data Quality Act, they've actually been lying about so-called global warming.[167]

As we have seen, the globe is not cooling but the canard is repeated without verification throughout denial ideology. Basing a lawsuit on such false information is risky. Courts could dismiss the suit as groundless.

Distinctions between climate change and economic development do not hold up when the reality of storms like Typhoon Haiyan strike poverty-stricken areas like Tacloban. Poverty exacerbated the damage because homes were flimsy and even the evacuation centers such as churches did not offer much protection.

Climate change and poverty are related in other events, such as severe hurricanes in Central America. "In 1998 Hurricane Mitch struck Honduras, killing at least 6,500 people and causing $ 2-4 billion in damage, an amount equivalent to 15-30% of gross domestic product (GDP). At the height of the emergency, donors pledged $72 million to the World Food Program for immediate humanitarian assistance. More than a year later, less than one-third of the promised funds had been delivered."[168] While some may insist that poverty has higher priority than mitigating climate change, when it comes to applying this priority to policy there is little follow-through. It would be more effective if those who want to assist, through humanitarian assistance, implemented policies that reduce the effect of extreme weather on poverty-stricken populations.

Discussion of responses to climate events raises the issue of adaptation. While most observers have noted adaptation is inevitable at this state of climate change, not all agree on its implications for climate policy. Certainly with the publication of the Stern Review [169] and other economic analyses of climate change, the costs of adaptation have been projected as rising sharply with delays in mitigation. What is more germane to the present discussion of poverty and climate change is the hypocrisy of denying climate science while promoting reduction of poverty. Adaptation will become unavoidable as extreme weather and other effects of climate change impacts exacerbate poverty and require increasing resources to manage disasters.

Treating poverty and climate disruption as polar opposites, where addressing one means neglecting the other, is a false dichotomy. In fact, they are two sides of the same coin: "Poverty reduction and climate change are linked," said Dr. Jim Yong Kim, the president of the World Bank, in a commentary this year. "We have powerful new evidence that even if climate change falls short of the much-discussed 4°C warmer world, we could witness the rolling back of decades of development gains and force tens of millions more to live in poverty." [170] Development experts understand that development versus emissions reductions is a false dichotomy.

Denial ideologues embrace this false dichotomy to argue against carbon emission reductions. One author states:

> What global warming hysterics want to fight is merely carbon dioxide. That's what plants breathe. CO2 may prove to be a problem, but we don't know that now. The world has *real* problems, though: malaria, malnutrition, and desperate poverty. Our

own country, although relatively rich, is deep in debt. Obsessing about greenhouse gases makes it harder to address these more serious problems.[171]

When someone talks about "obsessing about greenhouse gases" instead of addressing "real problems" he suggests that climate change is not a serious problem. Others such as poverty presumably are "more serious," and this suggests that climate change should be relegated to a lower priority. Some even go so far as to equate climate activists' alleged neglect of poverty with racism: "*I now believe global warming alarmists are unpatriotic racists knowingly misleading for their own ends.*"[172] Associating climate science with racism or lack of patriotism is a sweeping indictment with no basis in fact. It is an ideological assertion contrary to the facts.

When it comes to priorities, the U.S. Defense Department has some strong views. Reviewing the role of climate change as a "threat multiplier," the Quadrennial Defense Review of 2014 states: "*These effects are threat multipliers that will aggravate stressors abroad such as poverty, environmental degradation, political instability, and social tensions – conditions that can enable terrorist activity and other forms of violence.*" (emphasis in original) In other words, neglecting climate change will not alleviate poverty and other threat multipliers, but aggravate them.

Regardless of what the Defense Department says about it, some denial advocates do not want the department to address climate science. The U.S. House of Representatives passed a bill "banning the Defense Department from participating in climate change research. It was sponsored by West Virginia Republican Rep. David McKinley, who questioned the validity of climate science research generally but also argued that reducing the use of coal wasn't worth the harm it would do to the economy."[173] McKinley's statement reflects the interest of coal state representatives. Later in this chapter we will see how coal is becoming a "stranded asset" as power companies veer away from coal-powered electric generation.

The Defense Department conclusions are backed by findings reported by the IPCC: "**Climate-related hazards exacerbate other stressors, often with negative outcomes for livelihoods, especially for people living in poverty (*high confidence*).** Climate-related hazards affect poor people's lives directly through impacts on livelihoods, reductions in crop yields, or destruction of homes and indirectly through, for example, increased food prices and food insecurity."[174] In its report, the IPCC states that the problems of poverty and climate are mutually reinforcing, not contradictory.

Stranded Assets

Ironically, the denial ideologues who contend that climate action would harm the poor are the same ones who raise the specter of economic decline. Underlying their concerns is a fear of redistribution of wealth. Their fortunes have been accrued through economic activity that exploits cheap energy and ignores the true cost of fossil fuels and they are threatened by any policies that would raise the price of energy. Further, restrictions on extraction of fossil fuels would leave "stranded assets," reserves of oil and coal that could not be developed because their combustion would create conditions for runaway climate change. [175] These stranded assets have important economic implications: "…economic concerns about fossil fuels have raised the issue of value. There is a wonderfully evocative term, 'stranded assets,' to characterize the oil, coal and gas reserves that are still in the ground. Trillions of dollars in assets could remain 'stranded' there."[176] The first fear is that assets would become much less valuable under effective climate policies. "Powerful extractor nations and companies own oil, coal and gas reserves, many of which would need to be written-off or devalued if an ambitious global deal was struck. Industries, governments and households own plants, vehicles, boilers and other devices that need fossil fuels to function." The second fear is that losing access to cheap energy would reduce standards of living. "Ordinary consumers maintain or aspire to lifestyles that entail large carbon footprints, whether that means flying regularly or enjoying low-cost goods and services that take energy to provide.

All of this – and the stability of the whole global economy – may be at risk if world leaders decide collectively to phase out fossil fuels at the rate required."[177] Standards of living are threatened by restrictions on use of energy, leading some to consider the possibility of rationing.[178] This fear may be exaggerated, but it does affect discussions of climate policy and feeds denial ideology with justifications for stopping action.

Arguments that climate action will mean declining standards of living confuse two aspects of environmental action: Preservation and restoration. Preservation uses a model of stopping change to keep the environment static, to preserve its present condition. Restoration uses a model of restoring the environment to a sound state, while acknowledging that it cannot be perpetually kept in the same state forever. These two different approaches have significant effects on standards of living. "Restoring nature involves the active use of science and technology and thus, unlike preservationism's primitivist model, the restoration paradigm does not require repudiating these key achievements of civilization."[179]

When they accuse climate science of taking us back to primitive life styles, denial ideologues use the preservationist model. Most climate activists, however, are more oriented to the restorationist model, and few would advocate a "hunter-gatherer" lifestyle. This creates a mismatch between the arguments of denial ideologues about the negative impacts of climate action and the actual proposals of climate scientists for reducing carbon emissions.

There are hazards in the restorationist model, however. If we think of restoration as the only, or major, means of addressing climate change there will be overreaction. "Part of what is objectionable is the suggestion that nature as a whole has become dependent on our restoration activities, rather than particular elements and forms of nature being so dependent."[180] For example, in climate change geoengineering[181] would be an overreaction while energy conservation would be a tailored reaction. Climate science requires us to focus on the elements, such as energy, that are the principal causes of climate change. With effective action, some of those elements such as fossil fuels will become stranded assets.

With regard to stranded assets, some have estimated that reserves of fossil fuels including coal, oil and gas are five times the amount that could be safely burned if temperature increases are to be kept within 2 degrees Centigrade.[182] If corporations were restricted to selling only 20% of reserves that they have, energy use would have to be reduced to the point that lifestyles as well as balance sheets might suffer. This raises the specter of recession, another fear exploited by denial ideology.

Regardless of the compelling evidence that fossil fuel companies have more than enough reserves, they continue to explore. "The 2012 exploration and development expenditures of 200 fossil fuel companies listed on stock exchanges worldwide are estimated at $674 billion. (This compares to renewable energy investments of $244 billion the same year.)"[183] Not only are fossil fuel companies squandering $674 billion a year to find new reserves that cannot be developed, they are listing as assets existing reserves that cannot be burned. Those assets will have to be written off, drastically reducing the value of the companies and their stock. About 60% of the asset value of oil companies, for example, would be lost if they could use only one-fifth of their reserves.

One of those potentially stranded assets, coal, is a major source of contention in American politics. Many denial ideologues accuse the Obama administration of a "war on coal." The Senate majority leader, Mitch McConnell, used an interview with the *Cincinnati Enquirer* to voice his version of denial: "While lamenting how the Environmental Protection Agency has threatened the coal industry, McConnell on Friday said he doesn't believe in man-made climate change. "For everybody who thinks it's warming, I can find somebody who thinks it isn't." [184] McConnell uses the alleged disagreement among scientists to justify his denial of climate change. Fed by a few contrarian scientists and many denial ideologues, this "climate of doubt" gives cover to politicians who want to roll back any effective climate policies. It is based on misinformation that is useful to politicians.

McConnell raised another issue that is repeated throughout denial ideology: jobs, jobs, jobs. "President Obama's war on coal won't have any meaningful impact on global carbon emissions. What it will do is ship American jobs overseas, raise the cost of living substantially for middle and working-class families and throw thousands more Kentuckians out of work."[185] It is dubious to claim that the so-called war on coal won't have any meaningful impact on global carbon emissions, as it will reduce American contributions to those emissions by a considerable amount if coal fired power plants are closed. It could also reduce the opposition of other countries to reaching a worldwide agreement that includes developing nations like China. It is also dubious for McConnell to assert that jobs will be shipped overseas if the coal jobs (shrinking in any case) are replaced by jobs installing renewable energy facilities or improving building efficiencies. Those jobs cannot go overseas.

One interesting analogy about developing and using fossil fuel reserves is offered by Jared Diamond in his book, *Collapse,* about societies that exceeded the carrying capacity of their environment. He asked in the book, what was the Easter Islander who cut down the last tree thinking of? The answer may have been "Jobs, not trees!" If fossil fuel companies are going to develop and use the last barrel of oil or ton of coal, we might ask if they are thinking, "Jobs, not climate!"

You can look at fossil fuel reserves in two different ways: as assets or problems. Using an economic paradigm, they are assets, but using an ecologic paradigm, they are problems. Referring to the Alberta tar sands, Avery says, "They cannot exist simultaneously. Either the forest and the habitat become overburden and tar or they stay forest and habitat. Either the *economic* paradigm prevails, or we shift to the *ecologic* paradigm. There is precious little ground in between: the earth is not both alive and dead at the same time."[186]

An interesting argument used by skeptics is that even with regulations on coal, there will be little effect on the climate. "In fact, the costly anticarbon regulations that the Environmental Protection Agency is developing will by the EPA's estimate address a mere 0.18% of world-wide carbon emissions."[187] While this is technically true of the initial drafts of the regulations, they are a basis for scaling up when the government decides to address climate change more aggressively. At present, that is not politically feasible, given opposition by denial ideologues. Fossil fuel interests are likely to resist any policies that threaten their assets. For coal, oil and gas companies, effective climate policies are an existential threat. Their stock prices, and indeed their continued viability, depend on maintaining "reserves" at a ratio as high as their production levels. These "reserves" are assets will must be developed for them to survive.[188]

Is it any wonder that leaders are reluctant to come to an agreement that would effectively address climate change? Denial ideology gives them license to avoid unpleasant and unpopular decisions. They prefer to believe that energy use is an unmitigated good: "...it has been the many inventions that utilize the energy sources the Greens want to 'leave in the ground' that have totally transformed the lives of Americans and others throughout the world."[189] Mother nature is not so cooperative, however. As effects of climate change, particularly extreme weather, become more frequent and unavoidable, a different calculus may become necessary. Energy use is necessary, of course, but the source of energy is the problem that must be addressed. Fossil fuels are not the only source of energy, and substitution of other sources may leave them stranded.

The issue of stranded assets is one that must worry investors in fossil fuel companies. "Investors, even those unmotivated by stewardship of the planet, have reason to be suspicious of the fossil fuel companies. Right now, they are seeing their investment dollars diverted from paying dividends to doing something downright insane: searching for new reserves." As one looks at the energy industry, one wonders why so much is invested in what will become stranded assets. "Globally, the industry spends $1.8 billion a day on exploration. As one longtime energy industry insider pointed out to me, fossil fuel companies are spending much more on exploring for new reserves than they are posting in profits. Think about that for a second: to stay below a 2 degree Celsius rise, we can burn only one-fifth of the total fossil fuel that companies have in their reserves right now. And yet, fossil fuel companies are spending hundreds of billions of dollars looking for new reserves.[190]

Are investors making this calculation? At the time of this writing, only a few institutions, including eighteen foundations, twenty-seven religious institutions, twenty-two cities, and twenty colleges and universities, have divested from fossil fuel company stocks. [191] Universities, in particular, have been the locus of divestment campaigns by groups such as 350.org. There are more than 4000 colleges and universities in the U.S. Even if colleges and universities were all to divest, fossil fuel companies would have plenty of capital to thrive. In addition, about twenty-five North American cities committed to divesting fossil fuel stocks, as well as forty religious institutions. The divestment movement would have more success when mutual funds, hedge funds and Wall Street investors start to see the futility of investing in fossil fuels with unusable reserves. This will come only from concerted action to limit the emissions of fossil fuels to 565 gigatons of CO2 emissions (out of 2795 gigatons from proven reserves). Indeed, divestment should extend to stopping the high rate of investment in finding new reserves.

A radical view of the relationship between wealth and poverty is the concept that rich nations are imposing costs on poor nations out of a flawed model of energy use in capitalism. Ricoveri expresses this most clearly:

> Global warming and climate change are the most relevant problems of our time, as life on earth is possible only if the temperature remains around the average value that has been kept through centuries, 15 degrees centigrade. Global warming has many causes – mainly greenhouse gas emissions, caused by

the generalized use of fossil fuels and by deforestation – and many once a common good that everybody could enjoy has now been taken over by the oil, coal, mineral, energy, steel and cement companies, as well as by car traffic, all of which use the atmosphere as a 'private' space to get rid of their polluting waste, emitting into the atmosphere climate-altering gases that exceed the absorption capacity of the ecosystems.[192]

Ricoveri is expanding on the concept of "enclosing" common areas, generalized to the atmosphere. As a "common good," the atmosphere has been illicitly appropriated by oil, coal, mineral, energy, steel and cement companies that use the atmosphere as a "private" space when emitting greenhouse gases. He then applies this analysis to show how it deprives poor people of clean air: "The accumulation of carbon dioxide in the atmosphere deriving from the use of fossil fuels has deprived humans and animals of their share of clean, non-polluted air, producing global climatic changes of which the poor are the first, innocent victims. It is in fact the poorest, who have contributed the least to the degradation of the atmosphere and the destruction of the capacity of the planet to absorb carbon dioxide, who are paying the most for this new enclosure."[193]

This, then, is the most forthright argument against the false dichotomy of climate science versus poverty. While based on a radical view of capitalism, it does identify the principal issue in addressing both climate change and poverty: the deleterious effect of the effects of climate on poor nations and peoples. It further identifies this as a "North-South" issue: "Global warming is a double injustice for the South because its principal cause lies in the emissions that have been accumulated by the industrialised North in the past. But the main victims are the most vulnerable populations in the South, who are more affected by rising sea levels, the melting of glaciers, changes in rainfalls, floods, droughts, hurricanes and coastal storms, with direct repercussions on food production, water supply and the spread of diseases."[194]

Although this analysis is anti-capitalist, it is by no means pro-Marxist.[195] Ricoveri is in fact anti-Marxist and his analysis criticizes the Marxists as much as the capitalists for their similar Promethean views, i.e. "man over nature." Nevertheless, analyses such as this have been used by denial ideologues to accuse climate science (or, specifically, policies derived from climate science) of Marxism.

A columnist for the Pittsburgh Post-Gazette characterized the September, 2014 climate action march in New York as follows: "As more scientists say there is no crisis, alarmists must rely on the chronically ill-informed such as … the motley crew of Marxists in the "Peoples Climate March" in New York last Sunday to spread their increasingly hysterical message."[196] It is difficult to find "more scientists [who] say there is no crisis," but it is relatively easy to find denial ideologues that consider climate activists "Marxists."

Not all denial ideologues agree, however. Delinpole contends "Indeed, were Marx alive today, he would be fighting shoulder to shoulder with capitalists against eco-loons."[197] His term "eco-loons," of course, refers to climate scientists and environmentalists who would dare suggest that unbridled growth might affect climate with carbon emissions. We will see more discussion of Marxism and climate change in Chapter 4.

Growth as an economic/environmental issue has long plagued discussions of climate change.[198] (More on growth below.) Some commentators would like to blame environmentalism for impeding growth: "…environmentalism [is] a view that did not see the Earth and the fullness thereof – in the Biblical turn of phrase – as ours to develop for human benefit. Rather, it castigated people as a disease infecting the planet, best treated with the antibiotic of massive human depopulation and opposition to development and economic growth."[199] Here, the argument goes beyond suggesting that environmentalism impedes growth and suggests that environmentalists are "anti-human" and sacrilegious because they would dare to suggest that man does not always have dominion over nature.

When environmentalism is seen as "anti-human," any action by environmentalists to address climate change relies on a manufactured "crisis." "Sustaining robust anti-humanism requires a perennial crisis. Inspiring hatred of self requires a parade of horribles. We certainly have that when it comes to global warming alarmists. They offer up a never-ending parade of supposedly imminent catastrophes that will destroy us unless we immediately cap the greenhouse gas spigot. In other words, to keep from killing the planet, we have to cease and desist from most of the normal human activities and enterprises that have made modern life so rich and fulfilling."[200] These enterprises that *"have made modern life so rich and fulfilling"* may depend on free markets, free of constraints on carbon pollution because the air is *"free"* to use without regard to climate consequences.

Capitalism has had a long run of "free market" economics, backed by economists such as Hayek and Friedman, but the effects on climate change have not been positive. Planning and regulation became unpopular, but the cycle may be turning back as more and more economists and policy makers recognize the "market failure" of climate change.[201] Whether capitalism can continue in its present form or change direction is a major issue of climate change.[202] One example is the question of how fossil fuel assets can be managed in a diminishing market. That market will shrink drastically if the management of fossil fuels requires their rapid decline.

Graphically, the ratio of reserves to the amounts of fossil fuels that can be burned safely is depicted as follows:[203]

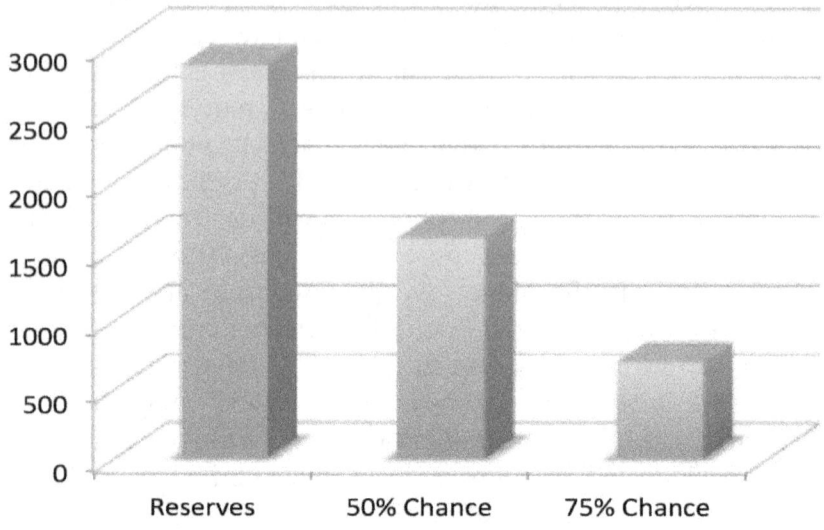

In this graph, the amounts are shown in gigatons (billions of tons) of carbon dioxide emitted by fossil fuels, including coal, oil and gas. The amount shown in the "reserves" bar, about 2800 gigatons, is the total proven reserves of these fossil fuels. The second bar is the amount, 1500 gigatons, that can be burned if we want to keep total emissions low enough to have a 50% chance of stabilizing warming at 2 degrees Centigrade, while the third bar shows the amount burned if we have a 75% chance of stabilizing warming at 2 degrees, just over 500 gigatons. We need to leave at least half the reserves in the ground for the 50% chance of stability and more than three-fourths for a 75% chance. Each of these would require immediate and drastic adjustments in energy use. Such adjustments would make the reserves of fossil fuels stranded assets, unusable resources counted as part of the possessions of fossil fuel companies. These assets would become valueless if their extraction and use were disallowed.

Another take on this issue of stranded assets was expressed by the leading economist of the International Energy Agency, who said that "about two-thirds of all proven reserves of oil, gas and coal will have to be left undeveloped if the world is to achieve the goal of limiting global warming at two degrees Celsius."[204] While he did not use a probability number, this would fall in between the probabilities of 50% and 75% mentioned above.

Case Study: Coal Trains

Management of stranded assets becomes a prominent issue in decisions about the supply of fossil fuels for energy production. In the United States, the demand for coal supplies has been waning as power plants have switched to natural gas. Mining companies such as Peabody have sought alternative markets overseas. Coal trains from the coalfields of the Powder River Basin are routed through the states of Wyoming, Montana, Idaho, Washington and Oregon, and the province of British Columbia, for export of the coal to Asia. At the time of this writing, only one port, Point Roberts in British Columbia, is in operation. Others have been proposed in Longview and Bellingham Washington. They would require up to 30 trains per day for supplies. Permits for building each terminal are pending. Permits for Longview and Bellingham are undergoing environmental review and will be subject to hearings on the drafts, and then will be subject to lawsuits if approved.

Environmental impacts of these coal trains are severe, not only along the tracks where coal dust is a major pollutant, but also in the waterways such as the Columbia and Puget Sound in Washington. The railroad, Burlington Northern Santa Fe, has been sued because of the effects on waterways.

Decisions about export of coal also involve environmental impacts on the atmosphere of Asian countries such as Japan, Korea, India and China. Coal-fired power plants in these countries, particularly China, have created major pollution crises. Pollutants such as mercury, nitrous oxides and carbon dioxide have crossed borders, drifting as far as the U.S. west coast. China is now the world's leading source of greenhouse gases, largely due to the use of coal-fired electricity generation.

How are such decisions to export coal made? In the case of coal trains, the U.S. Army Corps of Engineers controls the waterways such as the Columbia River and Puget Sound. The Corps can restrict its consideration of environmental impacts to the waterways, taking into account only possible spills or congestion of vessel traffic. When hearings about the scope of environmental impacts of coal trains were held in Washington State during 2012 and 2013, the Corps opted for restricting the scope to these waterway impacts. The Washington State Department of Ecology, on the other hand, called for a wider scope – including climate change impacts. How this will be resolved is still pending at this writing, because the environmental impact statement is still in draft. If the coal is shipped to Asia, impacts may include typhoons such as Haiyan. Increasing use of fossil fuels, particularly coal, may be linked to the conditions that create these increasingly severe storms.

Coal trains represent a real-life case of stranded assets. As opposition mounts – and over 100,000 people sent comments against approval of the terminals – the value of the coal diminishes. Prices per ton dropped from $142 per ton at the outset of the terminal review process in 2011 to $77 per ton in 2014. China has also indicated that it may reduce its demand for coal. Investors in the coal companies may be having second thoughts about the value of their investments if the asset is losing value. Goldman Sachs pulled out of one of the projects. Eventually, the coal in the ground may be worth nothing, particularly if China and India address their pollution problems by phasing out coal plants.

Activists in the Pacific Northwest are doing their best to make sure that the coal in the ground will be worth less. One observer, K.C. Golden of Climate Solutions, has observed, "The great Pacific Northwest is not a global coal depot, a pusher for fossil fuel addiction, a logistics hub for climate devastation. We're the last place on Earth that should settle for a tired old retread of the false choice between jobs and the environment. Coal export is fundamentally inconsistent with our vision and values. It's not just a slap in the face to 'green' groups. It's a moral disaster and an affront to our identity as a community."[205]

Environmental activists in the Pacific Northwest have a lot of clout and tend to be backed by local and state governments.

Why do we need to worry about coal trains, terminals or power plants? They are the infrastructure that continues to support high levels of carbon emissions, and they need to be retired or prohibited. "The more high-emissions infrastructure we build in the next few years, the more we'll have to scrap in the next few decades, so we need to stop as soon as we can. That means no more new coal plants [and] no new shipping terminals to move coal overseas." Stopping the terminals and plants is "politically difficult," as we will see shortly, but "once built it will be even harder to shut them down, so it's better that they never get built in the first place."[206]

Coal regulation by the Environmental Protection Agency has aroused political opposition.

Fifteen GOP governors say President Obama's signature climate change regulation on carbon pollution from existing power plants "exceeds the scope of federal law." In a letter to Obama, the governors from states including North Carolina, Alaska, Arizona and Wisconsin said the rule, which requires the nation's fleet of existing power plants to cut carbon emissions 30 percent by 2030, is an overreach of authority. The governors argue that the Environmental Protection Agency (EPA) cannot regulate a source under two different sections of the Clean Air Act; because the EPA already regulates existing power plants under another section of the law, it cannot do so again under section 111(d), the governors argue.[207]

There have been many attempts to limit EPA authority under the Clean Air Act,[208] and this is yet another one. While legal scholars and others argue that the Clean Air Act does indeed cover coal use, denial advocates will continue to attack EPA and try to roll back its legal authority.

Coal regulation does arouse opposition from some local officials, even in Washington, but they do not get very far. When protestors fought against coal ports in Washington State, one local official, Vancouver City Council Member Bill Turlay, said he was not convinced about climate change. "Turlay, who does not believe human behavior contributes to climate change, said instead of rushing to a moratorium he wants a public debate about whether carbon dioxide causes climate change. His comments prompted laughter and groans from the audience." [209] In Washington state, any suggestion that fossil fuels are unrelated to climate change tends to provoke derision.

Extreme Weather and Climate Change Denial

Climate scientists have been debating links between extreme weather and climate change, and there are different findings about some extreme weather events. Nevertheless, the general tendencies are evident.

> In other words, climate change has fundamentally altered the atmospheric environment in which all weather takes place, and has very likely increased the frequency and intensity of various types of extreme weather, including more intense flooding events, more extensive continental drought, more extreme heat and more intense storms. Just because an event hasn't been positively "attributed" to climate change in a formal "detection & attribution" study does not preclude speaking about the role climate change may have played, when the event is (a) consistent with expectations in a warming world, and (b) part of a larger trend. [210]

Scientists have examined the causes of extreme weather very carefully, and while cautious about individual events they have found that there are energy factors in the weather. Climate change disrupts normal energy flows; "This energy-flow disruption changes ocean, wind, rainfall and weather patterns –

causing increased frequency and intensity of hurricanes, tornados, droughts, floods and crop failures."[211]

While scientists are unwilling to state flatly that any one extreme weather event is linked to climate change, and consider it necessary to test any propositions about linking extreme weather and climate change, denial ideologues have no such qualms. Denial ideology tends to dismiss any connection between climate change and extreme weather. A meteorologist, Joseph Sobel of Accuweather, expressed it this way:

> It has been claimed that global warming is responsible for an increasing number of tropical storms and hurricanes, but here is a reason that the number of storms is increasing that has absolutely nothing to do with global warming…any increase in the number of hurricanes observed over the last 100 years is only the result of the fact that we have more ships at sea, more people living on coastlines, and satellites to see storms now that would have gone unrecorded 50 or 75 years ago.[212]

Another meteorologist, John Coleman, formerly weatherman of KUSI-TV of San Diego and co-founder of the Weather Channel, said, "Heat waves have actually diminished, not increased. There is not an uptick in the number or strength of storms (in fact storms are diminishing). I have studied this topic seriously for years. It has become a political and environment agenda item, but the science is not valid."[213]

These meteorologists are stating opinions that have no support in climate science. Scientists have found that, while hurricanes have not increased in number in recent years, they have increased in intensity. "When tracked from the 1970s until today (that is, during the period in which anthropogenic global warming has been most prevalent), there is a clear increase in the power of hurricanes. This trend is the result of both longer-lasting storms and more-intense storms. [214] While you may hear meteorologists discuss hurricanes in weather reports, you probably will not hear an explanation of why their intensity is increasing. They are sometimes more likely to deny that there is any link to climate change than to explain it.

Meteorologists often have problems dealing with climate change. Although they work as respected communicators on weather issues, they may not choose to, or want to, communicate climate science.[215] One reason meteorologists dislike climate science is the history of the emergence of climate science as a major discipline. In the 1950's, "Climate science was a new field, without an acknowledged place at the table or its own dedicated funding streams. It was emerging from meteorology, a traditionally low-status field, but it relied on computer modeling, a new, expensive, potentially high-status endeavor, but one that was not well understood outside the community."[216] Because climate science used some of the same methods but utilized computers more intensively, it seemed to take resources away from meteorology. "Climate science was the new kid on the block, often viewed as threatening established fields and disciplines by exorbitant resource demands that it justified in terms of its own importance."[217] As a result, meteorologists may have disdained its importance.

Worse, meteorologists may actively discourage consideration of climate science by dismissing it. "The frequently-mentioned extreme weather events cannot be attributed to global warming, because there has been no global warming for so long – simple as that."[218] This view combines the canard that there has been no warming with denial of a link to extreme weather.

Most scientists are cautious about making the link between climate change and specific weather events because the probabilities are complex. The clearest colloquial expression of this is "stacking the deck." "Weather is inherently chaotic and governed in part by randomness, like a hand of blackjack. But that doesn't mean that there's no connection between extreme weather and climate change. By warming up the planet with our carbon dioxide emissions, we're stacking the deck against ourselves. We're influencing the risk factors for these extreme weather events, and this will result in a trend of more extreme weather over time.[219]

James uses a similar metaphor in discussion of probabilities: we have changed the spots on the dice so that when we roll them, the chances for a double six are increased. We have put sixes on three faces of each die.

Critics assert that some of the extreme weather covered in Chapter 2 may be unrelated to climate change. At least one scientist dismisses any connection between climate change and hurricanes Sandy and Haiyan: "...the typhoon in the Philippines that dominated the UN climate change talks in Warsaw last November and that many people put down to climate change – it turned out it had no detectable evidence. And the same goes for Hurricane Sandy." [220] But other scientists question these arguments. [221] The difficulty of assigning responsibility for extreme weather plagues climate science.

Some commentators consider linking climate change and extreme weather as an indication that climate science is defective. "Their emphasis on 'extreme weather' is an especially tired piece of foolishness. Whatever the human impact on climate, the overwhelming reason storms are becoming more destructive is the simple fact that more people and property stand in their way." [222] Such a statement confuses the effects of weather, "storms are becoming more destructive," with the economic impacts. Storms can become more destructive regardless of whether "more people and property stand in their way." This statement seems to equate destruction with property loss. Destruction of uninhabited areas without property value to humans still means destruction of nature, such as habitat with ecological services, including wetlands, wilderness areas and forests.[223]

Ecological services are critical to sustenance of human survival, and their destruction will mean our destruction. "If we are in the situation where a quarter of the terrestrial species might be at risk of extinction from climate change – people often use the phrase 'being like canaries' – if we've changed our biological system to such an extent, then we do have to get worried about whether the services that are provided by natural ecosystems are going to continue. Ultimately, all of the crops we grow are biological species."[224]

An intense version of this view is offered by Avery: "Like every other form of life, we are an expression of the earth, and we build our economy within the living world. The economy is a wholly owned subsidiary of the ecology." [225] While acknowledging his point about building our economy within the living world, many denial ideologues would find it difficult to consider the economy a wholly owned subsidiary of the ecology. That would force them to see climate change in a way that threatens their worldview of growth.

Forests are particularly vulnerable to climate change, partly because of increasing vulnerability to fires, and in part because of the infestations of beetles (pine bark beetles, spruce bark beetles, etc.). While natural climate cycles have impacted trees before, the effects have never been so widespread as during the past few decades. John Muir, a pioneer environmentalist and founder of the Sierra Club, made an observation that would apply well to denial ideology: "Through all the wonderful, eventful centuries since Christ's time – and long before that – God has cared for these trees, saved them from drought, disease, avalanches, and a thousand straining, leveling tempests and floods; but he cannot save them from fools." [226] Some have referred to denial ideologues as "fossil fools," a term that would seem to fit Muir's definition well.

Denial of climate change links to extreme weather can take two forms, active and passive. "Those in what we might call active denial insisted that the extreme weather events reflected natural variability, despite a lack of evidence to support that claim. Those in passive denial continued life as they had been living it, unconvinced that a compelling justification existed for broad changes in industry and infrastructure."[227]

While active denial can be addressed by debunking the pseudoscientific claims that underlie it, passive denial is a more difficult proposition. Addressing climate change requires significant changes in energy production and use, and many people find it uncomfortable to deal with and grasp any straw to try to avoid action. When scientists admit to uncertainties in their findings about linking climate change and extreme weather, as they must, passive denial feeds off these uncertainties.

Passive denial also feeds on the desire of people to return to normality after a weather disaster. "People yearn for normality and safety, and no one wants to be reminded of a growing global threat. As they rebuild their lives, they invest their hopes along with their savings in the belief that the catastrophe was a rare natural aberration." [228] Even if they are victims of weather disasters, people want to put the experience behind them and start over with the illusion that "it can't happen again."

Many people will simply tune out climate change because it seems so overwhelming. "The reasonable man just wants to be left alone and is content to go with the flow, accepting that just as many species have gone extinct so will we, taking many others with us, as this is a law of nature. The unreasonable man points out that we know all that, we are dominant and in control, we know what is happening and could change direction in a global paradigm shift." [229] It will take many *unreasonable* people to overcome the inertia of "letting nature take its course," when nature is being thrown off course by human activities. Such unreasonable people tend to get on the nerves of *reasonable* people who do not want to hear the story of climate change once again.

When they think about the possible relationship between extreme weather and climate change, people can become discouraged if they do not see opportunities for solutions. "Where solutions are not readily apparent, people tend to focus on the obligations of their daily lives and avoid worrying about what may or may not happen in the distant future. Over time, this can feed a sense of political apathy and despair about the future, fostering a climate that ultimately helps advance the false populism of the ultra-right."[230] Some of this "false populism" involves denial ideology, which can exploit the political apathy and despair by offering an alternative narrative that avoids all of the vexing problems of climate change.

Denial ideologues can exploit "passive" forms of denial. The *Wall Street Journal* reported that although residents of California support that state's cap and trade policies, many of them do not know what it entails. Even though Californians have received rebates on their energy bills, they do not realize that prices of all goods are increased by business passing along the higher costs of energy. "In sum, public support in California for anti-carbon regulations rests on the delusion that there are no economic trade-offs. You might say that Californians suffer from climate-change denial."[231] Using a play on words, the *Wall Street Journal* suggests that Californians are denying climate change because they do not recognize the costs of dealing with it.

Something the writers of the *Wall Street Journal* might consider instead is "the big pivot," an idea that business can deal with the consequences of climate change by changing its orientation to sustainable growth. "To make this kind of pivot...we need radical innovations in resource efficiency (particularly energy and water) and in material science. We also need heretical innovation in how business operates...toward business models that help reduce consumption."[232] Convincing business to make such a pivot would be easier if the *Wall Street Journal* were to report accurately and fully on climate change.

Insurance companies have made a pivot, but some states in which they operate have not. Rick Scott, governor of Florida, has stated that he is not "convinced" that there is man-made climate change. (See Chapter 7) Recently, however, his constituents have become more and more convinced as insurance against extreme weather becomes less and less available. "One example of where Florida is hurting now is how property and construction have become too risky for insurers. According to the state-created storm risk management center, a growing number of insurance companies have exited the market entirely. Climate change and its related extreme weather both factored into that decision."[233] When insurance companies assess risks, they cannot afford to deny climate change.

Even if insurance companies get it, not everyone dealing with Florida politics does. Commenting on a briefing of Governor Scott by climate scientists, the *American Spectator* rants: "If elected officials on the right side of the political equation, Scott included, would spend less time hiding under their desks when the subject of climate change comes up, and familiarize themselves with the very weak evidence this computer-model house of cards is built on, there would be a chance we could head off one of the biggest frauds in the history of the planet."[234] The *"house of cards"* to which the *American Spectator* refers is a series of data showing that temperatures have increased. It is hardly a *house of cards*. The data indicates elevated risks for Florida, particularly sea-level rise and storms. Among those risks are flooding from storm sewers in Miami, where salty seawater gushes up through street drains as higher sea levels reverse their flow. Scott was briefed on this data and tutored in the science by climate scientists, but showed little interest in following up. He did not ask a single question during the 30-minute briefing.

Extreme weather is likely to increase in frequency and severity with climate change, even though individual storms are difficult for scientists to link directly to global warming. A good way to think about the link was articulated by James Hansen: "Would these events have occurred if atmospheric carbon dioxide had remained at its pre-industrial level of 280 ppm, an appropriate answer in that case is 'almost certainly not.' That answer, to the public, [means] humans probably bear a responsibility for the extreme event."[235]

Climate change is a factor in many different weather events. For example, there is 4% more moisture in the atmosphere over the ocean from global warming. Although this sounds like a small amount, it is enough to increase heavy precipitation and other effects of extreme weather. Many of these changes are complex and difficult to link to specific events. The trends are discernible, however, as the *National Climate Assessment* makes clear: "There has been a substantial increase in most measures of Atlantic hurricane activity since the early 1980s, the period during which high-quality satellite data are available. These include measures of intensity, frequency, and duration as well as the number of strongest (Category 4 and 5) storms. The ability to assess longer-term trends in hurricane activity is limited by the quality of available data."[236]

Increases in hurricane intensity and frequency are under scrutiny in climate science, and there are some questions about how directly related they are. Scientists have become cautious about making bald statements about extreme weather. Some have cautioned that trying to link extreme weather to climate change can backfire: "There is every reason to believe that efforts to raise public concern about climate change by linking it to natural disasters will backfire. More than a decade's worth of research suggests that fear-based appeals about climate change inspire denial, fatalism and polarization."[237]

While it is true that fear inspires denial, fatalism and polarization,[238] it is not the case that more information about the consequences of climate change will inhibit public concern. The problem is in how the information is presented, particularly with regard to the link between global warming and extreme weather.

It would seem that extreme weather would be like alarm bells to alert people to the dangers of climate change. Many activists have seized on extreme weather as a means of raising consciousness. In the run-up to the climate summit at the United Nations in New York on September 22, 2014, a number of speakers at a climate change rally invoked extreme weather. "Many panelists at the event spoke about the devastation wrought by Sandy, and a leader for typhoon victims said that the upcoming march would also be for the Philippines where Typhoon Haiyan struck late last year."[239]

Even if scientists did educate the public about the indirect relationship between climate change and extreme weather, public opinion might still be swayed by linking it directly to the weather. This can have both positive and negative implications. Research at the University of British Columbia, reported by Simon Donner and Jeremy McDaniels, found that public opinion is dependent on reactions to different kinds of weather: "While many factors affect climate change attitudes – political views, media coverage, personal experience and values – the researchers suggest that headline-making weather can strongly influence climate beliefs, especially for individuals without strong convictions for or against climate change." The research does indicate that this influence cuts both ways: "Our study demonstrates just how much local weather can influence people's opinions on global warming. We find that, unfortunately, a cold winter is enough to make some people, including many newspaper editors and opinion leaders, doubt the overwhelming scientific consensus on the issue."[240]

There are times when talking about climate change and extreme weather could be counterproductive. Right after a disaster such as a hurricane or wildfire that destroys homes, people may not be in a mood to hear about climate change. "These are times when people are most inclined to seek common ground and actively suppress the divisive and partisan issue of climate change. To talk about it seems inappropriate and exploitative."[241] Climate change is not something that can be used to blame someone for the disaster; it requires a cautious approach in linking climate change and extreme weather.

Unfortunately, the denial ideologues are not cautious about denying the possibility that extreme weather might be linked to climate change. "The suggestion that extreme weather events of today are linked to human activity is pure propaganda promoted by the IPCC and its supporters of catastrophic man-made global warming."[242] It seems rather harsh to talk about scientific statements with caveats as "pure propaganda," but that is the view of those who think that anything about man-made climate change is wrong.

Even self-described neutral observers try to avoid the connection between climate change and extreme weather. Bryce contends: "We can argue about whether severe weather is caused by carbon dioxide – and whether or not such weather is increasing in frequency or intensity – until the cows come home. The hard reality is that we must make our cities and systems more resilient. Whether those weather events are related to anthropogenic carbon dioxide doesn't matter."[243] *Doesn't matter?* Of course, we will have to make cities and systems more resilient, but we also have to address the causes of climate change and its relation to extreme weather. Ignoring the impacts of climate change on the weather will leave us uninformed, and make us more vulnerable to extreme weather events.

With regard to the Midwest and Western Droughts, some contend that they are not new. "When alarmists think of drought, they must only be considering the period from the 1970s to present, because that trend is rising. But we could drop back to the 1930s to show a decrease in droughts. Then again, based on the dotted linear trend line, there has been little change in droughts since 1900."[244] This statement is based on the canard that the 1930's were the warmest and driest on record, a point that has been refuted by measurements of temperature and precipitation (see Chapter 1). The warmest and driest years are in the twenty-first century, not the twentieth.

In their critique of climate science, some denial ideologues go beyond describing the science to characterizing it as "alarmist." One author uses as an example a research paper by two respected climate scientists:

> …it is a prime example of the typical peer-reviewed paper written in alarmist terms. Just look at the title "Climate Extremes and Climate Change: The Russian Heat Wave and Other Climate Extremes of 2010." "Extremes" appears twice in 15 words. "Record" as in "highest on record" or "record breaking" appears more than 25 times throughout the paper, and "extreme" more than 15 times. For most

readers, such repeated magnification tells them that the main intent of the paper is climate extremist propaganda.[245]

While noting that the paper is peer-reviewed, this author also describes it as "alarmist" and "climate extremist propaganda." Apparently if one uses *"extreme"* in describing weather or climate, one is guilty of spreading propaganda. Peer review does not get the authors off the hook. Denial ideologues argue that the peers who review climate research are all part of a clique of climate scientists who will approve publication of papers regardless of their merit. If scientists "tell it like it is," apparently they are alarmists. Kerry Emanuel argued "...those interested in treating the issue as an objective problem in risk assessment and management are labeled "alarmists", a particularly infantile smear considering what is at stake."[246]

From these examples, it is clear that denial ideology rejects the concept that extreme weather may have some relationship to climate change, however qualified that concept. Contending that extreme weather is unrelated to climate change leads politicians to deny the need for research that might either confirm or refute the connection. They apparently do not want any research that might contradict their predetermined views. In a statement for the Committee on Science, Space and Technology of the House of Representatives, Rep. Lamar Smith (R-TX) said "Unfortunately, this Administration's science budget focuses, in my view, far too much money, time, and effort on alarmist predictions of climate change. For example, the Administration tried to link hurricanes, tornadoes, floods and droughts to climate change."[247] Of course, the Administration is not itself doing studies to link extreme weather to climate change; scientists are doing the research that would verify or disprove any links. The Administration is complying with a law passed by Congress that requires periodic climate assessments. These assessments are based on scientific research.

One of the ironies of climate change denial is that denial ideologues are often anti-government, and their resistance to climate policies can lead to increased government activity in the future. Henry Paulson, former Secretary of the Treasury under George W. Bush and a staunch Republican, published an op-ed in the New York Times in June 2014 in which he noted: "In a future with more severe storms, deeper droughts, longer fire seasons and rising seas that imperil coastal cities, public funding to pay for adaptations and disaster relief will add significantly to our fiscal deficit and threaten our long-term economic security. So it is perverse that those who want limited government and rail against bailouts would put the economy at risk by ignoring climate change."[248]

As Paulson notes, it is not only the climate that is at risk from inaction; the economy is also at risk from extreme weather, flooding, droughts and other effects of climate change. As risks multiply, governments will be called on more and more frequently to provide disaster relief. Thus those who deny climate change while railing against government bailouts generate the paradox of a self-fulfilling prophecy. Paulson understands risks, as one of the principal players in the 2008 financial crisis.

Regardless of his impeccable credentials as a conservative Republican with a business background, Paulson is a target of attacks by denial ideologues. An op-ed in the *Wall Street Journal* attacked Paulson for presuming that some of the projections of climate models might actually be valid. "Their unnaturally specific forecasts of rising sea levels and heat waves are based on the same speculative climate models that do such a poor job of explaining even the present and recent past – and whose limits the report doesn't even mention in a footnote. The principals clearly want their assertions about the future to be taken as facts, not as extrapolations from simulations whose credibility they are wholly unprepared to defend."[249] Climate models are a favorite whipping boy of denial ideologues, as they conflate predictions and projections. Models often use "scenarios," based on variations in some of the input variables, which can show different outcomes. Nevertheless, denial ideologues will insist that these scenarios are "*forecasts*... assertions about the future to be taken as facts." This is a totally fallacious reading of climate science.

Being anti-government is an ironic feature of denial ideology. When ideologues try to reduce government spending, they find that the extreme weather events require emergency spending that either bloats government budgets or depletes accounts for other government services. "During good times, it's easy to deride 'big government' and talk about the inevitability of cutbacks. But during disasters, most everyone loses their free market religion and wants to know that their government has their backs. And if there is one thing we can be sure of, it's that extreme weather events like Superstorm Sandy, Typhoon Haiyan in the Philippines, and the British floods – disasters that, combined, pummeled coastlines beyond recognition, ravaged millions of homes, and killed many thousands – are going to keep coming." [250] Government spending is not only necessary for recovery from weather disasters, but also renewable energy. Because of the profit motive in energy production, most private utilities are reticent to invest in renewable energy with its high upfront costs. Public utilities are less reticent and may take the lead.

In the United States, state and local governments often lead the way in enacting climate policies. There is a good reason for this: "The push for state-level policies could rise, say experts, if there is a significant increase in extreme weather like droughts and flooding, which contribute to higher adaptation costs for state and local governments."[251] California is already leading the way, reacting to its drought with more stringent controls on emissions. It has also led the way in innovations for renewable energy such as leasing arrangements for solar panels on houses.

The *National Climate Assessment* describes one kind of extreme weather that seems to be linked to climate change.

In recent years, sudden, intense rains have caused extensive damage. For instance, large parts of Nashville were devastated by floods in 2010 after nearly 20 inches of rain fell in two days. Last year, parts of Colorado flooded after getting as much rain in a week as normally falls in a year. This March, a landslide killed dozens after heavy rains in Washington State. Just last week, widespread devastation occurred in the Florida Panhandle from rains that may have exceeded two feet in 24 hours; the exact total is unclear because the official rain gauge at Pensacola was knocked out by the storm. Scientists are reluctant to attribute any of these specific events to human-caused climate change, but they say that such heavy rains are consistent with what they expect in a warming climate.[252]

Here again we can see that scientific caution limits the attribution of specific events to climate change, but the trends are clear. "Precipitation patterns are changing, sea level is rising, the oceans are becoming more acidic, and the frequency and intensity of some extreme weather events are increasing. Many lines of independent evidence demonstrate that the rapid warming of the past half-century is due primarily to human activities."[253] Each storm has unique characteristics, but in aggregate they demonstrate the trends of changing climate.

Extreme weather has an effect on public perceptions of climate change: "Changes in extreme weather events are the primary way that most people experience climate change. Human-induced climate change has already increased the number and strength of some of these extreme events. Over the last 50 years, much of the United States has seen an increase in prolonged periods of excessively high temperatures, more heavy downpours, and in some regions, more severe droughts."[254]

Because of the difficulty of linking events to an overall trend, one climate scientist, John Wallace of the University of Washington, has cautioned that highlighting extreme weather is not a good way to alert the public to the dangers of climate change. "If the polling results are any indication, it would require a series of extreme weather events much more disruptive than the ones we've experienced during the past decade to bring about a real sea change in public opinion on climate change. I don't think we can afford to wait for that to happen. Raising public awareness of the multiple threats to our planet's life support system is too important to be subject to the whims of the weather."[255]

It would be unfortunate if the public is aroused by some extreme events, and then lulled into lethargy when such events diminish in frequency or intensity. Nevertheless, public opinion does tend to shift with the weather: "by a 2-to-1 margin, the public says the weather has been getting worse, rather than better, in recent years."[256] When this poll was released in 2012, the weather had indeed been somewhat strange, and since then some of the concern has abated.

At times it seems that the effects of climate change come and go, and worries recede as the weather improves. Nevertheless, the threat of climate change is immediate, constant and needs to be manifest in public awareness. It can be presented in a more nuanced manner, suggesting that while specific events are not necessarily linked to climate change, the general trend of more and stronger weather events is. One of the more serious of these trends is drought.

Drought is a complex phenomenon, and the Midwest and California droughts are caused by a number of factors. Can we attribute drought solely to climate change? No, but as a group of climate scientists noted, climate change exacerbates the drought:

> The current drought has certainly been exacerbated by climate change for one simple reason: Temperatures in California are now higher today, as they are globally. This alone increases water demand by crops and ecosystems, accelerates snowpack loss, and worsens evaporation from reservoirs. There are other complicating effects, but the influence of higher temperatures on drought is already real and cannot be ignored. We are now unambiguously altering the climate, threatening water supplies for human and natural systems. This is but one example of how even today we are paying the cost of unavoidable climate changes.[257]

What, exactly, are those costs? The President's Council of Economic Advisors has tried to put a number on climate costs: "the cost could climb by about 0.9 percent of global output per year if countries miss a target of limiting global warming to 2 degrees Celsius above preindustrial levels and stabilize global temperature rise at 3 degrees Celsius instead. For the 2014 U.S. GDP, that would mean an additional cost of $150 billion."[258] While an extra degree of heating seems miniscule – after all, temperature can increase four to five degrees during the course of a normal day – the increase in global average temperature can have profound effects. Extreme weather is one of those effects. Over the long term, climate costs can mount up: "Scientists now expect more frequent and expensive climate-related disasters in the future: disaster experts forecast that these disasters will cost more than $7 trillion in the next 75 years."[259]

Growth

Considerations of cost and stranded assets drive much of the fear that denial ideologues exploit. In the broadest terms, the fear stems from perceived loss of wealth, or declining living standards. Because twentieth-century economic growth was largely fueled by cheap energy, the denial ideology corollary of high energy prices is impoverishment. Some go so far as to say any effective climate solution would be "the final nail in the coffin of the American middle class."[260] Such a view is simplistic but must be addressed to overcome the effects of denial ideology. Alternative energies, tax systems for refunding some of the higher energy costs to consumers, and other policies can address these fears once the initial hurdle of denial is overcome.

Basically, the problem of growth is the dilemma of increasing wealth while dealing with limits on resources. "Put bluntly, the dilemma of growth has us caught between the desire to maintain economic stability [through growth] and the need to remain within ecological limits... Admittedly, the dilemma of growth isn't helping much, looking as it does like an impossibility for lasting prosperity." We know that we cannot continue to exploit resources at our current level of growth but do not like to face the consequences of climate change. "Perhaps at some instinctive level, we have always understood this. Maybe we're haunted by the subconscious fear that the 'good life' we aspire to is already deeply unfair and can't last forever."[261]

Measuring growth has always been a tenuous exercise. As Charles, the Prince of Wales, points out, measurement of GDP tends to ignore pollution:

> GDP [does not] reflect the huge costs that come with clearing ancient forests, depleting fisheries, or loading carbon dioxide into the Earth's atmosphere. Worse still, all these are the result of activities that at the moment increase economic growth. The clear-up of a major pollution incident contributes to growth; so does the sale of the complex drugs needed to treat our twenty-first-century health problems like cancer, heart disease and widespread allergies. While all of these things count positively towards GDP growth, they are at the same time either signs of diminished natural capacity or reduced human welfare. This is why I think there is now a very strong case to conclude that we are measuring the wrong things.[262]

GDP can measure growth but does it measure human welfare? Some writers think it is not only the wrong thing but also a misleading indicator that still has dominance. "Public decisions of great consequence continue to be made on the basis of shallow and misleading indicators such as gross domestic product (GDP), rather than on the basis of broader considerations such as quality of life or impacts on fundamental planetary systems."[263] Nevertheless, GDP will continue to inform decisions about climate change because it is the only measurement used by many decision makers.

Growth is particularly problematic from the standpoint of resource depletion. "The current mode of operating – the pursuit of consistent and compounding growth – is frankly incompatible with physical reality."[264] Economists would like to model economic growth on the basis of increasing populations using unlimited resources. "Unfortunately for those economists – and for us, as long as the system works their way – on a finite planet, an economy dependent on constant growth is no more perpetual than a chain letter or pyramid scheme, which always needs more people buying in. Eventually, there aren't any more, and everything collapses. Or the raw stuff to make whatever's being sold grows scarce, and the substitutes aren't as good, or they run out."[265]

In many ways, the current growth trajectory "bakes in" the use of fossil fuels as an engine of growth. If we measure only increases in GDP, we overlook the externalized costs that will detract from that growth. Climate change is a major externalized cost when the engines (literally) of growth produce CO2 emissions that warm the planet.

Some observers question the very concept of growth, which is embedded in a "free-market economy" ideology. Labeling it a "growth dogma," Warren Johnson notes "the growth dogma is inevitably encountering the barriers that, in a dogma-free world, would have led to questioning growth long ago. Instead we are working harder to keep the growth economy on track, taking on more debts and organizing more of our lives around the needs for jobs, profits, and tax revenues. We spend money freely to encourage growth and expand the global economy, both to increase our consumption here and spread our ways worldwide. Both reinforce our pride in the ways we have created, but also leave us more dependent on an integrated global economy of ever greater size and complexity, and makes it too dangerous to consider whether the economy would be better off with less consumption. Such thoughts could even trip up the economy to send it downward."[266] He identifies one of the most threatening aspects of climate change: the belief that anything that impedes growth, such as limits on greenhouse gas emissions, would destroy the prevailing belief systems by which we live.

Consumption is a problem for solutions to climate change, as many people do not want to change their consumption patterns to reduce the burden of carbon emissions on the atmosphere. "If saving the planet depends on changing acquisitive human nature – meaning, among other things, bucking the vast budgets of commercial advertising – the Earth will likely be thoroughly sacked long before that's ever accomplished."[267] It will be a tough nut to crack and few policymakers are up to confronting human nature. It makes denial a more inviting prospect.

Consumption patterns are a source of denial, not only for those who want to promote consumption for their own profit, but also for all of us who want to maintain or increase our standard of living without worrying about climate change. "We are being kept in denial about the seriousness of these major global issues by powerful business lobbies and timid politicians, but also by our own reluctance to disrupt the most comfortable lifestyle that any people on Earth have ever enjoyed."[268] It is this reluctance that often leads people to embrace denial ideology when it offers alternatives to the harsh realities of climate change.

Looking for an escape from this dilemma, some will try to use popular ideas to deny climate change. Many denial ideologues will cite cold winter weather as a refutation of climate science. A congresswoman, Marsha Blackburn (R-TN), told NBC listeners "What we have to look at is the fact that you don't make good laws, sustainable laws when you're making them on hypotheses or theories or unproven sciences."[269] Blackburn is vice-chairman of the House Energy and Commerce Committee, which has oversight of policies on public health, air quality and environmental health, and energy. In the context of a debate with Bill Nye, the "science guy," about the frigid weather in the eastern United States during January and February 2014, Blackburn repeated the denial canard about "unproven sciences."

The Indiana Assistant Commissioner of the Department of Environment echoed her sentiment, saying "anyone who says global warming is obviously suffering from frostbite."[270] But the frigid 2014 weather about which they spoke was limited to one region of a country that has only 2% of the surface area of earth. "For the earth as a whole, it was the fourth-warmest January on record. It was, in fact, the 347th consecutive month with temperatures above the 20th-century average."[271] It was warm not only in the southern hemisphere, where January and February are summer months, but also in California and other western U.S. states with winter temperatures well above normal.

Much of the confusion about extreme weather, particularly frigid weather, comes from the reporting by journalists. One climate scientist, John Wallace of the University of Washington, cautioned that this reporting could mislead the public about climate science: "Many of the reporters who write stories about our research don't recognize the distinction between the broad scientific consensus on climate change and the various unsubstantiated hypotheses relating to extreme weather events. When the public becomes confused, the carefully considered scientific consensus becomes vulnerable to attack by the apologists for economic growth at all costs. It didn't take them long to learn that poking fun at the notion that global warming could lead to extreme cold is an effective tactic."[272]

Nevertheless, unusual weather does arouse public interest. It can be linked to climate change in a general way.

Extreme weather is not just an abstract concept. It is a reality that affects people across the country. In 2013, two out of three Americans said weather in the U.S. has been worse over the past several years, up 12 percentage points since spring 2012. Many (51%) say weather in their local area has been worse over the past several years. Not surprisingly, then, the gap between what we know as scientists (that global warming impacts are here and now) and what Americans perceive is narrowing: about six in 10 Americans already say, "global warming is affecting weather in the U.S."[273]

When unusual weather occurs it sometimes stimulates discussion of climate change – not always in the most scientific vein. But it is important that people understand the probability of unusual weather becoming more common, and the tendencies toward extreme weather becoming more probable. Unfortunately, one effect seems to be that denial ideologues are becoming more extreme.

Chapter 4:
Extreme Denial

"Climate change is a plot invented by a bunch of old hippies who have been on drugs for a long time." Verne, quoted by Garrison Keillor, *A Prairie Home Companion, The News from Lake Wobegon, December 1, 2012.* Verne is of course a fictional character created by Keillor to provide a foil for his musings.

At times climate change denial can seem like fiction. Indeed, it is: A sarcastic novel with the title "Global Warming Revelations" states denial ideology with one fictional passage:

It's a decades-old plan to take over European and American governments by using the threat of catastrophic climate change as the leverage to control the economy and society. While there was slight global warming from the 1970s to the late 1990's, there has actually been global cooling since

104

then. The main thing is that human-caused heat is all a hoax, a scam, a fraud. It's all done by manipulating the computer models, the simulations. Those pushing it are deceiving the population to strip them of their rights.[274]

Fiction is a useful way to convey misinformation that cannot be stated in a verifiable manner.[275] As we have seen in Chapter 1, statements such as "there has actually been global cooling since then" are fictional. In this chapter, we will see why "human-caused heat" is called "a hoax, a scam and a fraud." Rejection of climate science and its explanations of severe weather tend to go to extremes. This is not to say that all denial ideology is extreme, but examples illustrate how it can be taken to extremes. Illustrations of extreme denial include "global warming scam," "eco-tyranny" and "totalitaria."

Global Warming Scam

Many denial ideologues have made serious accusations about climate scientists – that they are perpetuating a hoax,[276] bamboozling governments and foundations to obtain grants, or misleading the public to enhance their reputations.[277] Among the baldest expressions of this ideology is a statement by the late Hal Lewis, formerly Professor of Physics at the University of California, Santa Barbara.

> It is of course, the global warming scam, with the (literally) trillions of dollars driving it, which has corrupted so many scientists, and has carried APS before it like a rogue wave. It is the greatest and most successful pseudoscientific fraud I have seen in my long life as a physicist.[278]

In this statement, APS refers to the American Physics Society, one of many scientific associations that endorsed climate science. Lewis resigned from the APS over the issue. Using the term "fraud," he accuses the APS of cobbling together a statement on climate change in secret, and foisting it on the membership.

Lewis hints at a conspiracy of the APS leadership in framing the statement.

> The appallingly tendentious APS statement on Climate Change was apparently written in a hurry by a few people over lunch, and is certainly not representative of the talents of APS members as I have long known them.... APS appointed a secret committee that never met, never troubled to speak to any skeptics, yet endorsed the Statement in its entirety.[279]

Perhaps the global warming "scam" was written on napkins during that lunch and foisted on APS members without their consent. If so, it would have been ripped up and down by that membership, which is not known for its blind adherence to statements from on high. But that has not happened.

Lewis' statement also refers to another "fraud" perpetuated by scientists, as revealed by the "Climategate" emails. "Climategate" is a buzzword for a series of purloined emails that allegedly show fraud among climate scientists. Those scientists whose emails were hacked have been cleared by scientific academies of any wrongdoing.[280] Nevertheless, Lewis alleges that "...the ClimateGate scandal broke into the news, and the machinations of the principal alarmists were revealed to the world. It was a fraud on a scale I have never seen, and I lack the words to describe its enormity."[281] In this vein, denial ideologues are prone to see nefarious motives in scientific work that brings unpleasant realities into focus. Because the science seems unacceptable, the scientists must be perpetuating a scam. Ostensibly, the e-mails reveal this scam:

> What they reveal is that the scientists who've been scaring us for the last two decades with terrifying tales of a man-made climate apocalypse simply cannot be trusted. The entire edifice of the great global warming scam is built on a foundation of lies, corruption, and junk science.[282]

Climategate has led other denial ideologues to argue that climate science is a fraud. "[Climategate] vindicated the suspicions of thousands of sceptics around the world that CRU [Climate Research Unit] is the architect of the biggest scientific fraud in history. The only problem is that the media almost completely ignored it."[283] It is dubious to argue that the media have ignored the skeptics. Many journalists try to "balance" their reporting by quoting skeptics. But it was a disappointment to denial ideologues when the media did not find conspiracies in the alleged fraud:

> This is baffling considering the scale and implications of the scandal, which one might reasonably assume would be taken up eagerly by the media, which thrives on controversy. However, for the media to pay too much attention to the scandal would also mean having to debunk the hobgoblin of the century: human-induced climate chaos and global warming, which are supposedly threatening the planet. Such a message reads well in the press and makes great television with images of collapsing ice cliffs, wild fires in Australia and sweltering heat waves in Russia. Disaster porn. Climategate was nothing in comparison to the planet on the brink of Armageddon, so it faded into the background."[284] Now the media are considered part of the fraud, because they are not "debunking" the "hobgoblin of the century.[285]

"*Disaster porn*" is a colorful way of describing something as tame as tentative statements about the possible relationship between extreme weather and climate change (see Chapter 2 for some of the caveats scientists use). Apparently the media are not sufficiently vigilant to detect the fraudulent "*hobgoblin of the century*," whatever that is.

"Journalistic balance" is sometimes an excuse for not checking the validity of denial ideology. "In the case of the debate on global warming, the main distortion occurs when space is opened for the skeptics and deniers, which is clearly disproportionate to the actual contribution that they make to the scientific discussion."[286] As the denial ideology spreads in the popular press, it undermines the credibility of the scientific findings. Scientists are handicapped by being positioned on the same level as the deniers, when their findings are at an entirely different level of validity. This is one of the principal reasons that scientists dislike denial ideology (more in Chapter 6).

Media outlets affect public perceptions of climate change. Fox News is an example of a *"fair and balanced news"* source that is anything but fair and balanced. In one of its internal memos, revealed by the *Washington Post,* a Fox executive said "We should refrain from asserting that the planet has warmed (or cooled) in any given period without IMMEDIATELY pointing out that such theories are based upon data that critics have called into question. It is not our place as journalists to assert such notions as facts."[287] For scientists, to assert that "data" should not be reported as facts is infuriating. Of course, it is reasonable that critics call data into question, but they must do so with data. Fox should report all the data, not as *"notions"* that journalists can conveniently ignore if they do not like them.

Misapplication of the words "skeptics" and "critics" can be found throughout denial ideology. "In this sense, those who call themselves 'skeptics' of global warming are generally misusing this concept, since most of them do not participate effectively in the process of scientific consensus on the issue. They actually work within the public sphere to confuse 'scientific uncertainty' with doubt."[288] By conflating the term "skeptic" with denial ideology, the ideologues not only do the public discourse a disservice, they also besmirch the reputation of genuine skeptics. It is more accurate to label them *ideologues* because what they say is based on ideology, rather than science.

Doubt is a powerful weapon in the hands of denial ideologues. Some consider it a concomitant of the profit motive among fossil fuel companies: "Merchants of carbon-based fuels are *the largest corporations in the world.* Their vision is so clouded by money that they seize and magnify any shred of evidence that casts doubt on climate change – and there is plenty of it."[289] Sheppard goes so far as to label climate scientists "hucksters." He repeats one of the denial canards and accuses scientists of seeking money by falsifying the science:

> Simply stated, we've been swindled. We've been set up as marks by a gang of opportunistic hucksters who have exploited the naïvely altruistic intentions of the environmental movement in an effort to control international energy consumption while redistributing global wealth and (in many cases) greedily lining their own pockets in the process.[290]

Sheppard represents the type of denial ideology that considers climate science a racket, fabricated by a group of *"hucksters"* who are deluding environmentalists. He then extends the accusation to inculpate them for "controlling international energy consumption and redistributing global wealth. This seems a rather broad plot for a group of politically innocent scientists. Of course, to denial ideologues, scientists are not very innocent. They are part of a vast conspiracy, including environmentalists and politicians who are deluding the public.

One might ask, why would such a scam have any traction with governments or the mass media? Denial ideologues conveniently provide the rationale.

> For the government, saving the planet is also about securing popular support and hanging on to power. So it takes a brave politician to swim against the tide even if s/ he smells a scam like AGW [anthropogenic global warming]. The mainstream media fan the flames of fear by bombarding the uncritical masses with one side of the issue – the side with the more exciting story to tell. This is why few if any media providers are willing to publish more than a token number of

109

articles sceptical of human-induced climate change.[291]

But of course, denial also makes great copy. Many journalists have been lured into presenting a "balanced" story of climate science by lurid and colorful language used by denial ideologues. This is one of the problems caused by denial ideology, that it provides a rationale for people to ignore the problem because "scientists don't agree." In fact, 97% of climate scientists with peer-reviewed publications do agree on "AGW," the bugaboo of denial ideologues.[292] By contrast, about 81% of the "experts" quoted by denial ideologues, who disagree with climate science, have few or no credentials as climate scientists.[293] Unfortunately, because of *their* influence, only 32% of Americans "believe that global warming is happening, and that human beings are responsible for it."[294] There are many others who agree that the climate is changing, but do not hold humans responsible. It is this confusion about climate change that inhibits effective action.

A number of denial ideologues have labeled climate science a "hoax." Among the most well-known is Senator James Inhofe (R-OK), who uses the word in the title of his book, *The Greatest Hoax*. Even some who abjure the word "hoax" tend to downplay climate science and emphasize costs of climate policies: "It's not a hoax, but it's not proven science either. But you don't dismantle America's power and energy on a maybe. We need to be energy independent first. We need to do it better, which we can, but it is not a settled science."[295] Putting energy independence ahead of climate policies is a recipe for disaster, as the energy will become a major source of greenhouse gases, the effects of which can render energy independence moot.

In an ironic twist, one jokester perpetrated an actual hoax in which denial ideologues could believe:

> The results from 'an important new study' were posted on the Internet. Referring to a new scientific paper in the Journal of Geoclimatic Studies,

the post suggested that undersea bacteria were mostly responsible for the build-up of carbon dioxide in the atmosphere and not fossil fuel emissions from human energy generation. Within a few hours, maybe even minutes, this new scientific finding was appearing on blogs and circulating around the world on email lists, finding a particularly receptive audience among groups and commentators who were skeptical of the human influence on climate. The story was of course a hoax, with the perpetrator being British novelist and journalist David Thorpe.[296]

Thorpe was not a climate scientist but a fiction writer, which explains why he was skillful at perpetuating a hoax in which denial ideologues could believe. Much of their own belief system is based on fiction.

One prominent social critic identifies the term "hoax" as a characteristic meme for denial ideologues. "Today there is a significant cohort of voters in many countries who care passionately, even obsessively, about climate change. What they care about, however, is exposing it as a "hoax" being perpetrated by liberals to force them to change their light bulbs, live in Soviet-style tenements, and surrender their SUVs." The issues of lifestyles and redistribution of wealth infuse denial ideology, as we saw in Chapter 3. Sometimes these issues are linked to other hot-button political issues: "For these right-wingers, opposition to climate change has become as central to their belief system as low taxes, gun ownership, and opposition to abortion. Which is why some climate scientists report receiving the kind of harassment that used to be reserved for doctors who perform abortions." [297]

While it is provocative to identify climate denial with low taxes, gun ownership and opposition to abortion, it does suggest that the concept of "*hoax*" drives a type of mindset that is closed to reason. If one can dismiss climate science as a "hoax," one can then dismiss any information that would undermine the belief system. With plenty of contrarian scientists' "facts" to seize upon, the denial ideologue can simply rule out any data that does not support denial.

Denial ideologues continue to argue that scientists disagree on climate change. John Christy of the University of Alabama cites a survey by the American Meteorological Society where only 52% of meteorologists agree that there is anthropogenic climate change. Presumably, although he does not spell it out, the other 48% either do not agree or are neutral.[298] While meteorologists do have a wider range of opinions than climate scientists, their involvement in climate research is less oriented to climate change and more to weather prediction.

A number of meteorologists have echoed the denial ideology, some calling climate science a hoax.[299] This form of denial carries little weight in the scientific community. It does, however, carry weight with Republicans in Congress. "Just last week, Republicans in the House tried to pass a bill introduced by climate-change denying Congressman Jim Bridenstine of Oklahoma, that would have forced NOAA, the National Oceanic and Atmospheric Administration, to quit studying climate change and its effects so much, and instead just study and discuss 'weather.' This was, of course, to help 'the economy' – Republican code phrase for fossil fuel barons like ExxonMobil and the Koch Brothers."[300] Apparently, predicting weather is OK as long as you don't admit that the climate has any effect on it. Republicans are not all denial ideologues, but some seem to think it is necessary to make denial statements in public to keep their jobs.[301]

Why would denial ideologues label climate science a fraud, and accuse climate scientists of perpetrating a scam? It is highly doubtful that all the leading climate scientists would participate in a tight conspiracy to defraud world leaders and the public – they are more likely to attack each others' scientific findings if there was even a hint of fraud. Denial ideology is a narrative that serves the purpose of denying reality and supporting a myth: that earth is cooling, any changes are natural, and humans are not responsible. That is a more confortable scenario than the one that climate science portrays. It enables believers to ignore the ramifications of climate change, both for their own futures and for societies at large. Energy use can continue on the same path – business as usual – and growth can proceed without hindrance from government regulation or taxation. If the government is involved, according to this view, it will take over the economy.

One of the more bizarre statements about growth is that it resolves the problem of overpopulation and therefore would alleviate the threat of population pressure on resources.

> The problem for Gore, the Club of Rome and Agenda 21 is, it is in direct opposition to their solutions. Their predictions were wrong but more important another pattern had emerged. It is known as the Demographic Transition Model... It shows that populations decline with economic development – the very thing the entire Strong orchestrated agenda was designed to oppose.[302]

In this statement, Tim Ball wraps together the Club of Rome (which produced the "Limits to Growth" series of books), Al Gore ("Inconvenient Truth") and Maurice Strong (Chairman of the Rio Summit). The *"Strong orchestrated agenda"* refers to the UN Framework Convention on Climate Change and other activities designed to address climate change. It is doubtful that "populations decline with economic development," although they may grow more slowly. The U.S. population has not declined with economic growth, but that is partly due to immigration. Some countries in Europe, and Japan, are declining but many developing countries are growing rapidly.

Apparently, according to denial ideology, government is not the only institution bent on taking over the economy through exploitation of fears about climate change. One author has made the connection between General Electric – which produces wind turbines – and the Weather Channel, which it owns (as part of NBC – the National Broadcasting Company). According to this view, the Weather Channel has been frightening people with reports on extreme weather and climate change, so General Electric must be encouraging fear to sell more wind turbines.[303] I doubt that any GE executive has been able to concoct such a nefarious plot.

All of these examples indicate that when denial ideologues assume, as a matter of basic belief, that climate change is a scam, they will come up with some rather bizarre conclusions. Some of these are simply unrelated to reality, but others go beyond this point and develop fantasies of tyranny and totalitarianism.

Eco-Tyranny

One of the most egregious expressions of climate change denial is a book titled "Eco-Tyranny" by meteorologist Brian Sussman. He develops an argument based on equating environmentalism with Marxism:

> Despite the suffering Marxism has unleashed on the planet, we are continually lectured – by politicians, government bureaucrats, professors, environmental groups, and movie stars – that the world's foremost enemy is pollution, particularly greenhouse gas emissions. Our greatest challenge, they insist, is curtailing such discharges into the atmosphere and restoring the global environment; if we don't, they claim, the earth's ecological system will die. It's all a lie. There is no such planetary crisis. It's a concocted calamity churned out initially by Marx himself, and furthered by his modern devotees. It's what I have named the "green agenda.[304]

Associating climate science with Marxism seems rather old fashioned, but Sussman seems to think it will frighten enough readers to have some effect on their opinions. Marx's "modern devotees" are environmentalists, in Sussman's eyes, and their work is a radical "*green agenda.*" Climate science is "all a lie," and those who use its findings to call for a green agenda will by definition become Marxists.

Marxism is often used as a straw man for attacking climate science, but at least one commentator, Rupert Darwall, regards Marxism as the opposite of environmentalism. [305] Marxism, after all, perpetuated the old myth that "man has dominion over nature." But denial ideologues persist in equating them. As Marxism has declined, according to Darwall, climate alarmism has thrived, based on the concept that climate science has somehow replaced communism. When communism collapsed, some writers suggest that former communists moved into the environmental movement:

> One result of Communism's collapse was that the former Communists and their fellow travelers in the West found a new ideological home in the environmental movement and moved on to promoting the global warming hoax as a wealth redistribution exercise, via a network of UN agencies.[306]

Equating climate activism with communism provides two themes for denial ideology: activists are radical believers in a secular religion, and they are intent on redistributing income. These themes recur through denial ideology.

More profoundly, the "anti-Marxist" argument suggests that environmentalism is the opposite of Marxism. This argument starts with the "Promethean" view of man's domination over nature associated with Marxism, a view formerly associated with religion. In other words, Marxism tended to view human capabilities (rather than God's power) as omnipotent, able to overcome any challenge from nature. Now, however, Marxism has lost credibility and nature is seen as more powerful. This means that there is less restraint on those who question the Marxist Promethean view. Since environmentalists question the ability of humans to control nature, they are ultimately anti-Marxists.

The entire legacy of Marx is under challenge by climate change. "[The] ecological crisis – that humanity has to go a whole lot easier on the living systems that sustain us, acting regeneratively rather than extractively – is a profound challenge to large parts of the left as well as the right. It's a challenge to some trade unions, those trying to freeze in place the dirtiest jobs, instead of fighting for the good clean jobs their members deserve. And it's a challenge to the overwhelming majority of center-left Keynesians, who still define economic success in terms of traditional measures of GDP growth, regardless of whether that growth comes from rampant resource extraction."[307] The glib assumption that modern societies can grow out of their problems, whether they are poverty, pollution or inequality, is now under severe strain as the consequences of growth fueled by fossil fuels become vividly clear.

While anti-Marxist, this point of view is by no means a defense of capitalism. Globalization and multinational corporations are held responsible for the destruction of nature. It is rather a critique of the "free market" ideology that ignores the external costs of growth. Further, the "free market" may actually undermine the possibility of economic growth that is the bedrock of modern society. "The transition toward sustainable will occur regardless of what our feelings are about it, but how smooth or rough it will be will depend on how well we respond to the challenges of creating a clear, manageable path toward sustainable ways of life."[308] The inevitability of the transition toward a sustainable society is a frightening prospect for denial ideologues. It will require major changes in production and use of energy. It is often the fear of this transition that drives denial ideology toward extremism.[309]

This fear of a transition to a sustainable economy also drives government policy.

> Although successive federal and state governments have had energy-efficiency policies for many years, and some have even pledged action on climate change, their more prominent objective

continues to be to promote growth in the economy. This is seen as the only way of providing the public with improvements in quality of life and an extension of choice. Any downturn in the economy is seen as a serious cause for concern because it is assumed that only out of the wealth created from economic growth can the essential basic services of health, housing, education, and defense be provided. It would seem that the essential services of an ecologically balanced climate system provided by the planet are taken for granted...At the heart of the matter lies the belief that rising material prosperity through economic growth is a nonnegotiable aspiration.[310]

Growth becomes an end in itself in many countries, and the consequences of growth on the natural balance of the world are ignored in preference for other objectives such as health, education and defense. This is as true of Marxism as it is of denial ideology.

For denial ideologues, equating environmentalism with Marxism is not a viable indictment of climate science, so they must try other lines of attack. Brian Sussman tries to show that climate science is anti-human:

> Unfurling the flag of eco-tyranny, the left is engaging in a devious twofold process. On the one hand, they are deploying an aggressive, eco-based propaganda campaign designed to convince the majority of Americans that mankind's presence on Earth has irreparably harmed the planet, and the only way to prevent the environment from destruction is to create laws that will dramatically reduce greenhouse gas emissions and protect all manner of species. As we have learned, though, the spokespersons for this movement deliberately use junk science, blatant lies, propagandized school curricula, and religious institutions to sell their radical rubbish.[311]

A rather broad condemnation, this statement combines moral arguments about "mankind's presence on Earth" to political statements about *"junk science, blatant lies, propagandized school curricula and religious institutions."* Sussman seems to regard climate science as a completely reprehensible set of rules and activities that threaten his view of humanity.

Sussman's use of the term "eco-tyranny" is reminiscent of Michael Crichton's novel, "State of Fear."[312] Crichton attributes tyrannical motivations to an environmental movement that seeks to influence world leaders. The leader of the movement surreptitiously tries to generate a tsunami and kill thousands of people to fake an ecological crisis. While tsunamis have nothing to do with climate change, Crichton uses the rhetorical device of fake crises to frame his narrative of climate change denial ideology. Presumably scientists seeking to gain power fake all of the findings of climate change. This is a mirror image of what is actually the case: denial ideologues fake expertise to gain influence.[313]

A variation on the term "eco-tyranny" is "eco-fascism." Perhaps because a tyranny requires a belief system to support it, the eco-tyrants will invoke this kind of fascism. One expression, according to denial ideologues, is Agenda 21, the statement of principles that came out of the same Rio Summit (1992) that produced the UN Framework Convention on Climate Change. Here's one take on Agenda 21:

> You pay your local government for the basic amenities and services you need – trash disposal, street lighting, road maintenance, etc.- not because you want it to solve Third World poverty, eliminate sexual inequality, *combat climate change*, address overpopulation, or redistribute income. Yet, behind the scenes, this is exactly what Agenda 21 is being used to justify. You didn't vote for it. You weren't consulted. Yet these values— which may be alien to everything you believe in – have now been

absorbed, as if by osmosis, to form a key part of your local government's policy. That's Agenda 21: the blueprint for green tyranny.[314]

It is a long way from local trash collection to an international tyranny, but denial ideologues can make the leap just by listing a group of ideas that presumably are part of a fascist plot.

Other writers have expressed similar sentiments when it comes to environmentalism. Larry Bell has attributed sinister motives to environmentalists:

> The global warming rubric has served as an ideal platform to enable the UN to advance large philosophical visions, wealth distribution agendas, and world governance goals under a banner of global environmentalism. Dangerous climate change and attributing its cause to human activities serve as pretenses for a much broader global environmentalism doctrine aimed at defeating capitalism and free market choices.[315]

Bell expresses the common denial argument that environmentalists seek to impose wealth distribution and world governance under the *global warming rubric.* He quotes one academic as describing "the environmentalist's dream of an egalitarian society based on rejection of economic growth in favor of smaller populations eating lower on the food chain, consuming a lot less, and sharing a much lower level of resources more equally."[316]

Laframboise has reduced the issue to the following formula: "Less emissions = less fuel = less of nearly everything." She goes on to say, "While most parents hope their kids' futures will be filled with opportunity, emissions reduction is all about restricted, limited, impoverished lives." [317] This captures the denial concept that addressing global warming will inexorably mean drastically reducing our living standards, a concept disputed

119

by most environmentalists. While societies may have to change their consumption patterns, the change is not necessarily in the direction of impoverishment.

Changes are inevitable, regardless of whether the world prepares or not. The later the changes in energy use start, however, more likely that human welfare will be reduced. That dilemma is exacerbated by the "energy dogma," a corollary of the "growth dogma," by which modern society maintains its belief in the good life. "The energy dogma has not been challenged as openly as the debt dogma, in part because neither political party would benefit from something that nobody wanted to know about, such as the stabilization of world oil production and climate changes."[318]

With regard to the *"free market choices"* that denial ideologues advocate, an economist, William Nordhaus, tends to agree that addressing climate change might not support unlimited "free markets": "There is no genuine "free-market solution" to global warming. We need new national and international institutions to coordinate and guide decisions about global warming policies. These mechanisms can use the market, but they must be legislated and enforced by governments."[319]

Does this mean that climate policies must be "socialist" or anti-capitalist? No more so than military security, traffic safety and other government activities that protect a population. None of these has a free market arrangement with calculations of profit and loss. Like them, climate change is not subject to the same economic rules as free markets.

Climate change has an additional component that arouses the ire of those who see "eco-tyranny" in climate science. Because industrial societies have grown during the past 250 years along with rapidly increasing consumption of fossil fuels, the very question of economic growth is a core issue in climate policies. Growth is an issue fraught with emotion and misunderstanding.[320] Postulating that growth and climate stability are incompatible leads to false dichotomies and denial tendencies even among reasonable observers. Nordhaus provides a good metaphor for resolving this false dichotomy: "Should we conclude … that our problem is too much economic growth? That we should aim for zero economic growth? Few people today draw this conclusion. It would be like throwing out all the groceries because the milk is sour. The appropriate response is to fix the market failure by repairing the flawed economic externality involved in climate change. Throw out the sour milk and fix the faulty refrigerator."[321]

"Market failure" is a useful concept for addressing economic growth and climate change. Because the production and consumption of energy involves externalities such as pollution, producers and users do not pay the full costs of energy. Carbon pollution is the main issue in climate change, and production of electrical energy, transportation and so on create the dilemma of dangerous growth. Resolving this dilemma will require better management of economic growth, not blaming climate policy for stopping growth. What is that dilemma? It is a stark choice: "the choice we face is between taking unimaginable risks with the planet and leaving vastly valuable fossil fuels in the ground."[322]

Even if markets were not failing, there would be questions about how to evaluate the "externalities" caused by energy use. Very few markets now measure the cost of carbon emissions and assess a cost or tax based on their possible harm to ecosystems or economic systems. Extreme weather can be measured in terms of costs, but scientists are not assigning responsibility for any one storm or drought solely to climate change. The trends are clear, however. If markets were to assign costs according to these trends, it might be possible to argue that an economic system could account for costs of climate change but with markets that exist now that is a dubious proposition.

Some commentators will go so far as to accuse climate scientists of "terrorism." Ben Stein, a commentator for Fox News, said "Well, there is no cost that is too high to pay to save the Earth. The real problem is, do we really know that this is hurting the Earth? The science is not a hundred percent unanimous, despite what the global warming skeptics and terrorists will tell us, or global warming terrorists will tell us, the science is not clear on this. I just don't think we should be going all out on this until the science is completely clear." [323] *"Global warming terrorists?"* What kind of rational discussion of climate change does that engender? Stein is echoing the approach taken by the Heartland Institute, which sponsored a billboard featuring Ted Kaczynski, the "Unabomber," with the statement "I believe in global warming, do you?" It is quite a stretch to accuse climate scientists of terrorism when they presumably advocate an approach to global warming that threatens economic interests.

With regard to the argument that environmentalists are leading us into "world governance," denial ideologues see the UN Framework Convention on Climate Change (UNFCCC) as an elitist instrument for destroying national sovereignty. They completely misread the UNFCCC process, where unanimous consensus is required for any watered-down proposal to pass. Anyone who has attended UNFCCC meetings, as I have, would realize that this body could hardly be a command post for black helicopters swooping in to take over our country.

There is a case to be made for global action on climate change since greenhouse gases generated separately in each nation diffuse throughout the world. But the mode of action does not have to be a unified governance structure; each nation might have its own modes of responding. There will be commitments to do something as extreme weather becomes more common, but they may come too late to avoid the more serious consequences of climate change.

Totalitaria

In a bizarre book on the role of the United Nations in climate change policy, Ian Wishart describes at some length the "Satanist" nature of UN bureaucracy and relates climate change policy to this Satanic religion:

> The criticism has often been made that climate change policy is almost religious in the way it is being rolled out. It is, and that's because it is

central to the Gaia Earth-worship and Lucifer "consciousness-raising" that the UN is trying to engender. Around half the planet "believes" in climate change, almost in the religious sense, including most of the mainstream media. They "believe" it because it is being pushed as a doctrine of faith, disguised as science, by the Lucis Trust and its followers worldwide. If you want proof of their power to persuade, and therefore the danger inherent in their ideas, it is staring you in the face.[324]

Climate Science as Religion

Many denial ideologues have compared climate science to religion, a kind of mirror image of their own ideological tendencies. Hence the accusation that science is practicing religion because its findings require that followers worship nature. Some have accused UN climate leaders of paganism.[325] But this is the first example that I know of where denial ideologues accused climate change policy of devil worship.

How can someone equate climate science and devil worship? The convoluted reasoning in Wishart's book proceeds from a description of a non-denominational chapel in the UN General Assembly building to argue that it is there for worship of a form of Satanism, and thence to the "totalitariocracy" of the UN staff that administers climate policy. Wishart throws in Masonry and the Illuminati as forerunners of this Satanic religion. He describes a "Lucis Trust" as a part of this thread, and this "Lucifer" trust allegedly maintains the chapel and instructs UN staff in spiritual matters. It is all a bizarre logic that defies understanding if one has any knowledge of how the UN works, but it might appeal to those who want to believe the worst about global governance.

Other writers made the same link between climate science and practice of an "evil" type of religion. Charles Krauthammer, a columnist for the Washington Post, said that climate scientists have become religious "whores:"

Climate-change proponents have made their cause a matter of fealty and faith. For folks who pretend to be brave carriers of the scientific ethic, there's more than a tinge of religion in their jeremiads. If you whore after other gods, the Bible tells us, "the Lord's wrath be kindled against you, and he shut up the heaven, that there be no rain, and that the land yield not her fruit" (Deuteronomy 11). Sounds like California. Except that today there's a new god, the Earth Mother. And a new set of sins — burning coal and driving a fully equipped F-150. But whoring is whoring, and the gods must be appeased. So if California burns, you send your high priest (in carbon-belching Air Force One, but never mind) to the bone-dry land to offer up, on behalf of the repentant congregation, a $1 billion burnt offering called a "climate resilience fund."[326]

The "climate resilience fund" to which Krauthammer refers is an Obama proposal to aid farmers and others in adapting to climate change. To refer to the president as the *"high priest"* and to scientists and/or environmentalists (it's not clear which he refers to) as *whoring "after other gods"* drags down the argument to a new low level: heresy. It is not clear what religion they are violating – perhaps Christianity or Judaism – but it is clear that they are substituting "Mother Earth" for God.

Denial ideology sometimes attributes direct heresy to climate science. One meteorologist, Chris Allen of WBKO-TV in Bowling Green, Kentucky, put it this way:

> If you don't believe in God and creationism then I can see why you would easily buy into the whole global warming fanfare. I think in many ways that's what this movement is ultimately out to do – rid the mere mention of God in any context. What these environmentalists are actually saying is "we know more than God – we're bigger than God – God

is just a fantasy – science is real…He isn't…listen to US!" I have a huge problem with that.[327]

This kind of heresy must come from the environmental principle that substitutes "ecological services" for "man's dominion over nature." The very idea that man might somehow be dependent on nature for ecological services such as clean water and a stable climate is heresy, where the "centuries-old acceptance that earth is man's domain has given a new strain of politically correct self-hatred and eco-guilt."[328] Man should be independent of nature if he dominates it. Of course, that would ignore the fact that ecological services are actually worth quite a bit to the economy of the world: It has been estimated that these services, such as flood control and absorption of carbon dioxide are worth about $120 trillion. That compares to a world product (sum of all nations' GDPs) of about $70 trillion in 2013.

Ironically, "dominion over nature" evokes a counterpoint argument, that man could not possibly change climate: "the idea that the Earth's climate is too powerful a system for us puny humans to upset holds a certain folksy—not to mention religious—appeal. Still, the Heartland crowd is careful to frame its arguments in terms of science and skepticism rather than dogma." [329] Heartland Institute, one of the leading denial organizations (see Chapter 5), is careful to avoid religious connotations in its ideology while accusing climate scientists of believing in religion. "…since environmental and climate activism has always been a matter of faith rather than science, perhaps such essentially religious formulations were inevitable."[330]

Along with devil worship and burnt offerings, climate science supposedly is promoting superstition. Climate research uses "billions of dollars spent in the United States, Europe, and Australia in re-creating medieval fear and superstition, and calling it climate science." [331] While many denial ideologues have criticized climate science for absorbing billions of research dollars, few have accused it of creating *medieval fear and superstition.*" Research funding for climate science is a small fraction of the research and development for extracting unconventional types of fossil fuel, much of which will have to be left in the ground as stranded assets (see Chapter 2). Especially galling to denial ideologues is that environmentalism "has replaced Christianity as the West's dominant religious philosophy."[332]

Accusing environmentalism of nature worship is a theme that pervades denial ideology: "...the treason against real science by climate alarmists should be no surprise to anyone who's aware of the extent to which the environmental movement is riddled with 'nature religion,' a mystical approach to nature that turns its back on the Biblical worldview that is the foundation of real science and embraces pantheistic, animistic, neo-pagan, and secularist naturalist worldviews instead."[333] Using this theme is handy for denial ideology, because it exploits the fear that some followers may have that their own religious views about climate change are questionable. They can dismiss climate science as a kind of rival belief system with no merit.

Climate science as a religion is such a pervasive theme in denial ideology that it deserves further analysis. In its purest form, religion is about beliefs in spiritual matters or entities that cannot be easily observed or measured. Science is the opposite.

Of course, religions do not confine themselves to immeasurable, non-empirical matters such as deities or souls. Religions do spill over the theoretical boundaries into ideology, where identifying and measuring something is feasible, but doing so is not welcome to the ideologue. If one wants to retain integrity of beliefs, one cannot allow for questioning those beliefs through measurement of their validity.

In climate issues, this rigidity becomes evident in denial. Subjecting any beliefs to testing would be heretical, so facts are not allowed to interfere with the beliefs. Those unpleasant facts can intrude, however, when nature does not behave according to the preconceived notions of the ideologue. When that happens, one approach is to treat any findings of climate science as expressions of an unorthodox belief system that competes with one's own beliefs. Of course, this simply reduces climate science to another belief system or religion, no more valid than any other (and to some believers, less valid because it is not their own belief system).

One of the most egregious examples of this is the charge that science is like a "cargo cult," a religion that was inspired by U.S. transport planes bringing cargo to a Pacific island during World War II. This comparison was used by Cornwall Alliance in one of its rants about climate science: "scientists and politicians use this environmentalist Cargo Cult Science to make the most incredible predictions of future doom."[334] As in many cases of denial ideology, there is an analogous counter-example that shows why denial is a cult in itself. "Climate-change denial [is] like a cargo cult. Introduced from the outside, corporate motives via conservative media. But now it's become fully identified with the icons of local culture, so it's no longer up for discussion."[335] In a folksy way, this describes how denial ideology develops popularity, a belief system that is imposed from the outside but takes on local color that seems to make it indigenous when it is not.

Some writers, such as the author of an article in the UK *Telegraph,* use a rather cheeky style to describe climate science as a religion. "So, for some years, we humoured the climate-change lobby, and nodded our heads gravely when experts told us we must help save the planet. But most of us behaved like churchgoers listening to boring sermons." *Telegraph* readers might be bored by climate "sermons," but for some readers the sermons are not so much boring as infuriating, and the *Telegraph* quotes Owen Patterson as saying that renewable energy is "the single most regressive policy we have seen in this country since the Sheriff of Nottingham."[336] Patterson is former Secretary for Environment who has made a reputation for himself as a climate denier.

Treating climate science like a religion is not only wrong, it is dangerous. "Having 'faith' in a set of 'facts' puts you on the wrong side of history, and in the company of tyrants and inquisitors. ...Surely we can elevate our conversation about climate change to the sphere in which it belongs. It is no more appropriately a matter of partisan politics than it is a matter of faith to be confessed aloud." [337] If one attempts to suppress climate science through religious conflict, the "faith" test will become an anti-scientific mechanism for quashing information in the name of religious purity. (More in Chapter 6)

One commentator sought to equate climate activism with religious practices. Writing in the *Wall Street Journal*, James Taranto describes some statements by Eric Holthaus, a science journalist, as follows:

> What Holthaus describes is a religious experience, which led him to engage in ritualistic self-denial. "For me, quitting flying is just another choice that brings me closer to living a life that's in line with what I believe," he writes. This is the language of spirituality, not science. Of course Holthaus has a right to pursue spiritual fulfillment in whatever way suits him, at least as long as it does not harm others. But there's no denying that his spiritual practices – in Year 2, he says, he may "move into a smaller house" – are highly eccentric. [338]

Taranto conflates Holthaus' use of the word "believe" with religion, when it has other meanings such as subscribing to a scientific theory based on facts. [339] Taranto further muddies the water by accusing Holthaus of self-denial, as if he is a religious ascetic.

Some commentators use the analogy of religious orthodoxy to describe climate science. From the historical example of Galileo, who was persecuted for asserting the earth revolved around the sun, they will assert that climate change denial is the equivalent of truth versus religious orthodoxy.

> Just as the Roman Catholic Church imposed its dogma on the people for centuries, and made

groupthink the order of the day, the United Nations and its supporters of catastrophic man-made global warming want to impose their dogma on the world using groupthink as a means of achieving their goal.[340]

Galileo's example was used by one 2012 presidential candidate, Rick Perry (former governor of Texas), to justify his rejection of the "scientific consensus" on climate change.[341] Many denial ideologues have argued that one scientist like Galileo, bucking the consensus, can make discoveries that would totally overturn climate science. What they conveniently ignore is the massive scale of research on climate that has independently and repeatedly replicated the basic findings. Consensus is indeed a factor in research, as one commentator has observed: "...the use of consensus is merely one (structured) way of distilling evidence – evidence which might be somewhat ambiguous, incomplete or contradictory or where there is latitude for genuine differences of interpretation – into an overall agreed statement on an issue of scientific or public importance."[342] Consensus is never a sole criterion for the validity of science, but more of a reflection of how science operates through replication of research and peer review of publications. (More in Chapter 6)

Nevertheless, some politicians will continue to argue that even with consensus the science is not "settled," and that uncertainty justifies inaction. Congressman Jeff Miller (R-FL), stated:

> I'm concerned with the truth. And the truth is, climate has been changing for a long time. They call it global warming, global cooling – now everybody wants to call it climate change. Yes, the climate is changing. But it has been doing that for centuries. **And for us to say that it is a settled argument right now I think, again, is a foolish argument to make, because there are scientists on both sides of the issue that say that's it's not settled.**[343]

Of course, there are scientists on both sides of the issues around climate change and science is never "settled" in the sense that any finding has 100% probability. But many climate findings are supported at the 95% level.[344] To ignore the overwhelming level of scientific certainty about these issues – temperature increases, sea level rise, extreme weather – would, however, be a much more *"foolish argument"* than to pay attention to them.

George Will, a commentator who often appears on network TV, has linked climate activists with both "socialism" and religion:

> Global warming is socialism by the back door. The whole point of global warming is that it's a rationalization for progressives to do what progressives want to do, which is concentrate more and more power in Washington, more and more Washington power in the executive branch, more and more executive branch power in independent czars and agencies to micromanage the lives of the American people – our shower heads, our toilets, our bathtubs, our garden hoses. Everything becomes involved in the exigencies of rescuing the planet. Second, global warming is a religion in the sense that it's a series of propositions that can't be refuted. It's very ironic that the global warming alarmists say, "We are the real defenders of science," and then they adopt the absolute reverse of the scientific attitude, which is openness to evidence. You cannot refute what they say.[345]

Why is environmentalism defined as religion? For some politicians, it is a convenient way of rejecting climate findings as religious beliefs. "What are the costs of us going on these crusades, these environmental crusades?" Alabama State Senator Trip Pittman, R-Fairhope, asked Bloomberg News. "We've elevated environmentalism into some kind of religion." Presumably, if environmentalism is a religion, other (competing) religious beliefs might be just as valid and one can ignore or reject environmentalism since it is not a "true" religion. On the other hand, environmentalism may not have anything to do with religion if the bases of environmental policies are scientific findings.

Some commentators equate environmentalism to nature worship and other doctrines of a new religion. "The origins of warmism lie in a cocktail of ideas which includes anti-industrial nature worship, post-colonial guilt, a post-Enlightenment belief in scientists as a new priesthood of the truth, a hatred of population growth, a revulsion against the widespread increase in wealth and a belief in world government."[346] This is quite a list of sins attributed to a "*new priesthood*" of scientists.

Climate science addresses changes in nature that follow from human activities, and that arouses the ire of those who oppose the new priesthood. "But how do you start a new Earth religion in a secular age in which religious appeals have lost much of their resonance? Establish what could be described as a materialistic theocracy. Okay. How to do that? Personalize 'nature', and grant 'her' human-like 'rights.'"[347] This is how one author explains the emergence of nature worship from climate science.

Among the "new priesthood" are also environmental activists in organizations such as the Sierra Club and Greenpeace. One commentator has called them the "degrowth crowd."

> The prescriptions put forward by the degrowth crowd are familiar. Nuclear energy is bad. Genetically modified foods are bad. Coal isn't just bad, it's awful. Oil is bad. Natural gas – and the process often used to produce it, hydraulic fracturing – is bad. Those things must be replaced by what the degrowth crowd claims are the Earth-friendly ones. Renewable energy, of course, is good.[348]

A diatribe such as this tends to gather a whole range of issues and use them to criticize climate activism – genetically modified foods and nuclear energy – as well as fossil fuels. Supposedly, they are blindly and unalterably against growth of any kind. Such analysis is more rhetorical than analytical.

A politician in Alabama, who has rejected findings that the state will be subject to flooding and extreme weather, had this to say about climate science:

> Trip Pittman, a Republican state senator who represents Baldwin County on the east side of Mobile Bay, calls federal research on climate change "bad science" and "fear-mongering." Spending millions based on such predictions doesn't make sense, he says. "What are the costs of us going on these crusades, these environmental crusades?" says Pittman. "We've elevated environmentalism into some kind of religion."[349]

His rejection of this *"religion"* because of costs may cost the state a lot more in the future. Ben Raines, executive director of Weeks Bay Foundation, a conservation group in Baldwin County, noted "People here are already dealing with a more extreme climate and with sea levels that are on the rise inundating properties more and more frequently," and politicians "are just going to have to deal with it, whether they like to or not."[350] Politicians like Pittman will have to resolve issues of extreme weather and sea level rise soon, with costs increasing each year that they delay action. "Delaying action is foolish and irresponsible."[351]

A CNBC commentator, Joe Kernen, says that climate science is like witchcraft and compares it to medieval religion: "It's almost like witchcraft. In the middle ages it was witchcraft. You would have attributed adverse weather events to witchcraft. Now we just have CO2 at this point."[352] He accuses scientists of *witchcraft* that magically uses CO2 as a cause of climate change when there is no scientific proof of causation. According to this view, Tyndall, Arrhenius, Revelle, Hansen and countless other scientists must be wizards whose work is based solely on magic.

Ian Wishart traces the origins of climate change agreements to the Rio Summit, and describes the religious nature of that summit and the subsequent agreements:

> The climate change Earth Summit at Rio in 1992 was kicked off in its preliminary session, a Sacred Gathering, with a prayer to Satan. It was the largest gathering of world leaders in history. Little wonder the climate debate has such religious overtones. An attempt to stir up the biggest changes in human consciousness in history is being done in the name of Lucifer. You could be forgiven for thinking the world truly is going to Hell in a handcart. Again, and this point cannot be overstressed: regardless of whether you believe any of the supernatural jargon, the people ultimately controlling this and driving the UN process do, and so far they're winning.[353]

Allegedly the UN leaders are religious as well as political leaders, and the religion they espouse is Satanism. The denial ideology treatment of climate change as a religious belief system is not a valid definition of religion, which involves beliefs about non-empirical concepts such as deities and the soul. One might ask, why would an author mischaracterize science or ideology as religion? Wishart provides a clue in his statement about the international implications of climate science:

> ...the issue of Climate Change has been used as the primary evangelisation tool to prepare the way for acceptance of global government, which is why the actual science on the issue is secondary to maintaining momentum for a new structure.[354]

It is clear from this quote that Wishart regards climate science as "secondary" to evangelism in promoting "*acceptance*

133

of global government." In other words, climate science has been hijacked by elites to justify taking global power.

What about the role of conventional religion in addressing climate change? The vast majority of religious traditions – Christian, Jewish, Muslim, Buddhist, and others – do not have any tendencies toward denial. Many embrace climate science and adopt moral stances in favor of reducing carbon emissions, including evangelical Christians.[355]

When believers in any religion, particularly monotheistic religions, attribute natural events to God's will, there will be theological problems with climate change.

> To my mind, any intelligence that bestowed a moral system on just our species among millions, plus the tools to wreck it all, would not be worth the term; and any god remotely satisfied with the results to date would be a risible god. But such a provenance is surely the handiest, when it comes to self-justification: when "God is on our side," anything goes.[356]

It would be irresponsible to hold God responsible for the human activities that cause climate change. Nevertheless, there are some who believe that God has bestowed man with dominion over nature and therefore man has the right to treat nature as instrumental to his own interests. It is likely that most religions would consider this an abomination.[357] Only those believers with a bent toward denial ideology can ignore the true nature of religion vis-à-vis nature.

Religious conservatives may also be political conservatives and that parallel often determines their view of climate science. "One reason is the resurgence of conservative religious groups that have chosen to support specific economic, political, and social arrangements and the political candidates who favor those arrangements. ...Science is seen, then, as a challenge to a world view and to an ideology."[358] When religion spills over the boundary from purely spiritual matters to scientific matters, it will take on features of an ideology. Then, if the proponents of ideology see climate science as a threat, they try to reduce it to their ideological level so that they can challenge it on an equal basis.

A variation on the theme that climate science is a religion is an assertion that climate modeling is a religion: "Hypothetical global warming has reached religious levels for some people.... The climate science community knows about these failings, but I doubt many persons outside their clique do."[359] Supposedly, the "clique" in the climate science community has such faith in the models that they have become a kind of catechism, not to be questioned.

Science writer Wendy Grossman wrote, "Science is not a belief system but the best process we have for establishing the truth. If the issue of climate change is one of competing religious beliefs, then those claiming impending doom can be safely ignored."[360] By defining climate science as a religion, denial ideologues seek to downplay its findings and convince people that it is not worth taking seriously.

Finally, after all of the strange forms of religion attributed to climate science, what about conventional religion? Some organizations such as Cornwall Alliance that profess an evangelical religious orientation are accusing climate science of paganism.[361] They also rail against any other evangelicals such as the Evangelical Climate Initiative that support climate science findings and call for a moral effort against climate change.[362] The fact that there are such conventional religious groups with the same orientation as some of the denial ideologues suggests that religion is irrelevant to climate science, although it may be relevant to the ethical issues of climate policies. "Man's dominion over the earth," a doctrine sometimes invoked by denial ideologues, is not a justification for ignoring climate science. On the other hand, a doctrine common to many religions, "stewardship," is a doctrine that would provide a moral basis for addressing climate change.[363]

Climate Science and the UN

Another of Wishart's themes is the totalitarian nature of the UN. Denial ideologues show considerable animus vis-à-vis the UN.

> It turns out that UN...officials don't come from nations that encourage them to behave in a circumspect manner. These people don't believe they are answerable for their transgressions, or that the rules even apply to them. We can be sure that some of these people will end up deciding the fate of billions of climate-related dollars. [364]

The UN is a favorite whipping boy for denial ideologues. Often they assume that the UN controls climate science or climate policies through its bureaucracy. [365] The opposite is true. Scientists from many countries control findings of climate science, published in numerous journals, and then aggregated in UN reports under the aegis of the IPCC. The IPCC does not set climate policies; individual government members do. The "bureau" of the IPCC, a term that has bamboozled many denial ideologues, is actually an elected body of volunteer climatologists from many countries, not a large bureaucracy of civil servants.

Denial ideology seems to encourage the notion that this bureau is somehow a large office of "tyrannical" bureaucrats plotting global governance. Why would bureaucrats want to govern the world? The *Wall Street Journal* provides a rationale: "The IPCC also turns out to have an agenda that's less about climate change than income inequality and redistribution." [366] Presumably the IPCC bureaucrats want to control the world economy to end inequality, a proposition that is laughable if one knows anything about how the IPCC is run. [367]

Why is the UN such a whipping boy? The UN irritates climate ideologues because it seems to call for control over sovereign nations:

The other agenda Greens agree upon is that the government should own and control every square inch of the nation's (and world's) landmass. That is why climate change is part of the United Nations' intention to become the single world government. It is home to the Intergovernmental Panel on Climate Change that has clung to the global warming hoax since they invented it in the late 1980s.[368]

It is not unusual for denial ideologues to refer to global governance as a consequence of climate science findings. There is a kernel of truth in the assertion that climate change policies may require some global governance. The UNFCCC, for example, is an agreement among 194 nations to avoid "dangerous interference" by humans with the climate. Analysts have noted, "Those exasperated at the mismatch between the glacial progress of the global governance of climate change and the urgency of the problem sometimes long for more effective centralized global authority. That is not realistic (though that doesn't stop the fear of such an authority driving the paranoia of American denialists)."[369] It is not realistic because of nationalism and a fear of losing national sovereignty, a fear exploited by politicians such as Senator James Inhofe (R-OK). Any hint of international policies to address climate change will set off fiery denunciations by denial ideologues.

A documentary film with the title "Global Warming or Global Governance" was produced by Exploration Films for use in school classrooms. Its synopsis attributes the governance efforts to the UN:

> The DVD provides evidence that the global warming agenda is being funded with tens of billions of dollars as a mechanism to create global governance. Hear from congressmen, experts and even well-known news broadcasters how global governance puts global institutions, especially the United Nations (UN), that are not accountable to the

American people in control of every aspect of our economy.[370]

There is a school of thought in denial ideology that regards the motivation for climate science as power usurpation through international actions. Because greenhouse gases do not respect national borders, and emissions reduction actions by one country can be annulled by others that do not match such actions, the issue is inherently international. That is why some denial ideologues such as Senator Inhofe hint of threats to U.S. sovereignty as he speaks of "anti-sovereignty internationalists."[371]

The idea that the United Nations can somehow take over the U.S. and impose its will is bizarre: "there exists no plausible mechanism through which global authoritarianism could be established."[372] The UN is limited by the need for consensus. In the UNFCCC (UN Framework Convention on Climate Change) meetings, for example, all agreements have to have consensus to take effect, and even then the enforcement of any provisions depends on the authority of the individual member states. Those of us who have observed the prolonged arguments at meetings of the UNFCCC consider the rants of the denial ideologues ridiculous.

From scam to totalitarian rule, extreme denial becomes more and more wacky as ideologues seek ways to discredit climate science. As they find it difficult to refute the science, ideologues turn their attention to attacking the scientists. They start by accusing them of "scams" and fraud, then proceeding to "tyranny," and finally to "totalitarian" rule over society. Portraying climate science as a scam perpetrated by religious zealots with a thirst for power is a standard narrative of denial ideology. Examples in this chapter are more extreme than most, but the themes illustrated here are pervasive in the denial literature.

Chapter 5:
Denial Fanatics and Climate Costs

"Climate change sounds very much like a dead Hippie's revenge." *Houston Chronicle, December 10, 2012*

Many observers have compiled the costs of climate change, and the latest IPCC report makes these costs very clear.[373] Referring to that report, Secretary of State John Kerry said "There are those who say we can't afford to act. But waiting is truly unaffordable. The costs of inaction are catastrophic."[374] Nevertheless, there are denial ideologues who would have us wait, or do nothing about climate change, until those costs are unaffordable. Costs are now estimated at $85 per person for each ton emitted in the U.S. At that level, the total costs for the U.S. population would be $544 billion.[375] What could we do better with that money? Perhaps we could ramp up renewable energy.

Denial ideologues maintain their stance in the face of such costs. They find ways to deny the effects of climate change, including extreme weather. Two of the most vociferous advocates of denial, Larry Bell and Brian Sussman, have maintained their positions in the face of the droughts and superstorms. Brian Sussman made the following comment about Superstorm Sandy:

Let's stop here and apply some science. While it's true that a hurricane can only form in water 82 degrees (F) or warmer, there is no data to suggest that water warmer than 82 degrees increases the intensity of a hurricane or frequency of hurricanes. In fact there have been numerous studies indicating that in periods of actual global warming, hurricane formation is sub-average.[376]

Sussman is attempting to deflect the argument that the increasing warmth of the Atlantic strengthened Superstorm Sandy. He repeats the denial argument that such events are a "natural function of the atmosphere." He cleverly avoids the issue of warmer water so late in the season and so far north by use of an extraneous argument: *there is no data to suggest that water warmer than 82 degrees increases the intensity of a hurricane or frequency of hurricanes.* The issue is not whether the water is warmer than 82 degrees, but what role that warm water played in sustaining the storm and enlarging its scope. Many scientists have noted that during the months preceding Sandy, temperatures in the Atlantic became unnaturally warm further north than before.

Rejection of climate change as a factor in Sandy is echoed by Tisdale, who claims "Hurricanes are fueled by the seasonally warmed waters of the North Atlantic. What alarmists failed to understand – or they elected not to disclose – was that the sea surface temperatures of Sandy's storm track haven't warmed in 70-plus years, not since the Great New England Hurricane of 1938."[377] This canard is similar to the other statements about warming in the Twentieth Century, that claim that the hottest decade on record is the 1930's (see Chapter 1 for the refutation of this canard). Here is one example of scientific refutation of the sea temperature canard: "Over the last century, temperatures along the northeastern U.S. coast have warmed at a rate 1.8–2.5 times the regional atmospheric temperature trend."[378]

Issues surrounding droughts in the Midwest and the West have also provoked denial ideology. Larry Bell has commented on drought. In his discussion of the Midwest drought, Bell suggests that it is primarily a figment of media frenzy.

> How can there be any lingering doubt about global warming? Right? In other words, this means [Obama] will further energize his EPA's war on fossil energy, and double-down on his "green energy" subsidy agenda. If this doesn't help to fix the economy, that priority will just have to wait. Premised upon recent weather in some U.S. regions, the global warming crisis narrative has been driving lots of media traffic.[379]

Bell first dismisses any link of droughts and storms to climate change, and then goes on to suggest that it is a "war on fossil energy" that will preclude Obama from "fixing the economy." In other words, he tries to shift the argument with a *non sequitur,* dismissing the link between drought and climate change and making a segue to energy policy. He just doesn't think that it is necessary to conduct the "war on fossil energy" because there is global cooling, not warming.[380] This argument is found in many denial publications that set up a false dichotomy between climate change mitigation policy and economic recovery policy.

Bell introduces one of the main tactics of denial ideologues: creating doubt in the minds of readers and listeners. By asserting that climate science is uncertain, denial ideologues raise questions about whether unpleasant actions would be necessary. Creating doubt is the same tactic for climate change as it was for smoking. If you cannot disprove the science, raise doubts and those who do not want to accept the science will have excuses to ignore it.

Many denial ideologues have attacked climate science on the issue of whether extreme weather is related to climate change. John Christy, a climatologist at the University of Alabama, has characterized extreme weather as follows:

141

Recently it has become popular to try and attribute certain extreme events to human causation. The Earth however, is very large, the weather is very dynamic, especially at local scales, so that extreme events of one type or another will occur somewhere on the planet in every year. Since there are innumerable ways to define an extreme event (i.e. record high/low temperatures, number of days of a certain quantity, precipitation total over 1, 2, 10 ... days, snowfall amounts, etc.) this essentially assures us that there will be numerous "extreme events" in every year because every year has unique weather patterns.[381]

He then goes on to dismiss the Midwest drought, Colorado wildfires and other weather events as natural phenomena unrelated to anthropogenic climate change. He attributes all to natural causes. This is a standard argument of the denial ideology. We can afford to ignore human sources of climate disruptions because these events are only "natural" and will occur more or less randomly irrespective of human influences.

Of course, it is comfortable to attribute extreme weather entirely to natural causes. Relieving humans of the responsibility for climate change alleviates society from addressing the problems of energy and environment that underlie climate disruption. Some members of Congress were probably happy to hear the good news from John Christy.

A variation on this argument of natural causes is that volcanoes can cause more climate change than human sources. Senator Lisa Murkowski (R-AK), said "The emissions that are being put in the air by that [Iceland] volcano are a thousand years' worth of emissions that would come from all of the vehicles, all of the manufacturing in Europe."[382] It is inconceivable that someone in her position could have the facts so wrong. She is chairperson of the Senate Energy and Natural Resources

Committee, and her views will have an effect on how the Senate views climate change.

The Rhetoric of Denial

Denial has been expressed in numerous ways.[383] Many social movements have developed denial ideology through the establishment of certain principles. They have tried to (1) reinterpret reality to suit their particular world view, a principle I call "counter-mythology;" (2) promote leaders who offer contrasts to the elites of society, a principle I call "counter-elitism;" (3) criticize dominant practices as wrong for society, a principle I call "alienation;" and (4) offer their members absolute beliefs, or "absolutism."[384] With regard to climate change, these principles tend to shape the rhetoric of denial movements.

Counter-Mythology: Energy, growth and climate are a volatile mixture for ideological formation. Fossil-fueled growth in the past 250 years creates a major dilemma for modern societies: continue on the same path or make a paradigm shift to renewable energy. This dilemma often leads to some absurd analyses of the effects of energy on political and social change by denial ideologues. An illustration of the rhetoric of denial ideology is the book *"Energy and Climate Wars"* by Glover and Economides.

> We know from our history that an irrational fear of "climate apocalypse" and the arbitrary actions of the "weather gods" has driven nature-worshipping green ideologues' fears in every generation. Being inherently anti-capitalist in our day, they care little whether their demands threaten to bankrupt modern economies, or deny poorer nations the same hydrocarbon-powered path out of poverty taken by the industrialized developed nations.[385]

Attribution of a mythology involving fear of "climate apocalypse" and "weather gods" to environmentalists is a classic form of counter-mythology used in the denial movements. It projects a kind of religious motivation on climate science and policy (see Chapter 4). There is irony in this form of argument, since many denial ideologues invoke religious beliefs such as "man's dominion over nature" or a "Biblical viewpoint on the environment" in their ideology.

When one considers this facet of denial ideology, one can better understand the problems faced by climate science in countering what has become the dominant motif of the modern world. Even those who are well educated or knowledgeable about nature sometimes tend to ignore human dependence on the environment. "Even more astonishing, perhaps, is that among those who are aware, many hold the view that climate change and massive biodiversity loss will not really impinge on human well-being. This is not just about tendentious climate change skepticism. (Biodiversity loss skepticism is, interestingly, much rarer.) It is firmly rooted in another critical flaw in the industrialized worldview: the portrayal of human beings as somehow separate from the rest of the natural world."[386] As we have seen before, this worldview is pervasive in denial ideology.

Even among those who are aware, the effect of energy use and other facets of industrialized society seem somehow exempt from natural laws. We can continue "business as usual" without worrying about effects on nature, because human beings are "somehow separate from the rest of the natural world."

Counter-Elitism: Arguments against acknowledging the harmful effects of greenhouse gas emissions are common in the denial ideology, and they often depend on attacking climate science for its influence on public policy. Climate scientists are portrayed as an anti-democratic elite whose attempts to grasp power must be strenuously resisted.

One expression of counter-elitism is the argument that the environmental elites are trying to control public spending, something that vexes denial ideologues. Instead of spending money on alternative energies or efficiencies, they argue, it should be spent on poverty alleviation and economic development. This type of rhetoric depends on a false dichotomy: we can alleviate global warming, or alleviate poverty, but we cannot do both (see Chapter 3).

Invoking one of the canards of denial ideology, "global cooling" (see Chapter 1), the rhetoric accuses climate elitists of causing the public to panic about global warming and "peak oil."

> Driven by panic-inducing UN IPCC theory over the alleged threat from man-made CO2 - after a decade where the scientific data shows a downward trend in global mean temperatures and supplemented with irrational fears over early peak oil theories, Western politicians and others remain consistently inured to the economic energy "facts of life.".... Meanwhile, the political energy disconnect has fuelled an almost ethereal, religious vision among those who seek to appease the earth and climate change.[387]

Climate science is portrayed as "panic-inducing UN IPCC theory," presumably perpetrated by elitist scientists. Political leaders are blamed for succumbing to panic from IPCC "theories" based on irrational fears promulgated by scientific elites. Ideologues describe these elites as a *priesthood* "who seek to appease the earth and climate change." This may seem absurd, but sometimes such statements spook political leaders. Other commentators, such as Joseph Bast, president of the denial organization Heartland Institute, have criticized IPCC on scientific grounds: "Ethical standards have been lowered, peer review has been corrupted, and we can't trust peers in our most prestigious journals anymore."[388]

Tim Ball turns the concept of peer review, a principle of science, against climate science by accusing scientists of elitism:

> I became suspicious when people were classified and derided by the Palace Guard and others for the number of "peer reviewed" articles

145

they published. It was an extension of the attempt to isolate themselves as an elite group. They were the only people qualified and it is similar to their use of phrases like, working climatologist or active climatologist.[389]

Obviously, Ball is using the phrase "*Palace Guard*" to imply that climate scientists are somehow defending an elite group through peer review. He argues that the "Palace Guard" has closed off the discussion of climate science to others such as himself, who can be a counter-elite that can refute findings of temperature increases and other aspects of climate science.

Another view of elites comes from Richard Lindzen, Emeritus Professor of Meteorology at MIT, and a favorite source for denial ideologues. He describes the "decline" of popular support for climate science as follows:

> It is, therefore, no surprise that polls show that support for climate alarm is rapidly evaporating among the population at large, but continues to engage the fevered enthusiasm of the privileged. For the privileged, it matters little whether energy is provided by modern fuels or the sweat of the common man.[390]

This view of elitism shifts the attack from scientists to "*the privileged*," presumably those who are rich and powerful enough to command "*the sweat of the common man*." Perhaps this would play on fears of losing status under climate change, where the population at large might be reduced to manual labor.

Whom do denial ideologues prefer for their elites? Hamilton identifies the preferences of denial ideologues as follows:

> Previous work has shown that individuals with individualistic and hierarchical values are prone to dismiss the risk of global warming because accepting the danger would be an indictment of

146

social elites they respect, and require limits on the free market.[391]

They prefer "true" scientific elites, i.e. those who agree with the denial ideologues, to counter mainstream climate science with "scientific data that shows a downward trend in global mean temperatures," a canard circulating among denial ideologues. Whenever a "scientist" states that the globe is cooling, it reassures those who do not want to face the possibility that action is required to reduce global warming. At the same time, such a "scientist" drives followers further and further away from the truth.

John Christy and Richard McNider of the University of Alabama attribute nefarious effects of the use of climate science for policy.

> "Consensus" science that ignores reality can have tragic consequences if cures are ignored or promising research is abandoned. The climate-change consensus is not endangering lives, but the way it imperils economic growth and warps government policy making has made the future considerably bleaker. The recent Obama administration announcement that it would not provide aid for fossil-fuel energy in developing countries, thereby consigning millions of people to energy poverty, is all too reminiscent of the Sick and Health Board denying fresh fruit to dying British sailors.[392]

In this rather convoluted statement, the use of "*energy poverty*" to describe the effect of climate science mixes metaphors with "*denying fruit to dying British sailors.*" The reference to British sailors harks back to a time when the admiralty officials resisted efforts to treat scurvy with fresh fruit.

Scientists are often viewed as elitist, a view that feeds into counter-elitism in denial ideology. "It is true that some scientists are barely disguised elitists, impatient with process and politics, and apparently confident that if they could get their hands on the machinery of governance, then whatever problems we face could be solved before dinner." This impatience sometimes stems from a realistic view that the pace of climate change demands immediate action, but such action is not occurring yet. Scientists are reticent to insist on rapid changes in energy use (see Chapter 7), but they are aware of the costs of delay. "In my opinion, however, scientists have largely behaved admirably in bringing climate change to public attention, and in doing what they can to motivate action in ways that are consistent with their professional responsibilities."[393]

Even if they are impatient and brusque in dealing with climate change denial, scientists can hardly be considered in the same vein as political elites. Indeed, many of them avoid the political limelight, recognizing that they would be subject to attack if they wandered outside their areas of specialization. A few have dared to confront denial ideology, as we will see in Chapter 7, but they have often paid dearly for their "transgressions."

An issue analogous to climate change that arouses counter-elitist tendencies is the issue of smoking and health. When the Surgeon General first reported the health effects of smoking in 1964, many smokers and tobacco companies attacked the report as an elitist document. Climate science may be at that stage now, where IPCC documents or the National Climate Assessment can be seen as representing only an elitist point of view. If the same dynamics as smoking come into play, there may be a gradual drift away from this counter-elitist view. "In the end, smoking became unacceptable. That was not a legal statement. It was a social statement, and consensus was broad and has held for a long time. Maybe you can get there on carbon emissions, but right now this is an issue for the elites," according to economist Douglas Holtz-Eakin.[394]

A number of observers have noted the analogy between smoking and climate change denial. Some of the same "scientists" who tried to prove that second-hand smoke does not have health effects are now denying climate science.[395] This denial may sustain the counter-elitism of the denial movement for a time, but if it follows the course of the smoking denial movement, the views of the elites may become socially acceptable and isolate the climate denial ideologues.

Alienation: At its root, alienation means separation from something, as when a person is "alienated" from his or her property and can sell it without losing a sense of self. In the context of climate change denial, alienation means a separation from natural laws, "man's dominion over nature," signifying a lack of responsibility for the fate of nature. In ideological terms, this takes the form of denying scientific findings about nature.

Denial ideologues regard climate science as a fraud, and the climate scientists are viewed as elites perpetrating their hoaxes on the public.[396] This line of reasoning relies on a version of "common sense," in which those without a scientific degree can understand climate as well as any scientist. It often invokes the concept of climate as an extension of weather:

> The theory of global warming is a gigantic weather forecast for a century or more. However interesting the scientific inquiries involved, therefore, it can have almost no value as a prediction. Yet it is as a prediction that global warming (or, as we are now ordered to call it in the face of a stubbornly parky 21st century, "global weirding") has captured the political and bureaucratic elites.[397]

This is a complete misreading of climate science, which uses projections, not predictions. These projections are "scenarios" in which different variables are tweaked to provide estimates of varying outcomes, not unchanging predictions of specific outcomes. Confusing weather and climate is typical of denial critiques of climate science.[398]

In its most sophisticated form, alienation takes the shape of a critique of "popular science."

> And yet, it is the erroneous blind faith - very different from reasoned faith - in the viability of renewable energy as a future energy "solution" that is currently driving massive public investment in alternative energy projects. ...it is equally pertinent to other notions of popular science, especially alarmist predictions associated with the twin issues currently panicking us in the direction of the global "quick-fix" renewables revolution. They are: peak oil (the theory that the oil will quickly run out) and global warming/climate change alarmism (the theory that CO, from fossil fuel burning is catastrophically warming up the earth).[399]

Here the rhetoric seeks to criticize climate science as *"popular science"* and *"alarmist."* Climate policies such as renewable energy are considered a *"quick fix."* Many problems are said to result from peak oil theories and global warming *"alarmism."* All of these accusations distort the science and its prescriptions for change.

Some of this sarcasm about renewable energy and other climate policies is taken to an extreme in critical analyses. Discussing prominent environmental groups, Bryce suggests

> ...the Sierra Club, Greenpeace, and many other groups want to pave the world with low-density wind turbines. Not only do they insist on renewable energy; they want us all to live on homesteads equipped with a bedraggled organic garden, a compost pile, and maybe a few scrawny chickens.[400]

While facetious, this analysis suggests that environmental activists are not to be taken seriously because their proposed solutions are too unrealistic.

Many denial ideologues argue that the eventual effect of climate science is to remove human influence from the earth, ultimately by removing humans from earth.[401] This kind of argument attributes a kind of extreme alienation to climate science, a mirror image of the extreme arguments of denial ideologues about "man's dominion over nature." It is, of course, a complete fantasy on the part of denial ideology. More pertinent is the critique that by asserting "man's dominion over nature," denial ideology is encouraging alienation from nature. If man can dominate nature, it must be somehow separate from humanity and subject to subordination.[402]

If one rejects the dominion of man over nature, then one has to rethink the development of a fossil-fuel based economy. At times this leads to a criticism of the "vanguard" of climate activists as anti-everything:

> Unfortunately, the vanguard of the Green Left continues to promote an antibusiness, anti-innovation, antimodern energy, and in some cases, an anti-human outlook. The Green Left's romanticization of the past, along with its continuing claim that renewable energy and organic agriculture are the only way forward, ignores the deprivation, lack of social, intellectual, and economic mobility, and short life spans that dominated preindustrial societies.[403]

Now, the "Green Left" becomes an elite that is leading society back to a more primitive level, and is even showing "anti-human" tendencies. This is ironic, given the possibility that humans will be among the main victims of their own tendencies to pollute the atmosphere, tendencies against which the "Green Left" is expending so much effort. Such an approach makes climate activism into a kind of extreme alienation, attributing to it a form of nihilism that offends the optimistic nature of modern societies.

151

Absolutism: One of the clearest examples of absolutist rhetoric is "alarmism," a form of exaggeration that builds on any suggestion that there may be dangerous consequences of climate change. Denial ideology conflates climate science with "alarmism," and tries to link it to "global disaster."

> Over recent decades, the popular science-mass media axis has been wrong in its dire warnings of one global disaster after another. ...After so many failed predictions you might think they would wise up to the gulf that exists between real science and speculative "consensus" science. Now the same axis of alarmism is equally "sure" about global warming and the early end of our oil-driven civilization.[404]

Climate science is lumped with a bunch of other "*false prophecies*" as "*prophet-of-doom-induced mass hysterias,*" completely discredited by the absolute truth of "scientific hard facts." Climate science is depicted as an "alarmist house of cards."[405] This type of either-or thinking is illustrative of the absolutist nature of denial ideology.

Fanaticism in climate denial leads some to hold onto their beliefs in the face of contradictory reality. Even after the 2011 and 2012 droughts had major impacts on his state, Senator Inhofe maintained his denial posture. He released a report that describes how climate policy "spells doom for jobs and economic growth."

> Washington, D.C. - Senator James Inhofe (R-Okla.), Ranking Member of the Senate Committee on Environment and Public Works, today released a new EPW Minority Report entitled, "A Look Ahead to EPA Regulations for 2013: Numerous Obama EPA Rules Placed On Hold until after the Election, Spell Doom for Jobs and Economic Growth." This report enumerates the slew of environmental regulations that the Obama-Environmental Protection Agency (EPA) has

delayed or punted on before the election while President Obama is trying to earn votes; but the Obama-EPA plans to move full speed ahead to implement this agenda if President Obama wins a second term. As this report reveals, these rules taken together will inevitably result in the elimination of millions of American jobs, drive up the price of gas at the pump even more, impose construction bans on local communities, and essentially shut down American oil, natural gas, and coal production.[406]

The report contains many assertions about the deleterious effect of climate regulations on jobs and the economy, but nothing about the deleterious effect of climate change on future jobs or agricultural production.[407] It measures the costs of energy but fails to mention the costs of extreme weather. A report on climate change regulations that fails to mention the drought that devastated Inhofe's home state is hardly a meaningful analysis of a major issue facing the Congress and the country.

The issue of *"jobs, jobs, and jobs"* is one that has driven denial ideologues to ignore the long-term benefits of renewable energies versus the short-term benefits of construction jobs. One of the arguments used for building the Keystone XL pipeline is that it would create some jobs for construction workers. Research on the employment benefits of pipelines has shown, "if $5 billion is spent on a pipeline, it produces mostly short-term construction jobs, big private sector profits, and heavy public costs for future environmental damage. But if $5 billion is spent on public transit, building retrofits, and renewable energy, economies can gain, at the very least, three times as many jobs in the short term, while simultaneously helping to reduce the chances of catastrophic warming in the long term. In fact, the number of jobs could be many times more than that, according to the institute's modeling. At the highest end, green investment could create thirty-four times more jobs than just building another pipeline."[408]

Denial ideology often invokes higher costs and impacts on jobs and the economy, and extends these arguments to accuse "*alarmists*" of not justifying negative impacts. In this manner, the ideology converts fears about higher costs (and presumably a lower standard of living) to a critique of climate science. Scientists are not in the business of justifying negative impacts on the economy, however. They provide information about negative impacts on the environment that may indeed have negative impacts on the economy if nothing is done about the growth of carbon emissions.

On the issue of subsidies, denial ideology is vociferous about renewable energy subsidies but silent about fossil fuel subsidies. The International Monetary Fund (IMF) estimates that fossil fuel subsidies amount to $1.9 trillion a year, an amount that dwarfs any renewable energy subsidies and grossly distorts the market. Energy is not even priced for full cost, and the subsidies for fossil fuels further conceal the costs.

Documentation and Denial

Denial ideologues are prone to produce numerous documents to bolster their arguments without dealing with any of the major issues. They prefer to assert their positions without any substantiation of the facts. One of the most notorious expressions of denial is the "Oregon Petition," a document supposedly signed by 31,000 scientists.

> Global warming denialism is rife with fake experts. The Oregon petition and various other lists generated by climate change denialists are full of MDs, meteorologists, and the occasional AC repair man. These are not climate experts...when you have cranks like Christopher Monckton, who asserts he's a member of parliament when he's not (they even had to send him a letter telling him to stop), who routinely makes the same debunked arguments over and over... Cranks and denialists are probably incapable of judging whether someone is a legitimate source or authority. This is where crank magnetism comes from, as long as an "expert"

agrees with them, their otherwise ludicrous views and behavior have no bearing. Intellectual consistency and expertise in the field in question has no relevance in their eyes as long as they spout out BS that fits with their ideological biases.[409]

"Crank magnetism" is a rather vivid way of describing the tendency of denial ideologues to feed off each other's denial beliefs and misstatements, and to draw in followers who do not want to face the implications of climate change.

A further illustration of this tendency toward absolutism is the denial treatment of the "hockey stick" graph showing acceleration in temperature rise in recent decades. One writer claimed that "With no scientific evidence, the graph was fabricated to omit world-wide scientific recognition of Earth's previous recent natural cyclic periods that were far warmer. [The hockey stick] graph bypassed scientific peer review. [It was] Subsequently scientifically discredited world-wide."[410] In fact, it was subsequently verified by replication.

Global warming denialists are excellent at moving goalposts, they're still arguing about the damn hockey stick graph after all, despite its validation by multiple other methods. Some early criticisms which actually entered the literature might have represented a legitimate attempt to debate the findings scientifically, but after being affirmed by the NAS, replicated by other investigators, and expanded upon using other methods, the denialists still are not satisfied. They still will never accept the conclusions. No additional data, no worsening trend, no publication in the legitimate literature will ever make a dent. They reject the research because of ideological conflict, not because they have a legitimate scientific beef with the data.[411]

What can one do with extreme denial? We can begin with the acknowledgement that any one weather event does not prove climate change but that the trends are clear. This avoids the usual attacks that denialists levy on anyone that dares to suggest that weather patterns are changing. One can point to the undeniable increase in global temperatures (Chapter 1). Increasing temperatures have a number of effects, some of which will increase the severity of extreme weather. Sea level rise is a clear example of climate change, unavoidable to even the most closed-minded denial ideologue. He or she may quibble with measurements such as temperature or sea level, but will not be able to deny reality.

One undeniable reality is the refusal of insurance companies to insure vulnerable waterfront properties, coupled with deficits in government flood insurance programs.[412] When private insurance will not insure these high-risk properties, the government steps in and loses money. Liabilities for this insurance program amount to $527 billion, second only to Social Security for potential claims on government funds.[413] These economic realities are not scientific hypotheses.[414] Other realities are the billions of reconstruction dollars required to restore services in the cities impacted by superstorms, or billions of crop insurance dollars paid out to farmers in drought areas.

Insurance companies have not only reacted to climate science with changed business plans, they have aggressively asserted the need for governments to prepare for climate change. When floods inundated the Chicago sewer lines, one insurance company sued.

Farmers Insurance — on behalf of itself and other insurance companies and affected customers — has filed a suit against the city of Chicago and municipalities throughout Cook County for their failure to properly prepare for such weather eventualities in light of foreknowledge that such climate change-empowered storms may be possible. Farmers alleges that the city knew that its drainage systems were inadequate to handle a major infusion of floodwater, but did nothing to alleviate the situation.[415]

Heartland Institute, AFP, ALEC and the Koch Brothers

Organizations such as Heartland Institute and Americans for Prosperity (AFP) are making real progress in damaging acceptance of climate science in the general populace. Heartland sponsors conferences where "quack" scientists try to prove that mainstream climate science is wrong. [416] Americans for Prosperity, funded by the Koch brothers, sponsors legislation designed to derail climate policies.

> Foundations connected to the [Koch] brothers had, in the three-year stretch between 2005 and 2008, directed nearly $25 million to dozens of conservative think tanks, policy institutes, and advocacy groups that had challenged the existence of global warming. Exxon, during that same period, had contributed about $9 million to similar outfits. Charles and David Koch had outspent a public company with one of the world's largest market caps by nearly 3 to 1.[417]

AFP is counting on the uncertainty and lack of concern among American voters for its political strategies. According to Tim Phillips, president of Americans for Prosperity, "The left knows that the global warming agenda is a loser for them with the American people. Senators up for re-election have their sneakers on and are running from this. They know the issue doesn't matter with most Americans."[418] Phillips may have a point, since climate change is a low priority for American voters. If, however, extreme weather generates more interest, AFP may be on the losing side instead of the "global warming agenda."

AFP is an AstroTurf organization with grass-roots pretensions, and it does have clout in elections.[419] Speaking of Republican candidates in the 2016 presidential primaries, Phillips said, "They would be at a severe disadvantage in the Republican nomination process [if they supported climate science]. We would absolutely make that a crucial issue."[420] Making climate change a "crucial issue" means that AFP would apply a loyalty test to candidates, requiring them to take a position against climate science. At present, that test usually leads Republicans to say "I am not a scientist," sidestepping any commitments about climate policy (see Chapter 7).

Americans for Prosperity has lashed out at the EPA regulations on coal and the renewable energy mandates. "President Obama's E.P.A. is waging a war on traditional affordable energy through burdensome regulations and unrealistic mandates," the group's president, Tim Phillips, said in a statement. "It's time for the American people to stand up to this federal overreach, and send a message that they cannot afford to pay for Obama's environmental ideology."[421]

For Americans for Prosperity any hint of reduction of fossil fuels in the energy supply is anathema. Projecting dramatic increases in energy prices, from climate actions, is a standard tactic of denial ideology, as is ignoring the costs of inaction. Those costs of inaction have been estimated by the White House at $150 billion per year now, with escalation of costs in the future at the rate of 40% per decade. Many of those costs are associated with extreme weather. Senator Patty Murray of Washington state made this connection, citing that state's massive wildfires: "It's becoming clearer and clearer that if you care about the deficit, you need to care about climate change. We've got a responsibility to leave a stronger country for our children and grandchildren, and that means addressing climate change to help the environment, help the economy and help the federal budget."[422] The issue of costs extends beyond the narrow view of energy prices promoted by denial ideologues. When the National Forest Service and other government agencies are saddled with firefighting costs, the federal deficit increases or other programs must be cut.

Heartland is one of the leading denial organizations in the U.S., and ALEC is a group of state legislators funded by Koch brothers. [423] Together, they can sway a number of state

158

legislatures. James Taylor, Heartland's senior fellow for environmental policy, justifies their action in terms of short-run costs, ignoring the longer-run costs of extreme weather.

> Renewable power mandates are very costly to consumers throughout the 50 states, and we feel it is important that consumers have access to affordable electricity. We wrote the model legislation and I presented it. I didn't have to give that much of a case for it.[424]

Taylor would indeed have to give a case for it, if he would account for the full costs of electricity. Since power plants are allowed to emit carbon without paying for its costs, "affordable electricity" is cheap only in the short run. In the long run, its costs will be much higher.

What has been the role of Heartland Institute in climate change denial? In addition to sponsoring a number of conferences (as mentioned above), it also sponsors "studies" of climate change by the Non-Governmental International Panel on Climate Change (NIPCC), presumably a counterweight to the IPCC. These studies have, for example, attempted to refute IPCC findings by criticizing models used by climate scientists and downplaying the role of carbon dioxide in climate change.[425]

One rather insidious activity of Heartland, which parallels its efforts on state energy policies, is its role in attacking science education in various states. It has promoted policies of "teaching controversy," requiring schools to teach both "sides" of the climate debate. In other words, teachers are required to present denial ideology as the equivalent of climate science. When a set of internal Heartland documents describing these activities was purloined by Peter Gleick, a climate scientist, Heartland reacted with legal action and other measures.[426] One denial ideologist described this fight as follows:

> The left-liberal media was in no doubt that this was a very important story. Much bigger than

Climategate, certainly, to judge by their coverage. But those on the other side of the debate smelled a rat. This phrase about trying to stop "teachers from teaching science," for example. It didn't sound like anything a climate realist would say, but something more like the paranoid fantasy of a deranged alarmist engaged in a desperate smear job.[427]

Calling a climate scientist such as Gleick, whatever his slips, "a deranged alarmist engaged in a desperate smear job," is rather frenzied.[428] It is an example of the *ad hominum* arguments used in denial ideology when the science does not favor their views.

Despite the increasing costs, denial organizations continue to fight policies that might mitigate climate effects and cost less in the long run. Many states have passed "renewable portfolio mandates" requiring utilities to increase the amount of energy generated by renewable power such as wind and solar. Even this small move toward climate stability has generated denial opposition. Heartland Institute has teamed up with American Legislative Exchange Council (ALEC) to fight renewable portfolio mandates. ALEC is sponsoring legislation to reverse the mandates:

> The Heartland Institute, a libertarian think tank skeptical of climate change science, has joined with the conservative American Legislative Exchange Council to write model legislation aimed at reversing state renewable energy mandates across the country. The Electricity Freedom Act, adopted by the council's board of directors in October, would repeal state standards requiring utilities to get a portion of their electricity from renewable power, calling it "essentially a tax on consumers of electricity." Twenty-nine states and the District of Columbia have binding renewable standards; in the absence of federal climate legislation, these

160

initiatives have become the subject of intense political battles.[429]

ALEC's position paper on the renewable portfolio standard reads "As it pertains specifically to state-based renewable portfolio standard (RPS) programs, ALEC developed the *Electricity Freedom Act* which opposes government mandates that require utilities to generate a certain percentage of electricity from any particular source."[430] The model act itself has four proposed resolutions:

> **THEREFORE LET IT BE RESOLVED,** that the legislature of the State of _____ understands that a renewable energy mandate is essentially a tax on consumers of electricity that forces the use of renewable energy sources beyond what would be called for by real market forces and under conditions of real competition in generation resources; and
>
> **BE IT FURTHER RESOLVED,** that the State of {insert state} does not wish to discourage the marketing of "green" power and "green" pricing such that willing buyers and sellers of renewable energy sources are free to negotiate the terms and conditions of such sales, and no technology or class of technologies is given an unfair competitive advantage; and
>
> **BE IT FURTHER RESOLVED,** that this Act also recognizes the prudency and reasonableness of many of the renewable contracts and investments and allows for recovery of costs where appropriate; and
>
> **BE IT THEREFORE ENACTED**, that the State of {insert state} repeals the renewable energy mandate and as such, no electric distribution utilities and electric services companies will be forced to procure renewable energy resources as defined by the State of {insert state}'s renewable energy mandate.

It is generous of ALEC to suggest allowing marketing of "green" power at "green prices" by utilities, but utilities are not so willing as ALEC to let the markets work. In fact, encouraged by ALEC resolutions, utilities have been resistant to continued planning for renewable energy. Some have even tried to discourage it. There have been proposals such as one passed in

Arizona to require solar panel installers to pay extra for connecting to the grid. Although none has passed yet, they are having an effect.

A list of ALEC "model bills" includes a number that are directed toward stopping climate policies:

- Resolution in opposition to a carbon tax
- Resolution concerning EPA proposed greenhouse gas emission standards for new and exiting fossil-fueled power plants
- Resolution in response to EPA's plan to regulate greenhouse gases under the Clean Air Act
- Electricity Freedom Act [see above]
- The Market-Power Renewables Act
- Updating net metering policies resolution
- Resolution to retain state authority over hydraulic fracturing
- Resolution in support of the Keystone XL pipeline
- Resolution urging quick congressional action on the recommendations of the Blue Ribbon Commission on America's Nuclear Future
- Pipeline Replacement and Infrastructure Modernization And Enhancement Act
- Restrictions on participation in low-carbon fuel standards programs
- Resolution on alternative fuels[431]

While some of these resolutions are designed to support oil and nuclear power industries, most of them oppose state or federal efforts to reduce carbon emissions. The role of nuclear power in reducing emissions, for example, is hotly debated – a subject that will not be covered here. Other resolutions promote pipelines, hydraulic fracturing and other fossil fuel projects that would contribute to increasing carbon emissions.

Some state governments have followed the logic of ALEC and Heartland Institute and fought EPA regulations. The State Attorney General of Alabama, Luther Strange, said "EPA's proposed guidelines for existing power plant performance standards under Clean Air Act section 111(d) are simply the most recent example of the Federal Government usurping authorities properly delegated to the States." [432] He went on to justify opposition to EPA regulations by citing "low-income consumers in my state, or any other state, who will ask why they must pay more to reduce CO_2 emissions when those reductions cannot and will not impact the global climate." [433] This is a familiar denial argument: the control of emissions will hurt the poor the most, and besides it will not do any good. Not all state officials agree with this, however. Many states are implementing policies that would reduce global warming, even if their efforts contribute only small amounts to the total reductions in emissions needed at the global level.

Heartland Institute and ALEC collaborated on the "*Electricity Freedom Act*" proposed in 17 states with mandates. They have run into some resistance: "The solar and wind industries are lobbying hard against any rollbacks, since without mandates or other forms of coercion most of these companies would soon be out of business." [434] Some states might be surprised to see that their mandates are "coercion" as they have embraced the standards, which can save capital expenditures on fossil fuel plants that might be required if renewable energy is not installed. [435] The standards are examples of the "no regrets" policies that can be adopted regardless of the politicians' views on climate change.

ALEC has produced a position paper on climate change and renewable energy that is a masterwork of obfuscation.

> *Climate change is a historical phenomenon and the debate will continue on the significance of natural and anthropogenic contributions. ALEC will continue to monitor the issue and support the use of sound science to guide policy, but ALEC will also incorporate economic and political realism. Unilateral efforts by the United States or regions within the United States will not significantly decrease carbon emissions globally, and international efforts to decrease emissions have*

proven politically infeasible and unenforceable. Policymakers in most cases are not willing to inflict economic harm on their citizens with no real benefit. ALEC discourages impractical visionary goals that ignore economic reality, and that will not be met without serious consequences for worldwide standard of living.[436]

ALEC is correct in prophesizing that "debate will continue on the significance of natural and anthropogenic contributions," primarily because ALEC itself and its fellow travelers such as Heartland Institute continue to fan the flames of debate at the ideological level. It is not a debate about science *per se*. The scientific debate is more about timing and locus of consequences, not the significance of natural and anthropogenic contributions. As ALEC attempts to "incorporate economic and political realism," it tries to reorient the debate to political ideology by equating "realism" with its own views on how politics should ignore climate science. Science will continue on its own course.

ALEC has become a controversial organization as some of its supporters came to recognize its true character. Google, Inc., was one of those supporters. Executive chairman Eric Schmidt said that ALEC had been "literally lying" about the reality of climate change, "a fact that led Google to reconsider its financial contributions to the organization."[437] ALEC responded in kind: "It is unfortunate to learn Google has ended its membership in the American Legislative Exchange Council as a result of public pressure from left-leaning individuals and organizations who intentionally confuse free market policy perspectives for climate change denial."[438]

A number of other companies, including Coca-Cola, General Electric, General Motors and Microsoft, have also cut ties with ALEC because of its stands on climate change and other issues. Even an oil company, Occidental Petroleum, cut its ties with ALEC and found "other associations at the state-level that provide equal or greater value" than ALEC. When ALEC's denial ideology became apparent to these supporters, they withdrew their support. This seems to be a trend – a number of these same companies have withdrawn support from Heartland Institute as well. Nevertheless, ALEC and Heartland continue to have influence on climate policy.

Extreme weather and extreme denial collide in denial ideology conflation of "affordable electricity" with fossil-fueled generation. As coal-fired power plants increase carbon concentrations in the atmosphere further and trigger more extreme weather, their costs will far outstrip the costs of renewable energy. Nevertheless, ALEC has tried to get Congress to prohibit EPA from regulating power plant carbon emissions: "ALEC is very concerned about the potential economic impact of greenhouse gas regulation on electricity prices and the harm EPA regulations may have on the economic recovery,"[439] according to a resolution adopted by ALEC. Its concern about effects of climate change is considerably less prominent.

Impacts of Extreme Weather and Denial

One area where extreme weather has a direct impact in U.S. states is transportation. Recently, the American Association of State Highway and Transportation Officials, whose advice on the design and maintenance of roads and bridges is closely followed by states, formed a Sustainable Transportation, Energy Infrastructure and Climate Solutions Steering Committee. The Association's executive director noted that extreme weather events have many impacts.

There is a whole series of standards that are going to have to be revisited in light of the change in climate that is coming at us," said John Horsley, the association's executive director. In the latest and most severe example, Superstorm Sandy inflicted the worst damage to the New York subway system in its 108-year history, halted Amtrak and commuter train service to the city for days, and forced cancellation of thousands of airline flights at airports in New York, New Jersey and

Philadelphia…. Record-smashing heat from Colorado to Virginia last summer caused train tracks to bend and highway pavement to buckle. A US Airways jet was delayed at Washington's Reagan National Airport after its wheels got stuck in a soft spot in the tarmac.[440]

Across the country, heat and floods impact subways, trains, airports and roads. Planning now must include more frequent repairs and reconstruction to adapt to climate change. This means increasing costs at a time when cities and states are strapped for cash.

Debate and argument will continue on the causes of extreme weather, but extreme denial is likely to lose ground as more weather events follow current trends. The effect of fanatic denial can be summed up as self-delusion in the face of risk.

The paradox in waging a war against the weather and other extreme events is that we might very well be our own worst enemy. As individuals, we may decide to build in risky areas. As entrepreneurs in the private sector, we may decide to locate our businesses in these hazard-prone regions. As decision makers in the public sector, we may permit millions of people to reside and businesses to operate in these areas without requiring them to adopt appropriate risk reduction measures. In refusing to take steps in a proactive manner to reduce our vulnerabilities, the seeds for future disasters are created that will affect our future well-being and social welfare.[441]

We can fool ourselves that climate change is not threatening our coasts or our food security only so long before reality catches up. Those who deny this reality are living in a fantasy world where droughts, superstorms and climate science are irrelevant to their dreams of the future. The future will not be so accommodating to their dreams, however. The effect of climate change on food production is not always bad, but in general food security is less assured in a changing climate: "**For the major crops (wheat, rice, and maize) in tropical and temperate regions, climate change without adaptation is projected to negatively impact production for local temperature increases of 2°C or more above late-20th-century levels, although individual locations may benefit (*medium confidence*).** Projected impacts vary across crops and regions and adaptation scenarios, with about 10% of projections for the period 2030-2049 showing yield gains of more than 10%, and about 10% of projections showing yield losses of more than 25%."[442] In other words, while some regions may benefit from longer growing seasons with climate change, the net effect will be negative. Those who argue that climate change will improve food production are whistling past the graveyard. Even those who claim that more food can be grown in Canada or Siberia are overlooking a crucial factor: "...cheerful assurances that farming would expand poleward, turning northern Canada and Siberia into breadbaskets, failed to consider that acidic, conifer-covered taiga soils would take many millennia to adapt to the loamy demands of grains."[443]

One of the deleterious effects of questioning climate science is to raise doubts about societies' abilities to control emissions. This often takes the form of questioning the use of taxes or other economic policies to reduce carbon impacts.

> Very high carbon taxes or severely restrictive cap-and-trade policies might provide substantial motivation to conserve. These could reduce carbon-intensive consumption and motivate a switch to lower carbon power sources like nuclear. But these actions are undesirable because of their adverse effects on the economy. Research and development are worthwhile. But they can be wasteful and ineffective—recall Solyndra—and if R&D is to be government sponsored, all developed countries should participate in funding. Given these limitations on mitigating carbon emissions, it is important to study how to

167

adapt to climate change.[444]

While not denying climate change, this approach tends to delay or downplay mitigation, i.e. attempts to "reduce carbon-consumption and motivate a switch to lower carbon power sources," and then switch the argument to adaptation. But there is no reason why societies cannot pursue both, except a kind of fatalistic acquiescence that focuses on "adverse effects on the economy." Such a narrow view leaves out beneficial effects of switching to alternative forms of energy.

A variation on this theme is the argument that, even if we admit there is climate change, there is nothing we can do about it. "When you're discussing global warming, for example, the proper question is not whether man is causing global warming. The question is whether man can fix global warming – a question to which the universally-acknowledged answer is essentially no, unless we are willing to revert to the pre-industrial age."[445] This argument presupposes that there is nothing other than suppressing consumption for resolving climate change.

More insidiously, the effect of these kinds of denial is to legitimize indecision. Climate change seems to present a vicious conundrum: either we reduce emissions quickly and painfully, or we create conditions for economic, social and physical disaster. Diversion of GDP to develop and install renewable energy on a vast scale may have a painful impact on growth in other areas of the economy. Early investment at a massive level will reduce later costs but it also may inflict pain early on.[446] How it is managed is crucial to its effectiveness.

Growth has been associated with increased emissions of carbon, but it does not inevitably instigate global warming. To overcome the "dilemma of growth," as Tim Jackson terms it, there are models other than the current economic model that equates growth with prosperity. [447] Essentially, these models involve resolution of the conundrum of increasing use of resources and impact on the environment, by separating prosperity from unfettered growth of GDP (gross domestic product), the dominant current model. Measures of growth other than GDP can redirect economic activity toward long-term sustainable growth.

Even among leaders who accept the findings of climate science, this conundrum inhibits action. Denial ideology reinforces their delay because it reduces their scope of action. Fierce pushback in Congress and some state governments has been a major factor in the delay of action in the U.S.[448]

When considering the effects of climate change, decision makers need to take into account not only the immediate consequences, such as extreme weather, but also the long-term consequences such as sea level rise. It is difficult to make changes in the near term that will not have benefits until much later, and this leads many decision makers to avoid and delay actions. Adding to the problem is the uncertainty of climate science, which is small when it comes to attributing climate change to human activities, but enough to be exploited by denial ideologues.

In this sense, science is not the realm of "absolute and unquestionable certainty" – this is for ideologies and religions. Science, by contrast, works towards decreasing the degree of uncertainty in a given phenomenon or theory. Some level of uncertainty, however small, will always exist, especially when it comes to complex phenomena, such as global warming.[449]

Distinguishing between the absolute certainty of ideology and the nature of uncertainties inherent in scientific research on climate is important for understanding the disparity between them. While science is on one plane – reporting findings with some level of probability but not absolute certainty – ideology is on another plane, disseminating belief with unquestioning conviction.

While no scientist can clearly link individual extreme weather events to climate change, most scientists would advise decision makers that climate change would increase the probability of these events occurring more frequently. This should be reason enough for prudent decisions on energy. However, as we will see in the next chapters, there has been so much backlash against the science that decision makers are not prone to act according to long-term interests of society.

Chapter 6:
Ideology and Climate Science

There is a cultural disconnect in the quarrel between scientists and the denial ideologues. Ideologues view climate science as disdainfully as the scientists view denial. This disparity comes from the difference between science and ideology.

Why Scientists Object to Denial Ideology

Denial ideologues tend to dismiss most of climate science and treat it as irrelevant. Scientists take themselves and the science seriously and regard denial ideology as harmful, no matter how it is expressed. This difference comes from the way each views reality.

Scientists treat reality as a moving target, one that can be fixed only in "snapshots" that represent a slice of time. In climate science, the climate is always changing and the changes are the focus of attention. Denialists, on the other hand, tend to stick with dogma regardless of changes. In this respect, they are unlike either skeptics or contrarians: "Denialists, unlike both skeptics and contrarians, are dogmatists. They persist in espousing some particular view despite the evidence against it."[450]

171

In denial ideology, the climate remains static, or changes slowly, naturally and will return to stasis. Denial ideology does not admit of any human role in climate change that would require economic or social changes.[451] Some denial ideologues will admit that carbon dioxide concentrations are increasing – it is difficult for them to refute the Keeling curve – but they consider the effect of carbon dioxide as minimal or unrelated to temperature (see Chapter 1). Denial of human-induced climate change constitutes a cornerstone of the ideology and makes it adamantly absolutist in its approach to science.

Statements by denial organizations are almost entirely based on ideology rather than science. Scientists tend to view denial ideology as a political matter removed from their own work. "Climate change denial is about ideology."[452] Climate science is about research and data.

Heartland Institute is one of the more prominent denial organizations (see Chapter 5). Penn State University scientist Michael Mann, author of the "hockey stick," provides a description: "Heartland Institute was one of a number of these think tanks or front groups funded by industry or certain right-wing special interests to manufacture false controversy, to attack climate science and individual climate scientists. Heartland has actually admitted to [a] program to indoctrinate K-9 school children with climate change denial propaganda."[453]

Mann is referring to a program sponsored by Heartland Institute to "teach the controversy" by equating denial ideology and climate science. Scientists find this "balance" offensive because there is no valid science in denial ideology. They regard espousal of denial ideology as propaganda that should be disconnected from science education, not taught in a science classroom. Nevertheless, some states continue to require that denial ideology be taught along with climate science as two sides of a non-existent debate.[454]

A rather blatant example of success from the effort by denial ideologues to promote teaching the controversy it the McGraw-Hill teacher's edition of the sixth grade *World Cultures & Geography* text:

Scientists agree that Earth's climate is changing. They do not agree on what is causing the change. Is it just another natural warming cycle like so many cycles that have occurred in the past? Scientists who support this position cite thousands of years' worth of natural climatic change as evidence. Or is climate change anthropogenic—caused by human activity? Scientists who support this position cite the warming effect of rapidly increasing amounts of greenhouse gases in the atmosphere.

Yes, scientists do agree that climate changing but 97% also agree what is causing the change. How can McGraw-Hill imply that they do not agree? Citing "thousands of years' worth of natural climate change as evidence" is fine, and indeed climate scientists are fully aware of evidence of natural climate change and incorporate it in their findings. But that does not mean that current climate change is "just another natural warming cycle." Unfortunately, Texas seems ready to adopt this misleading approach to climate change for its public school teachers.

Joseph Bast, President of the Heartland Institute, has denied funding by some "right-wing special interests," especially the Koch brothers.[455] He contends that Heartland is supportive of authentic science.

The Heartland Institute is not "skeptical of climate change science." We are one of its leading supporters, having hosted seven international conferences (with an eighth one taking place in Munich this week) and published a comprehensive survey of the scientific literature in two volumes, with a third volume on its way. We spend more [money] *supporting* climate science than all but a handful of public policy think tanks.[456]

The claim that Heartland Institute is a leading *supporter* of climate science would surprise a lot of climate scientists. Most of them view Heartland's treatment of climate science as ideological, not scientific. What galls scientists is a suggestion that anything Heartland promotes is subject to the scientific method, such as testing of hypotheses and peer review of published research. Michael Mann observes: "In addition, in recent years, the Heartland Institute, a group that has been funded by both tobacco (Philip Morris) and fossil fuel (Exxon, Koch, Scaife) interests, has financed a series of one-sided conferences on climate change, featuring a slate of climate change deniers, many with no discernible scientific credentials, and most with financial connections of one sort or another to the fossil fuel industry or groups they fund."[457]

Here is the conflict: Bast claims that there is no Koch funding for Heartland Institute but Mann lists Koch among Heartland's fossil fuel funders. Bast claims that the Koch money is only for its "health-care reform" work but it would be unlikely that the Heartland Institute could separate the funding so clearly.[458]

Heartland is not the only denial organization that has been funded by fossil fuel companies: "Some legal analysts believe that fossil fuel producers could be vulnerable to fraud or civil conspiracy charges if it can be legally proved that companies like ExxonMobil and Peabody Coal spent millions funding climate-change-denying organizations like the Competitive Enterprise Institute and the Greening Earth Society, while internally acknowledging that the science supporting anthropogenic (i.e., human-caused) climate change was a settled issue."[459] It will be interesting to see if the lawsuits now underway will have the effect of discouraging further funding and if organizations such as Greening Earth Society will fade away. Heartland Institute seems here to stay.

Heartland has attacked climate scientists such as Michael Mann, sometimes in a rather facetious manner. "For a February 2011 video entitled "I'm a Denier" and hosted on the Heartland Institute Web site, they even employed a doppelganger to play me dancing around with a hockey stick ..."[460] The "hockey stick" to which Mann refers is the famous IPCC graph from its Third Assessment Report, to which Mann contributed. It has been the subject of numerous attacks by denial ideologues, which have little effect on the science but are highly offensive to the scientists. The research underlying the hockey stick graph has been reconfirmed many times.

Nevertheless, denial ideologues continue to attack Mann. Reacting to his book *The Hockey Stick and Climate Wars,* one reviewer said "Dr. Mann did not draw the proper conclusion when others tried to intimidate him into silence. Instead of recognizing that scientific progress requires the freedom to challenge and debate ideas, Dr. Mann apparently concluded that it is better to silence others than to be silenced. If his ideas are correct, then he should welcome challenges; ideas that withstand repeated criticism gain tremendous respect."[461] It is revealing that this critic admits that Mann *"did not draw the proper conclusion when others tried to intimidate him into silence."* This suggests that Mann should have been silenced by intimidation, rather than produce evidence that disproves his findings. In fact, Mann has maintained his conclusions in the face of brutal attacks.

One of the most egregious aspects of denial ideology is its attempt to place climate science on the same level by talking about "beliefs." This has had the effect of convincing people that climate science is based on beliefs. As noted by Melton, "So right away, you see that there is a fundamental problem here with the way our society is treating climate change. We are treating it like it is another belief; something that can be judged through morally appropriate behavior. Of course, it is nothing of the sort."[462]

The world *belief* is a slippery term in English, since it can be applied to religious or non-religious concepts. For example, one can say "I believe that it may rain today," stating a probability rather than religious devotion. It may only indicate affirmation of facts. Nevertheless, use of *belief* can be problematic for scientists. "As with so many of the arguments that surround climate change, this is not really about the word belief, but about the religious frames that it triggers and the false polarity it suggests between the rational brain and the emotional brain. In the struggles with deniers, the word belief has become poisoned, and many scientists see it as the antithesis of peer-reviewed science."[463] The "false polarity" is between ideology and science, a polarity of disconnected ideational systems where ideology is based on fixed beliefs and science on testable hypotheses.[464]

Denial advocates try to intimidate others who question denial ideology by believing in facts rather than ideology. "Lawrence Torcello, a philosopher at the University of Rochester, received more than 700 abusive emails and phone calls following an article he recently published on The Conversation website in which he said corporate funding of climate denial was morally wrong and criminally negligent."[465] If mere suggestion of corporate negligence were a cause for intimidation, what would happen if someone actually sued the companies that fund climate denial?

Especially galling to many scientists are meteorologists who deny climate change. Two prime examples are David Bernard of CBS4 of Miami, a consultant to CBS News on hurricanes, and John Coleman of KUSI-TV in San Diego. Bernard has been quoted as saying that the globe is cooling, and that climate policies are "global wealth redistribution."[466] Bernard is also a supporter of the Heartland Institute.

Coleman is quoted on the station's website: "We're talking about the greatest hoax in history, let's understand this. There is no man made global warming. The whole thing is a phony call for quick action."[467] Meteorologist Dave Dahl, at KSTP in Minneapolis, suggests that climate science is a "political theory" pushed by grant-hungry scientists.[468] Although trained in the science of meteorology, these TV weathermen are susceptible to the anti-scientific ideology of climate denial.[469] They may gain popularity by attacking climate science, but they are not contributing to an understanding of climate change among the public.

What denial organizations and weathermen have in common is a disdain for the scientific method. While they claim to support "true" science, they in fact promote an ideological view of climate science and reject the findings of most climate scientists. The feeling is mutual. Most scientists do not want to acknowledge the existence of denial ideology, but some have tried to grapple with it.[470]

Communicating climate science is difficult, given that scientists are cautious about overstating their case and careful to note any uncertainties in their findings. Nevertheless, in the case of climate science communication is crucial. One climate scientist who has indicated some caution about findings has emphasized the need for improved communication: "Climate science communication hasn't been very effective in my opinion. The dominant paradigm seems to be that a science knowledge deficit of the public and policy makers exists, which is exacerbated by the Koch-funded climate denial machine. This knowledge deficit then results in the public failing to act with the urgency that is urged by climate scientists."[471] Koch-funded organizations such as Americans for Prosperity may exploit this "knowledge deficit" by use of misinformation to fill in gaps in the public's knowledge.

Scientists recognize that there is widespread resistance to climate science. One of the earliest analyses of climate change in the scientific literature was made in 1938 by Guy Callendar, who expected that there would be resistance to his findings for a number of reasons:

- The idea of a single factor causing worldwide climate change seems impossible to those familiar with the vast complex of forces on which any and every climate depends.
- The idea that man's actions could influence so vast a complex is very repugnant to some.
- The meteorological authorities of the past have pronounced against it, mainly on the basis of faulty observation of water vapour absorption.
- Last, but not least, they did not think of it themselves![472]

Callendar was prescient when he wrote these words. He could see that climate science would become "repugnant to some" and that "meteorological authorities...pronounced against it." Denial ideologues have treated climate science as "repugnant" and some meteorologists still pronounce against it (see above).

Callendar felt it was important to "carry on" regardless of these objections to science.

IPCC has produced its fifth assessment report and it deals with the denial claim that climate change is all natural.[473] The report does acknowledge natural causes of climate change, the "noise" in which the "signal" of anthropogenic climate change can be discerned. The substantiation of human influences has been documented in research that produced the following graph tracing the difference between one natural source, solar activity, and temperature:[474]

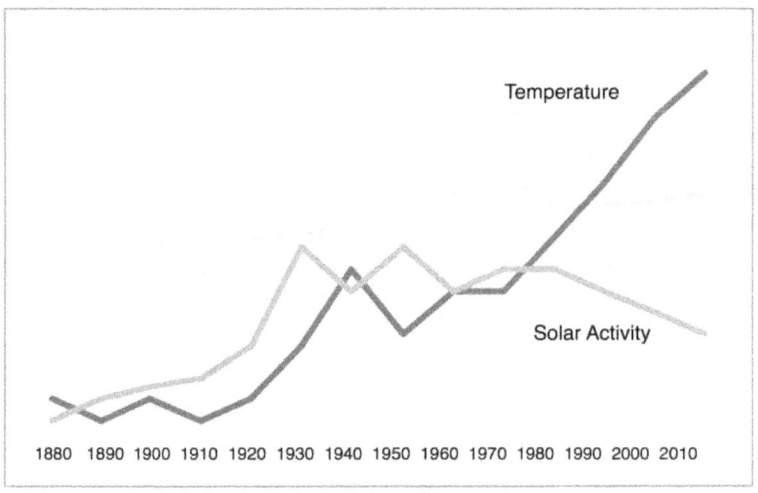

As the trend lines indicate, climate science has examined the natural sources of climate change such as solar activity (one of the most commonly noted factors in denial claims that there are only natural causes). One author summarized a critique of climate models with the following judgment: "Suppose the IPCC, because of the many failings of climate models, has mistaken a series of sunlight-fueled (not manmade CO_2-fueled) warming events for human-induced global warming. It's really not a supposition."[475] In other words, according to this ideologue, the IPCC missed solar activities in its models and thus has misstated the role of CO_2 emissions in global warming. Climate scientists would regard this critique as a gross misunderstanding of climate science.

Solar activity has been diminishing in recent years, while temperatures continue to increase. If the sun were the primary influence on climate change, this divergence would not be likely to happen. Researchers have concluded: "Hence, like many authors before us, we conclude there is no credible way that the recent rise in air surface temperature can be attributed to solar effects."[476] For a full explanation of temperature trends, it must also take into account CO2 emissions.

As this example indicates, climate science cannot consider all the relevant factors when reporting on causes of climate change. Nevertheless, some denial ideologues continue to claim that IPCC only reports on anthropogenic climate change and leaves out any consideration of natural climate change. This was elaborated by James Delingpole, who said:

> Breaking news from the US ... where a leaked draft of the IPCC's latest report AR5 admits what some of us have suspected for a very long time: that the case for man-made global warming is looking weaker by the day and that the sun plays a much more significant role in "climate change" than the scientific "consensus" has previously been prepared to concede.[477]

Climate scientists have reacted with criticism of the denial conclusions, and note that the leak mentioned by Delingpole resembles the "Climategate" leak of emails in 2009, in that it completely skews what scientists are saying. Some point to a breach of the confidentiality agreement that reviewers like Alec Rawls signed.

> I think the process of developing IPCC assessments should be more open in a number of ways. But as long as it is closed, I don't approve of anyone leaking drafts because, among other reasons, people like me who are involved in the process and feel obliged to follow the rules can't adequately respond to the ensuing confusion. But it will all come out in the wash in the end.[478]

Other scientists reject Rawls' and Delingpole's conclusions. Michael Mann reacted by pointing out that it violates the methodology by which scientists review and improve climate findings. He noted that one statement in AR5 about solar "forcing," or the effect of solar activity on earth's climate, is not a major finding. "So what climate change deniers are doing, assisted by a dishonest leaker, is to once again distort what climate scientists have actually had to say about the role of solar forcing to somehow make it sound as if there is some new development here. There isn't. There are only incremental developments in the science, all of which reinforce the conclusion that natural forcing, including solar forcing, cannot explain the warming we have seen over the past century."[479]

Some authors take a more optimistic view of how climate science can successfully overcome denial. "Let me repeat my little bit of good news here once again: the climate change challenge will be easier and cheaper to fix than we have been led to believe. All we have to do is start treating our environment like we treat our banks that are "too big to fail." Earth, after all, is too big to fail. Once the true nature of climate change is known by more than just our climate scientists, once we can overwhelm the "beliefs" of "those who would rather we not trust our climate scientists", the rest will be easy."[480] I don't think it will be as easy as this author claims, but certainly as climate science builds a consensus about the causes, effects and solutions of climate change, there will be more impetus for action.

Consensus and Climate Science

What, exactly, is the role of consensus in climate science? An often-cited figure is that 97% of climate scientists agree on anthropogenic climate change.[481] But is this enough? Are the denial ideologues right when they say that consensus does not matter, that any one scientist can "disprove" climate science just like Galileo disproved the earth-centered view of the universe?

As noted above, climate science is incremental, and the findings are subject to review by other scientists as soon as one scientist publishes them. In fact, with the Internet, the findings may be subject to immediate review as soon as they are on a blog site. As one expert on the scientific method has noted: "Consensus knowledge, by construction, will always allow experts to disagree, with knowledgeable opinion existing at either tail of the distribution of views. Such scientific consensus is not ultimate 'truth' and, on occasion, may turn out to be wrong. But the alternatives to the IPCC style of consensus-building are even less likely to command widespread authority within the worlds of science and policy."[482]

So consensus may not be the best system. As Winston Churchill said about democracy, it is the worst except for all of the others. Nevertheless, it has enabled some politicians to push their denial of climate policies to extremes. They fight against the idea that most scientists agree, for example, Senator John Boozman (R-AR) said that "the 97% statistic is a misleading tactic used to marginalize people who are concerned about hard-working Americans and oppose a all-pain, no-gain energy policy that's bad for our country and that won't change the global climate."[483]

Boozman is conflating the idea of 97% agreement on the science with 97% of all scientists. Not all scientists agree, but the question is not whether they are marginalized but whether the science they practice is relevant to climate science, and if so, how it is validated through the peer-review process. One of the scientists whom Boozman cites, for example, is Roy Spencer of the University of Alabama, Huntsville. "Spencer previously claimed in testimony to US Congress to be part of the 97% consensus, although his research actually falls within the less than 3% fringe minority of papers that minimize or reject the human influence on global warming."[484] His work (and that of his colleague, John Christy) has been reviewed as follows: "Spencer and Christy sat by for most of a decade allowing – indeed encouraging – the use of their data set as an icon for global warming skeptics. They committed serial errors in the data analysis, but insisted they were right and models and thermometers were wrong."[485] Spencer and Christy eventually admitted the errors but politicians continue to cite their earlier

181

work as valid. Does this mean that everything they say is valid? Some of it may be, but to rely on their findings would be risky.

Some ideologues have argued that using consensus as a criterion is equivalent to defining science as a "democracy." For those with this view science can never be verified by consensus: "...science does not work by democracy. A consensus does not make a theory more or less true. The data supporting the theory is what makes it more or less true."[486] Such an approach conflates consensus with voting. Scientists do not cast ballots on facts, but use replication and other means of verifying independently the validity of the facts. Scientific consensus is simply agreement on validity based on objective verification.

When it comes to scientific review of findings on climate change, consensus is not required. In fact, scientists will try their best to find reasons to disagree.

> To anybody with even a cursory familiarity with the climate science literature, the claim that it is impermissible to discuss uncertainties is laughable. There is hardly anything else scientists do, in climate science or elsewhere, besides dispute received wisdom and one another's findings. The reward structure in all of science favors those who overturn some widely accepted theory over those who just confirm or provide an elaboration on what is already known.[487]

Some have called scientific consensus on climate change a "meme." "The meme that 'the scientific consensus' should settle the matter completely not only contradicts the scientific method, but corrupts the way science is supposed to be conducted."[488] The term "meme" implies that climate science is a fixed belief or tradition that pervades the culture. Research on climate change is not fixed, but denial ideology does rely on fixed beliefs.

Naomi Oreskes, the historian of science who is the scholar who is most responsible for triggering the debate on consensus, said, "I didn't know it, but when I'd used the word 'consensus,' I'd hit a land mine. For those who claim that climate change is a myth, the term 'consensus' will – boom! – trigger a backlash. That's because their strategy is based on spreading the idea that the science is still unsettled. Why? Because if you don't know for sure there's a problem, you can't justify doing anything about it." [489] One might say that climate change denial is most threatened by the fact that scientists, despite their proclivity for lively debate, have completely agreed on human causes of climate change. In her seminal article on scientific research, published in *Science,* Oreskes famously found that 97% of scientific studies in peer reviewed literature agreed on the human influences on climate.[490] It is less well known that she also found that none of the other 3% of articles denied human influences; they simply did not mention them.

When denial ideology tries to refute the findings established by the pesky consensus, it usually comes up with a number of dubious claims.

> The fact is that CAGW [catastrophic anthropogenic global warming] alarmists constantly appeal to consensus not because it's real or even would be scientifically significant if it were, but because they're running scared. Observational science is torpedoing the modeling science on which they depend. None of the models predicted the cessation (whether short-term or long-term) of warming in 1997 (leaving us with no warming for at least the last 17 years and 10 months); all call for far more warming from 1980 to the present than has actually happened.[491]

Relying on canards such as "cessation of warming" is, as we have seen in Chapter 1, a recipe for defective analysis of climate science. Compounding the problem by attributing scientific consensus to fear – "they're running scared" – is a further distortion of the scientific method. Scientists are not "running scared" when they establish a consensus on climate findings; they are running toward the facts.

At times, the argument reaches extremes (see Chapter 4) and the claim that science is not "settled" by consensus is turned on its head. Denial leads some to say that the opposite conclusion is established: "Science is never settled, but the current state of 'climate change' science is quite clear: There is essentially zero evidence that carbon dioxide from human activities is causing catastrophic climate change."[492] *Zero evidence*? There is certainly enough evidence to reach the opposite conclusion if anyone other than these authors looks at climate science.

It is clear from these examples that denial ideologues will seize on anything they can to try to disprove climate science, and scientists have to refute the false information while continuing to pursue their research. As we will see in Chapter 7, there are approaches that might work in confronting climate change denial, but before going there we will look at the ideologues' views of science.

Why Ideologues Object to Science

Denial ideologues do not object to all scientists. They may in fact be enthusiastic about "contrarian" scientists such as Roy Spencer and Patrick Michaels. These are scientists whose work is used by denial ideologues to justify their denial of the main body of climate science.

Since they agree with only the "contrarians," denial ideologues find the vast store of climate science objectionable. They regard this science as a kind of "orthodoxy," and feel that scientists are excluding them from a dialogue: " [Climate science has] the orthodoxy on its side and delegitimizes the views of those who disagree, rather than engaging with them intellectually and showing them why they are wrong." [493] Why wouldn't scientists engage intellectually with denial ideologues? Mainly because scientists consider their views invalid in scientific terms. Many scientists do not find it useful to engage in debates with denial ideologues. They are unlikely to change any minds because the ideologues are not using the same approach to facts.

The "science" that denial ideologues believe in is not testable, so it does not follow the tenets of the scientific method. This is especially vexing for denial ideologues such as Heartland Institute's Joseph Bast, who says *the scientific debate is a source of enormous frustration.*[494] Translation: we do not have a good comeback to the requirement that our analysis of climate change is testable. We would rather keep it free of any hypothesis testing that might refute our theory.

Denial ideologues are unhappy with climate science. Denial ideologues are especially offended by what they call "politicized science," which seems to them to corrupt the scientific method.

> Too often the conclusions the scientists want seem to precede their actual study of the evidence. And then there is the attempt by some self-appointed "science advocates" to corrupt and co-opt the scientific method as a justification for a misguided philosophy known as scientism. Scientism mistakenly asserts that science can not only tell us the way things are and how things work, but also identify right from wrong.[495]

This statement distorts the roles of scientists. Scientists do discuss solutions, but their advocacy of positions is usually performed as part of their role as citizens, not as scientists. Solutions to climate change can be presented as alternatives, for example the Socolow/Pacala "wedges,"[496] and science can inform decision-makers about the efficacy of different alternatives. None of this constitutes cooptation or corruption of the scientific method. Accusing science of *scientism* is an attempt by the author to bring science down to the level of ideology, a frequent tactic of denial ideology. If science can be made to seem as no better than ideology, ideologues can attack science as an equal and opposite thought system.

Politicization of science is a sword that cuts both ways. As mentioned earlier, there are scientists with whom denial ideologues agree, and cite, when they want to deny climate change. Yet these same scientists are often those who are most likely to politicize climate change: "the politicization of science by a handful of climate change deniers and their patrons is extremely well documented, and continues to be a major obstacle to the United States adopting effective climate policy."[497] It may be that climate change is an issue that compels difficult policy decisions because of its pervasive nature, but that does not justify willful ignorance of valid science.

Much of the ideological animus against science comes from "free market" ideology, which contends that markets can best serve human welfare free of government intervention. "However, when environmental science showed that government action was needed to protect citizens and the natural environment from unintended harms, the carbon-combustion complex began to treat science as an enemy to be fought by whatever means necessary."[498] *Carbon-combustion complex* refers to industries and businesses that depend on sale and use of fossil fuels to sustain growth and profit. While business enterprises such as Exxon-Mobil have at least paid lip service to climate change issues, the think tanks and media that support this "carbon-combustion complex" continue to attack and deny climate science. They justify their attacks and denial on the basis of neo-liberal ideology that extols free markets and denigrates government action.

Ironically, the very same people who resist government intervention to prevent the worst consequences of climate change could be the people who bring about authoritarian systems that may be necessary to respond to climate change. They should be in favor of government intervention now: "So people who care about freedom should want to see early action to prevent catastrophic climate change. Delay increases the risk that authoritarian forms of governance will come out ahead in the end."[499]

186

Defining climate science as a religion, discussed in Chapter 4, is a method for denial ideologues to reorient their perspective on climate change and attack anyone who addresses it scientifically. "Many deniers harbor a deep hatred for all religion, seeking to smear climate change by association. To one business columnist, climate advocates are like "crazed American televangelists who predict that the Antichrist will come next Tuesday or that God will purge the land of homosexuals."[500] Treating climate scientists or advocates of climate policies as *"televangelists"* is a clever way for denial ideology to place them in a position of weakness. Many people are dubious about the motives of televangelists, after a number of scandals made them objects of ridicule.

Being a belief system itself, denial ideology also tends toward religion. "However, climate skepticism is, in a manner of speaking, a broad church, and it also includes those, especially among the American Christian right, who see climate change as a heresy that 'speaks to the inherent spiritual yearnings of human souls and seduces children in our classrooms through spiritual deception.'"[501] Use of this characterization of climate science as heresy denies the rationality and precision of the scientific method. It equates science with devil worship and other nefarious forms of religion as described in Chapter 4.

Leading the charge for denial ideology are several denial organizations, Heartland Institute, Americans for Prosperity and the Tea Party, described in Chapter 5. In general, climate scientists disdain these organizations[502] and denial organizations return the favor. They draw on the work of a few scientists who have "defied" the consensus on climate change. Heartland Institute is promoting more than denial ideology. Along with think tanks such as the Cato and Heritage Institutes, it carries the water for all kinds of neo-liberal causes such as low taxes, less regulation and economic freedom. This neo-liberal ideology leads these institutes to challenge climate science. "If the dire projections coming out of the IPCC are left unchallenged, and business as usual is indeed driving us straight toward civilization-threatening tipping points, then the implications are obvious: the ideological crusade incubated in think tanks like Heartland, Cato, and Heritage will have to come to a screeching halt." Think tanks that depend on neo-liberal ideology need to deny climate science. "And that is what is behind the abrupt rise in climate change denial among hardcore conservatives: they have come to understand that as soon as they admit that climate change is real, they will lose the central ideological battle of our time – whether we need to plan and manage our societies to reflect our goals and values, or whether that task can be left to the magic of the market." [503]

More than difficult to reconcile with their beliefs, climate science to many ideologues is unfair and threatening. "You can understand that, from their perspective, the scientific reality of climate change must seem spectacularly unfair. After all, the people at the Heartland conference thought they had won these ideological wars – if not fairly, then certainly squarely. Now climate science is changing everything: how can you win an argument against government intervention if the very habitability of the planet depends on intervening?"[504] When the implications of climate science seem so threatening to one's favorite ideology, the response can be very negative. Denial may be the only option when abandoning the ideology is unthinkable.

Ideology is the application of a fixed belief system to a changing reality. Denial ideology starts with the fixed premise that humans are not responsible for climate change, and attributes any changes in the climate to natural causes. When evidence is presented to the contrary, attack the scientists rather than the science.[505] Because denial ideologues' ideas are fixed, they do not acknowledge any "falsifiability" of their beliefs.

Personal attacks on scientists have a limited utility for denial ideologues, however. Scientists tend to work in groups, collaborating on research and publishing articles with multiple authors. Identifying any one author or researcher responsible for a finding is difficult. Sometimes denial ideologues will seize on "evidence" such as the hacked "climategate" emails from the Climate Research Unit in the UK and accuse scientists of conspiracy. [506] Social researchers have found that conspiracy ideology is "associated with rejection of climate science as well as other scientific propositions." [507] Unfortunately for denial ideologues, conspiracy theories have a limited public appeal given that so many different sources of information come to the same conclusion without any sign of collaboration.

A major line of attack is to accuse scientists and diplomats working on climate change of "alarmism," alleging that they exaggerate science. When describing the 2012 UNFCCC Conference of Parties (COP 18), denial ideology used heavy-duty rhetoric.

> Despite the embarrassing lack of any increase in planetary temperatures, climate-change alarmists and representatives from almost 200 governments and dictatorships are still assembled at the UN Conference of the Parties (COP18). They claim their mission is to save the planet from warming purportedly caused, in part at least, by human emissions of carbon dioxide – a byproduct of human breathing, an essential molecule to all plant life, and a fraction of one percent of all the greenhouse gases naturally present in the atmosphere. [508]

Such rhetoric reverses logic and claims that instead of endangering the planet, carbon dioxide is essential. Some denial ideologues exaggerate the effect of CO2 on plant growth, and make it seem beneficial: "On average, plant growth efficiency rises by 35 percent for every doubling of atmospheric CO2 concentration. From 1961–2011, increased atmospheric CO2 added \$3.2 trillion in food value, and it can be projected to add \$9.8 trillion more from now to 2050." [509]

This sort of rhetoric completely ignores the adverse effect of climate change on agriculture. Plant growth is subject to many variables, of which increased carbon dioxide is only one. "When [researchers] grew soybeans and corn in the sort of conditions expected to prevail in a future climate, with high temperatures or low water, the extra carbon dioxide could not fully offset the yield decline caused by those factors…Their work shows that when crops are subjected to temperatures above a certain threshold – about 84 degrees for corn and 86 degrees for soybeans – yields fall sharply."[510] Of course, if increasing concentrations of carbon dioxide had only one effect – increased plant growth, denial claims might be valid. When they ignore the other effects such as higher temperatures, droughts and extreme weather, they base their claims on unreality.

An absurd claim is made by one author, based on a canard that scientists want to remove all carbon dioxide, and all plant growth will cease and the biosphere will die.

> If we remove something from the atmosphere and the biosphere benefits, we have removed a pollutant. If we remove something and the biosphere suffers, that something is not a pollutant. If we removed all carbon dioxide, the biosphere would not only suffer, it would die![511]

Is anyone proposing to remove all carbon dioxide? This is a straw man argument used to suggest that climate advocates want to harm the environment rather than preserve it. With this point, the rhetoric shifts the argument from fossil-fuel based emissions to natural processes such as breathing and plant photosynthesis, which use CO2. No scientist denies these processes; indeed, many work to measure the effects of photosynthesis. Climate models take photosynthesis into account when measuring the effects of CO2 on climate. Deforestation, for example, is one of the factors in climate research because it reduces the effect of photosynthesis on carbon concentrations.

One version of denial of the role of CO2 is offered by one self-described scientist: "On cooling CO2 sinks quickly to ground and disappears out of sight… If CO2 is cut off from sunlight by hiding in the earth, how can it cause warming?" It would surprise a lot of other scientists to learn that CO2 sinks into the ground, when they have been measuring it in the atmosphere for decades (see Keeling curve, Chapter 1). Nevertheless, this so called "scientist" claims "*CO2 for global warming is utter twaddle.*"[512]

He criticizes the IPCC and climate modelers for using CO2 as a key variable.

The role of carbon dioxide of climate science is downplayed by denial ideologues. Joseph Bast, President of Heartland Institute, said "Carbon dioxide does not cause weather to become more extreme, is not causing polar ice and sea ice to melt, is not causing sea level rises to accelerate."[513] This flies in the face of scientific research as far back as the 1800s, in which the role of carbon dioxide in these phenomena has been documented many times. Nevertheless, the rhetoric continues and intensifies with an attack on UN agencies and documents.

In reality, however, according to experts and analysts, the real goals of the global summit bear little resemblance to the increasingly wild claims made by the UN and its allies. Evidence of that can be found in the global organization's own documents and, more recently, in the fact that there has been no global warming even as the hysteria peddlers continue to demand a planetary carbon-control regime to save humanity from a non-problem. The climate models were clearly wrong, yet the increasingly irrelevant climate alarmism marches on.[514]

Denial ideology tries to change the argument by claiming, according to UNFCCC documents, there has been no human-induced global warming. This is fallacious, as UNFCCC documents incorporate the findings of the IPCC, which has issued five assessment reports including the most recent, AR5. In its fourth report IPCC says *"it is likely that there is a discernible human-induced warming averaged over each continent..."*[515] In its fifth report it increases the probability estimate of human influence to "very likely," which is defined as confidence at the 95% level.[516] Climate science has established that there is a warming trend during the past decades, and this evidence is incorporated into UNFCCC documents.

Regardless of the trends, denial ideology continues to contend that there has been cooling. "As we have seen, over the past dozen years global greenhouse gas emissions (despite Europe's self-sacrificial efforts) have soared but temperatures have not risen. Numerous scientists have produced graphs showing the planet's temperature is either below or at the very low end of the range the IPCC's famed computer models predicted. If recent trends continue, the models will be totally off base after only 20 years."[517] Conflating models and misleading reporting of temperature trends are common themes of denial ideology. As described in Chapter 1, temperature trends are upward and closely follow some scenarios in the models.

When the UN scheduled a summit of world leaders in September 2014 to discuss a new climate agreement, one denial ideologue reacted sarcastically.

> UN Secretary-General Ban Ki-moon has invited world leaders…to create a world in which the developed nations agree to pass their wealth to developing (or not developing) nations (or the thugs who rule them) in exchange for reduced greenhouse gas emissions (even though regulations are way out of bounds now and have only negative effects). The result will be severe damage to the people, economies, and environments of developed nations (both with the cost of ridiculous emissions regulations and with redistribution of wealth), and to the people, economies, and environments of developing nations (continued prohibitive cost of electricity, high food and healthcare costs, etc).[518]

Much of denial ideology uses a critique of climate models to "disprove" climate change, while in reality those models are designed only to show different outcomes based on variable inputs. Nevertheless, the models have become objects of extreme opprobrium.

If the models cannot replicate real-world observations, they also cannot replicate future climate scenarios. Such models cannot even accurately predict the weather just one month ahead, let alone one week ahead. So, for governments to have believed in the IPCC predictions of extreme climatic events ten, twenty, fifty or a hundred years from now, and to have then formulated climate policies based on such predictions, it is tantamount to extreme ignorance, total stupidity, gross negligence, and gross irresponsibility of the highest order. This is particularly so considering that highly respected sceptic scientists have made every effort to point out why the IPCC has been wrong, only to have been constantly ignored, ridiculed, and dismissed for being out of line with the 'scientific consensus'.[519]

Accusing governments, along with scientists, of *"extreme ignorance, total stupidity, gross negligence, and gross irresponsibility of the highest order"* is a rather extreme response to attempts by scientists to project various scenarios. The "highly respected skeptic scientists" who are trying to point out that the IPCC is wrong are, for the most part, ridiculous ideologues. Nevertheless, most of the ridicule goes the other way, toward the scientists who are trying to understand the climate science and warn about consequences.

Denial ideology starts from the premise – a belief unrelated to scientific methods – that there could be no human-induced global warming, so any suggestion that there is amounts to *"hysteria"* and *"alarmism."* This view of climate science is totally at odds with most informed opinion, and serves to alienate denial ideology completely from science.

Meanwhile, recent efforts to exploit fear by climate alarmists and UN bureaucrats seeking to blame "global warming" for weather events like Hurricane Sandy, for example, are absurd on their face, according to Lord Monckton and a wide array of experts. In reality, these sorts of bogus claims are

193

nothing more than fear mongering aimed at drumming up hysteria and duping the public to facilitate a global agreement that would benefit the UN, power-hungry governments, dictatorships, and elements of "Big Business" — all at the expense of humanity, science, prosperity, liberty, national sovereignty, and real environmental problems.[520]

This quote is from *The New American,* the magazine of the John Birch Society, an ideological movement that has been more or less active for the past fifty years.[521] It accelerated its political activism recently, as a sponsor of the 2010 Conservative Political Action Conference (CPAC) and supporter of some Tea Party candidates for Congress in 2010 and 2012. This does not mean that the John Birch Society is identical to the Tea Party – they are totally separate organizations – but the ideology has led the John Birch Society to become part of denial movements. The John Birch Society has always railed against the UN, viewing it as a conspiracy of socialists attempting to take over the U.S. In this vein, it has become the enemy of climate science, which is associated with UN agencies like the IPCC and UNFCCC.

A more mundane line of argument used by denial ideologues is the critique of "skeptics" like Marc Morano, former aide to Senator James Inhofe (R-OK) and publisher of the "Climate Depot" blog. He took issue with physicist Richard Muller's work in the Berkeley Earth Surface Temperature (BEST) project, when Muller reconfirmed IPCC and other findings about temperature increases. Morano said:

Climate Depot since at least March of 2011 had been publicly warning that Muller's entire BEST project was a predetermined con set up to take down a straw man argument. On 3-23-11, Climate Depot wrote in group email to fellow skeptics: "This whole [Muller] project has to be a set up to screw skeptics. Who disputes warming has taken place? Why have we allowed Muller to set up a straw man argument to take cheap shots at skeptics? It appears Muller is incapable of running

194

this project. He has allowed leaks, media distortions, allowed [warmist activist Joe] Romm to publicly hijack project and Muller remains silent."[522]

Morano objects to Muller's research because it upsets the denial expectation that Muller would reject the dominant IPCC findings that the globe is warming. He accuses Muller of setting up *"a straw man to take cheap shots at skeptics."* He considers Muller incapable of running his project and allowing leaks, media distortion and hijacking of the project. In other words, the best strategy for denial ideologues is to attack the scientists rather than the science, because they will lose that argument.

Muller's work continues to be the object of denial attacks, several years after he presented it to Congress. One author reported on his work as follows:

> Muller makes it seem as if global warming necessarily implies human causation, thus neatly burying the debate. Only at the conclusion does he cover himself by saying, "How much of the warming is due to humans and what will be the likely effects? We made no independent assessment of that." In other words, if you make your way to the very end, you discover the BEST studies are irrelevant to the fundamental dispute. But if the BEST studies are irrelevant to the scientific debate, Muller has ensured they are not irrelevant to public perception of that debate.[523]

By cherry-picking a quote from the report the critique leaves out the fact that Muller actually confirmed that climate science accurately measures climate change and relates it to fossil-fuel emissions.[524] Ignoring the full report's conclusions is a convenient method of denying climate science.

When the IPCC came out with its 2014 report on policies to manage climate change,[525] the denial ideologues took umbrage.

Climate Depot, one of the denial web sites, summarized it as follows:

> **The United Nations (UN) has delivered its latest verdict on the measures necessary to save the world from global warming and the news is as grim as it is predictable and wearisomely familiar:** More regulation from "experts", technocrats and bureaucrats at supranational organizations, such as the one whose initials begin with U and end with N.
>
> - More taxpayer subsidies for expensive, inefficient renewable energy.
> - More nuclear power (with shale gas used as a transitional fuel to replace coal).
> - The abandonment of fossil fuels.
> - Less meat consumption.
> - A single, globally-regulated price for carbon dioxide.
> - More local-government-enforced walking, cycling and public transportation.
> - More back-door wealth redistribution from the West to the developing world in the name of "sustainability"
> - All at a cost to the global economy of up to 3.7 per cent of GDP by 2030, provided we act now.[526]

"Regulation from 'experts', technocrats and bureaucrats at supranational organizations" is a code phrase for the identification of UN agencies as elitist. This issue was examined more fully in Chapter 4. The rest of the points are designed to restate the IPCC report in provocative terms to elicit a negative response from the followers of denial ideology. Ideologues are not satisfied with simply restating the findings but they also like to add their own "spin" to them.

Another approach frequently taken by denial ideologues is to seize on the uncertainties of science to argue that since we cannot definitively prove climate findings, they are not valid. This approach has been used, for example, in discussing Superstorm Sandy. Kerry Emanuel, a climate scientist from MIT, explained the role of uncertainty in climate science:

> At its best, climate science deals in probabilities. This means that under ideal conditions, scientists can estimate how a given climate signal alters the chances of a particular event. For example, we can now begin to estimate how global warming changes the probability of destructive hurricane landfalls. But in the case of hybrid storms like Sandy, which combine hurricane and winter storm characteristics, science hasn't even progressed to the point of assessing probabilities.[527]

As Emanuel indicates, science deals in probabilities and there is a good deal of uncertainty at an early stage of assessment. This might lead some denial ideologues to dismiss any connection of extreme weather to climate change, however. "Although this point may seem straightforward, it is routinely spun and misinterpreted. My colleagues and I try to make concise statements such as 'Science has not established a link between hybrid events and climate change.' But often, such statements are spun by climate skeptics into *Science has established that there is no link between Sandy and climate change*."[528] Emanuel makes the incisive point that whatever scientists say can be twisted and distorted to fit the denial worldview, a common tactic of ideological movements. They take advantage of the fact that "political debate often demands clear, confident, fast answers and is unsympathetic to scientific caution.[529]

Uncertainty, as has been mentioned before, promotes the views of denial ideologues because they can be quite certain of their own views while denigrating climate science. This tends to confuse the public by suggesting an asymmetry between the certainty of denial and the uncertainty of climate science. "The denial industry has exploited these confusions on an industrial scale. It has developed strategies for systematically producing misinformation and misunderstanding."[530]

The main result of this exploitation of confusion is doubt. "Regardless of the archives full of reports, pseudo-science on climate change still gets a lot of play. This pseudo-science, which is often purveyed by industry-funded groups like the Heartland Institute, frequently gets set up against genuine science. The result—which presumably is what these groups are hoping for—is that the public ends up confused. 'The single most common myth about climate change among Americans is that there's a lot of disagreement among the experts,' says Ed Maibach, director of the Center for Climate Change Communication at George Mason University. 'And the reason why they think there is a lot of disagreement among the experts is because there was an intentional strategy to sow the seeds of doubt.'"[531] Ideologues are unhappy when research shows that 97% of climate scientists agree on the science, as has been described previously. The misinformation about disagreement serves their purposes, and it is in their interest to suppress any concept of scientific consensus.

When dealing with extreme weather, denial ideologues try to refute climate science by claiming that the cause of such weather is natural: "Climate change and extreme weather have always happened and always will no matter what we do. Therefore, instead of vainly trying to stop them from occurring, we need to adapt to such phenomena by hardening our societies to these inevitable events."[532] In other words, it is unnecessary to mitigate climate change through reduction of emissions and the only necessary response is to adapt to the extreme weather. This line of reasoning leads denial ideologues to use their own prejudices to define reality and reject the methodologies and conclusions of climate science: "While someday we may be able to meaningfully predict climate, it is not possible now. And actually controlling global climate will remain science fiction for the foreseeable future. That may not be a comforting thought for climate crusaders, but that is climate reality."[533]

Juxtaposition of *"climate reality"* with *"climate crusaders"* is a favorite theme of denial ideologues. By posing them as polar opposites, denial ideology seeks to make climate policy a fruitless endeavor, a "science fiction" approach to global warming. It also attracts attention from journalists who may want to find "balanced" opinions about climate science in their writings.

Denial ideologues often expand on this theme of "climate crusaders" by making a charge of "alarmism" and complaining about the "catastrophic" projections of global warming.

> The alarmist repertoire uses an inflated language, with terms such as "catastrophe", "chaos" and "havoc", and its tone is often urgent. It employs a quasi-religious register of doom, death, judgement, heaven and hell. It also uses the language of acceleration, increase, intractability, irreversibility and momentum.[534]

Here we see the familiar charges of "quasi-religious" projections of "*doom, death, judgment, heaven and hell.*" Since they cannot accept climate science as science, denial ideologues try to convert it into religion and attack its validity.

With regard to probabilities and projections, scientists and denial ideologues often talk right past each other. Scientists may consider their findings sound and their projections as useful even when the probabilities are not 100% certain. Denial ideologues, on the other hand, will regard anything less than 100% certainty as an admission of weakness and try to dismiss the findings as meaningless.

Scientists can drive denial ideologues crazy with the use of probabilities. Because science is self-critical and willing to change conclusions based on new evidence, it makes denial ideology seem rigid and unbending. Ideologues want certainty, but science does not provide definitive convictions for believers to latch onto. As one commentator noted, "Critical self-examination is the obligation of every scientist and researcher. The fact that the findings of the IPCC are almost always expressed in terms of probabilities and possibilities gives due recognition to the many uncertainties that exist, as well as gaps in our knowledge. Moreover, the scientists contributing research findings to the IPCC have differences among themselves about the progression of global warming and its likely consequences."[535] Denial ideologues often accuse the IPCC and climate scientists of "alarmism" because they project catastrophic consequences. In fact, the IPCC projects different scenarios based on various possibilities, including the possibility that things will not be too bad. But the probabilities are not very comforting.

When they see that climate science has credibility, denial ideologues become concerned that it will cause *"turmoil"* because of its implications for policy. This leads to accusations of collaboration among a host of actors who are *"spinning"* climate science into a *"trillion dollar bonanza."*

All of this turmoil will only result if we don't effectively address the current state of climate science. The crisis in climate science isn't the result of a natural catastrophe. It's manmade: A cadre of scientific specialists has won the support of an army of career politicians, bureaucrats, environmental and social activists, academics and educators, journalists, bloggers, technologists and consultants, and groupies of all stripes to spin a bit of understanding about the atmosphere into a trillion dollar bonanza.[536]

Eventual expenditure of trillions of dollars for cleaning up the consequences of using fossil fuels is more likely to result from neglect of climate science than taking it seriously. As the Stern report makes clear, costs will mount the longer that action on climate change is delayed.[537] Denial ideology attacks this extrapolation of climate science as a misuse of climate models: "Climate models are being used as marketing tools both for governments and for the environmental movement to try to force the free industrialized world to abandon fossil fuels and to keep developing nations from enjoying the benefits of inexpensive energy."[538] As we saw in Chapter 2, climate science is somehow guilty of keeping developing nations in poverty because it dares to suggest that there might be a problem with continued use of fossil fuels.

Sometimes this accusation of causing poverty goes beyond calling it a side effect of emissions reductions. One author considers it a deliberate polity of climate activists: **"Poverty is the answer to global warming.** The willingness to sacrifice human welfare is reaching a fever pitch among those who believe that global warming is a crisis of unimagined proportions."[539] It is a stretch to accuse climate activists of promoting poverty when the principal objective is to reduce emissions. As we have seen, that can be compatible with reducing poverty if implemented through improvements in social conditions generally.

At times, denial ideologues try to bring science down to their level by labeling climate science an ideology. When discussing the leaked IPCC AR5 report, James Delingpole says, "…this was never really a debate about science but is, and always has been, about ideology."[540] Another author has declared that climate models are "non-empirical evidence," an indication of ideological beliefs.[541] Still another author exonerates science but accuses activists of pursuing an unrealistic ideology: "What scientists say about global warming isn't the problem; the problem is what political professionals and ideologues say when they enter into the conversation. The public sees their dishonesty and reacts accordingly. This is why climate alarmists lose most objective voters." [542] Such attitudes demonstrate that denial ideologues do not recognize the role of climate science in challenging unfounded beliefs about climate. To establish what is ideology and what is not, one can ask whether the beliefs are testable. Denial beliefs, by this standard, are clearly ideological. By contrast, scientific findings are testable, and climate science is not ideological.

One self-described "agnostic" about climate science is Robert Bryce. He would not fit the definition of denial ideologue because he is open-minded about causes of climate change, and his primary emphasis is energy. Nevertheless, he feeds into the denial argument against climate science with statements such as:

There's no question that carbon dioxide is a greenhouse gas. What we don't know for certain is the ideal concentration of that gas in the atmosphere. I can't talk knowledgeably about polar vortexes, cosmic rays, ice cores, forcings, or aerosols. Nor can I be certain that the climate models being used are accurate. I've become bored by the arguments about "hockey sticks," proper thermometer siting, and whether temperatures have leveled off in recent years. In my view, the media and pundits are way too focused on climate models and not nearly focused enough on reactor, engine, and fuel cell models.[543]

"Models" are hardly the focus of too much attention; temperatures and extreme weather are more important. Bryce's disdain for arguments concerning temperature measurements is a telling point. He goes on to portray climate science as part of a "*slugfest*:"

Over the past few years, the discussion about climate change and carbon dioxide emissions has devolved into a hyper-partisan slugfest that's obsessed with tribalism. And that tribalism has obscured nearly everything else.[544]

While "*tribalism*" may fit the definition of denial ideologues, it is hardly appropriate for climate science. Tribes do have clear ideologies, while science is variegated into many contrasting and, indeed, competitive views. By positioning denial ideology and science on the same level, Bryce denigrates climate science.

Tim Ball provides a prime example of trying to turn climate science into ideology. His statement is a mirror image of the extremist denial statements described above in Chapter 4: "Extremism will increase as purveyors of prevailing views on climate and climate change try to defend the indefensible."[545] Ball considers climate science "*indefensible*" because he treats it as a

202

belief system rather than research, and he calls it *"extremist"* because the findings are so antithetical to his own belief system.

Why would denial ideologues hold so fast to their beliefs if they were demonstrated as wrong? Why would they refuse to put them to scientific test? There are many explanations[546] but they all boil down to one: *fear*. To some extent, it is fear of the unknown but even more likely it is a fear of future impoverishment. If fossil fuels are abundant denial ideologues may feel that future prosperity is assured. But if more than four-fifths of oil, coal and gas reserves must remain in the ground,[547] there is a fear that prosperity will be jeopardized.

Fossil-fuel companies would lose trillions of dollars of investments, and economies dependent on fossil fuels would be endangered (see Chapter 3). The sanguine view that the climate changes slowly, naturally and will return to stasis is bound to be frustrated in the future. Societies are likely to lash out as extreme weather creates more and more frustration with the denial ideologues' glib dismissal of climate science. Until that happens, however, denial ideologues will step up their efforts to combat the science and evade the true costs of business as usual.

Fear is a powerful motivator for denial ideology. "Our research joins past research in showing that people in general tend to deny the problem when the cure to that problem is scary. For conservatives, the cure to the climate change problem, at least the one everyone talks about, is particularly scary to them, so it makes sense that we see more skepticism on their part."[548] If you don't like the *"cure,"* you probably don't want to hear about the *"disease."* It is much more comforting to deny climate change than to deal with the consequences.

Chapter 7:
What can Scientists Do?

Chapter 6 outlined the mutual antagonism of science and denial ideology. Because of the inherent intellectual conflict between them, it is difficult to engage both sides in a joint discussion of their disagreements. Scientists would rather avoid any discussion as they regard ideology as a separate and irrelevant operation. Science does have a role to play, however, in addressing impacts of denial ideology by questioning its core beliefs. While many scientists would prefer to ignore denial ideology, some are beginning to challenge it.

It is virtually certain that in most confrontations between science and denial ideology, there will be a clash of opinions that makes reasonable discussion impossible. In a somewhat unusual case, however, there was such a confrontation and it did move the discussion along. The case in point was the testimony of Berkeley physicist Richard Muller before the House Committee On Science, Space And Technology on March 31, 2011.[549] At that time, the committee was chaired and staffed by politicians who questioned climate science, and a number of its members were climate deniers.

Muller's testimony directly confronted some core beliefs of denial ideologues. He dealt with the oft-expressed belief that scientists are not measuring temperatures correctly by detailing how his research had identified problems of measurement, dealt with these problems and confirmed other scientists' research. "Despite potential biases in the data, methods of analysis can be used to reduce bias effects well enough to enable us to measure long-term Earth temperature changes. Data integrity is adequate. Based on our initial work at Berkeley Earth, I believe that some of the most worrisome biases are less of a problem than I had previously thought."[550]

Much was made in the press of the fact that Muller's research was partly funded by David Koch, but that was the least significant aspect of his testimony. The fact that it was presented in a hostile committee setting was a more important aspect of this occasion. Scientists can sometimes win over denial ideologues by dealing with their questions directly. Whether Muller had much effect on the committee is hard to tell. The committee and the House of Representatives have continually passed legislation to strip the Environmental Protection Agency of its regulatory authority for controlling greenhouse gases under the Clean Air Act.[551] These bills have died in the Senate, however. It remains to be seen if they will succeed in the new Congress.

Muller's research has not had a large impact on climate science, but has a potentially large impact on denial ideology because some who do not understand how he could come to these conclusions view him as an apostate.[552] The reason they don't understand is that their fixed beliefs are not open to revision in the face of contrary evidence. As Upton Sinclair said, "It is difficult to get a man to understand something, when his salary depends upon his not understanding it!" Some denial pundits may be in the thrall of fossil fuel companies which fund their think tanks, but others may be true believers regardless of who pays their salaries. Hard-core believers do not allow for revision and will not be open to changing their views. A prime example of this is the classic research on cognitive dissonance, involving an "end-of-the-earth" prophecy that failed.[553] Believers continued to hold to their beliefs when the date of doom passed and nothing happened.

Dealing with Politicians

Muller testified before the House Committee on Science, Space and Technology, which has members who deny climate science. A similar example is the House Committee on Energy and Commerce. Representative Fred Upton (R-MI), who has said that climate change is not "necessarily" due to anthropogenic greenhouse gases, chairs that committee. Most of the Republican members of the committee are skeptical or outright hostile to climate science.

> House Republicans on the Energy and Commerce Committee demonstrated their commitment to science denial by unanimously voting down three separate amendments offered by Democrats to reaffirm basic facts about climate science. They then unanimously voted to pass the Upton-Inhofe bill to repeal the Environmental Protection Agency's scientific endangerment finding on greenhouse pollution.[554]

When it is difficult to get representatives to accept basic science, it will be impossible to pass legislation to deal with climate change. One Democratic congressman even used the phrase *"fact-free zone"* to describe the Republican-dominated House of Representatives.[555]

Science must confront this basic nature of ideology when dealing with denialism. It is not enough to present findings, even those "cleansed" by an identified skeptic like Muller, and expect a change of mind. Beliefs are often so rigid that they will not change easily. Scientists must also overcome the "conspiracy" accusations and the related attacks on UN agencies. These UN agencies, particularly the IPCC and the UNFCCC, are among the most transparent international organizations on the planet. They could not be further from the "black helicopter" stereotypes of the UN. Nevertheless, scientists are saddled with additional burdens of suspicion and false accusations because of international cooperation. Scientists need to fight back against this abuse of UN affiliation from which they benefit.

Perhaps one reason that scientists are reluctant to deal with politicians is the ludicrous nature of some statements they make. Republican state Sen. Brandon Smith made the following statement during a hearing convened by the Kentucky Interim Joint Committee on Natural Resources and Environment.

> I don't want to get into the debate about climate change. But I will just simply point out that I think that in academia we all agree that the temperature on Mars is exactly as it is here. Nobody will dispute that. Yet there are no coal mines on Mars, there's no factories on Mars that I'm aware of. So I think what we're looking at is something much greater than what we're going to do.[556]

Of course, Smith misstated the different temperatures of earth (57 degrees F) and Mars (minus 81 degrees F, a difference of 138 degrees). He is probably right in stating that there are no factories or coalmines on Mars, although it is difficult to see what relevance that has to climate science. Perhaps he is suggesting that Mars has no greenhouse gases generated by humans, but of course that does not explain the role of greenhouse gases on earth.

Other politicians make less preposterous statements, but many will hedge their denial with lack of knowledge. Senator Joni Ernst (R-IA) said "I don't know the science behind climate change. I can't say one way or another what is the direct impact, whether it's man-made or not. I've heard arguments from both sides, but I do believe in protecting our environment, but without the job killing regulations that are coming out of the [Environmental Protection Agency] which is what Congressman Braley supports."[557] (Congressman Bruce Braley was her Democratic opponent.) Although she "can't say" whether climate science shows a direct human cause, climate scientists can, and she needs to be informed by them even if she is not a scientist if she wants to protect the environment.

Perhaps some politicians are following the lead of Sarah Palin, the Republican candidate for vice president in 2008. She has made lack of knowledge about issues a badge of honor. It is no different in her view of climate change: "No one has proven that these changes are caused by anything done by human beings via greenhouse gases. There's no convincing scientific evidence for man-made climate change. The climate has always been changing."[558] Apparently she does not know about *"convincing scientific evidence"* for man-made climate change available from many sources, but that does not excuse her from finding out.

Paul Ryan (R-WI), a congressman from Wisconsin who ran for vice president in 2012, followed Palin's example when he responded to a question on human causation of climate change, "I don't know the answer to that question. I don't think science does, either."[559] Perhaps Ryan is not well informed enough to know the answer, but he certainly is ill informed to think that science does not know the answer. He is probably better informed about the possible consequences for his re-election chances if he confirms climate science. Such courageous action might cost him his seat.

House Speaker John Boehner used the "I am not a scientist" ploy to attack Obama Administration policies. "Listen, I'm not qualified to debate the science over climate change. But I am astute enough to understand that every proposal that has come out of this administration to deal with climate change involves hurting our economy and killing American jobs."[560] The strategy of many in Congress who deny any need for climate policies is first to abjure any responsibility for considering proposals and then change the subject to *"economy and jobs."* This is the equivalent of saying, "I am not a doctor," and denying any responsibility for protecting the American people from poison in drugs or E. coli bacteria in food. These politicians might consider abolishing the Food and Drug Administration because it might "hurt our economy and kill American jobs." Why not? Senator Joni Ernst (R-IA), who said, "I don't know the science behind climate change," wants to abolish the Environmental Protection Agency.

Lamar Smith (R-TX), chairman of the House Science, Space, and Technology Committee, dismissed IPCC reports in November, 2014, by saying that they are "nothing new." "Similar to previous reports, the latest findings appear more political than scientific. People are tired of the re-packaged rhetoric. It's time to stop fear mongering and focus on an honest dialogue about real options."[561] Perhaps he is tired of reading scientific reports on climate change because he is unwilling to act on them.

What about the leadership of the Senate? Majority Leader Mitch McConnell, running for reelection, made climate change a low priority in his issue pantheon: "I am not a scientist. I know there are scientists who think it is a problem and those who think it isn't a problem. There are differences of opinion among scientists. My job is to try and protect jobs in Kentucky now, not speculate about science in the future."[562] His job may also include learning about climate change if he is leader of the Senate.

There are two offshoots of denial ideology in McConnell's statement: the claim that there are scientists "who think it isn't a problem" and the priority on jobs over "speculating about science in the future." Of course, there are scientists who *say* it isn't a problem, regardless of what they think, and they are overwhelmingly opposed by those who say it is a problem. McConnell does not need to speculate about science in the future; it is already clear that climate change, and the science to explain it, are happening today. Scientists can inform him on these matters.

Some Republicans have criticized their leaders when they use the "*I am not a scientist*" alibi. According to Michael McKenna, a Republican energy lobbyist who has advised House Republicans on energy and climate change messaging, "It's got to be the dumbest answer I've ever heard. Using that logic would disqualify politicians from voting on anything. Most politicians aren't scientists, but they vote on science policy."[563] One Tea Party-supported politician who is slated to become chairman of the Senate Committee on Science, Ted Cruz (R-TX), has used the "misunderstanding" argument to denigrate climate science: "My view of climate science is the same as that of many climate scientists: We need a much better understanding of the climate before making policy choices that would impose substantial economic costs on our Nation."[564] Perhaps he does need a much better understanding of the climate, and it would be available if he invites climate scientists to testify before his committee. He might also get a better understanding of the *"substantial economic costs"* that climate change would impose on the world if he listens to economists like Herman Daly.

Tea Party candidates can be creative in their rejection of climate science. A Tea Party candidate running for the Senate in Louisiana, Rob Manness, said, "you know, if we don't really know how the climate changes and we aren't seeing any warming, I think it leaves that in doubt."[565] Perhaps he does not know how the climate changes if he screens out climate science, and he may not see any warming if he ignores reports from NOAA and WMO (Chapter 1). *"Not knowing"* is a bad sign for a candidate who aspires to be a senator. If "doubt is his product," he will lead people astray.

What can scientists do with the statements of these politicians? Scientists can challenge the more particular statements about politicians not understanding the science by offering one-on-one tutoring to political leaders such as Ryan, Cruz, Smith and McConnell. Even this, however, may not be effective in overcoming denial ideology, as we have seen in the case of Governor Rick Scott of Florida (see above). Politicians may try to ignore the science if it does not serve their purposes, but scientists may redress this ignorance through proactive approaches to politicians.

Cherry-Picking the Data

Scientists are sometimes accused by denial ideologues of cherry-picking, or selective use, of data. The opposite is actually the case. Denial ideology thrives on selective use of data. An approach to dealing with denial ideologues is to call them out on their use of scientific data. Scientists need to confront those who select data for ideological purposes and provide the data that refutes their claims.

A good example of how ideologues cherry-pick data:

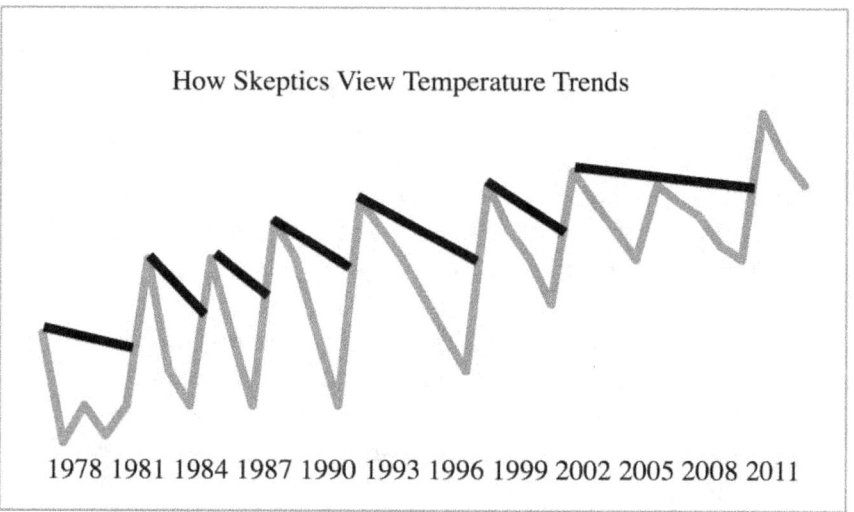

In fact, the trend line through the entire forty-three year period shows that the globe is warming:[566]

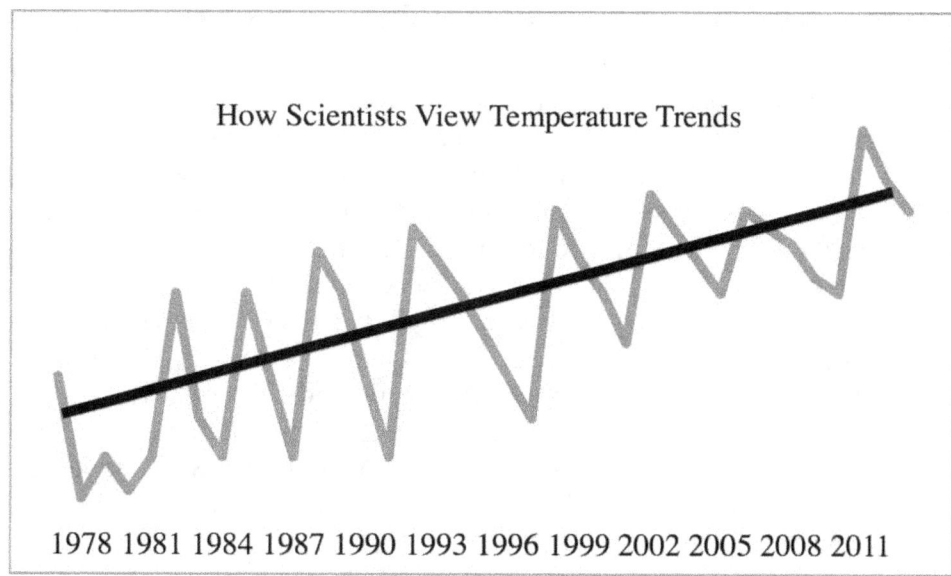

Bill Nye, the "science guy" on children's TV, debated Marc Morano (former aide to Senator Inhofe) and used this example of denial cherry-picking from skepticalscience.com. The misuse of temperature data shows how, by restricting their data analysis to limited periods, denial ideologues can "cherry pick" the data to show "cooling" during the past few years The data actually shows warming over a 43-year period.

While the misinterpretation of data seems like a trivial matter when it is handled this way, the effects are not trivial. An official publication of the State of Indiana, called "State of the Environment, 2011," makes the following false claims:

> Actual records of measured temperatures in the U.S. are relatively new (about 130 years), and reliable, worldwide temperature measurements from satellites are less than 30 years old. These short term temperature records show the earth both warming and cooling over this period, with no appreciable change since about 1998."[567]

By choosing terminology carefully, the Indiana Department of Environmental Management (IDEM) states *"short-term temperature records show the earth both warming and cooling...with no appreciable change since about 1998."* This statement cherry-picks the data and leaves out the long-term trend. It is not just that IDEM misstated climate data, but it also based policies on this misstatement: "Indiana's Commissioner of the Department of Environmental Management, Tom Easterly, laid out a plan to stall the US EPA global warming action in a power point clearly addressed to coal industry representatives at ALEC's meeting." [568] ALEC is the American Legislative Exchange Council, an organization funded by the Koch brothers with the purpose of defeating any climate policies at the state level and using state actions to counter the EPA. (See Chapter 5). Scientists must deal with these organizations when working at the state level.

Another example of cherry-picking is the statement that Arctic sea ice is not decreasing because the amount shown in satellite photos in 2013 was more than in 2012. If the entire period from 1979 to 2014 is plotted, there is definitive evidence of sea ice decrease.

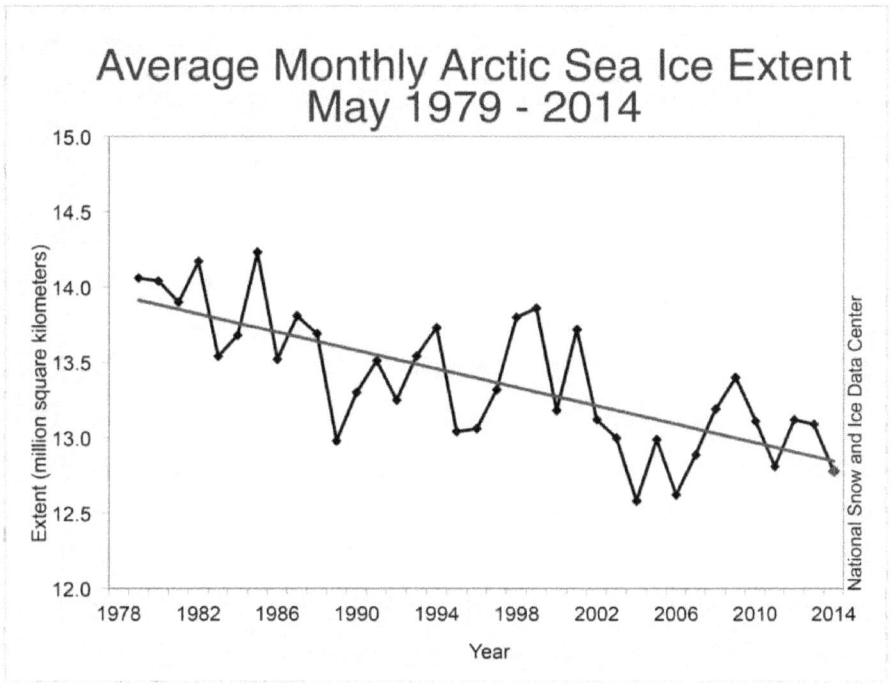

If you look only at the line between 2012 and 2013, it looks like sea-ice is increasing, but the overall trend downward is clear from the 44-year period.

Scientists find "cherry-picking" of data offensive. When they do, they can smoke out the perpetrators and call their bluff. An example comes from a debate between James Hansen of NASA and Patrick Michaels of the Cato Institute. In testimony before a House committee in 1997, Michaels used the high temperature scenario projected by Hansen in 1988 testimony before a Senate committee, not the two lower scenarios Hansen had also used. The graphs below show the different scenarios and the one that Michaels extracted for his testimony.

Hansen's graph from his 1988 testimony:[569]

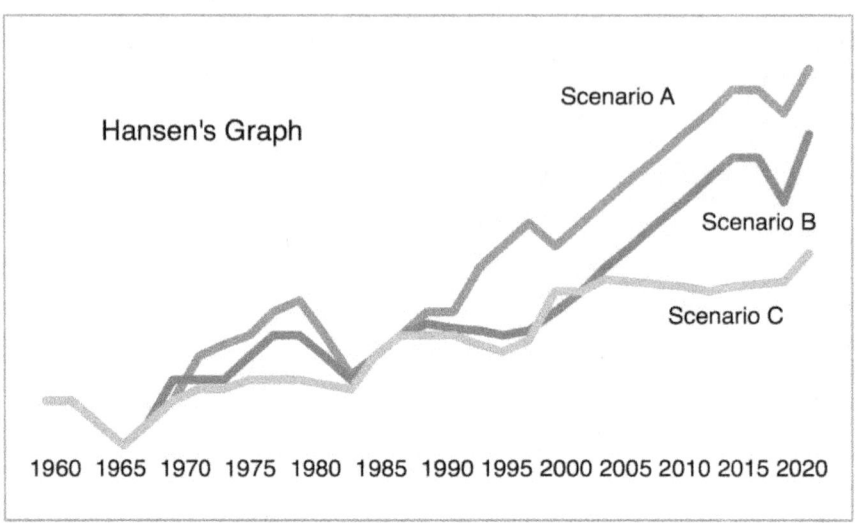

In this graph, Hansen's Scenario B (business as usual) tracks the observations closely, while the high (A) and low (C) scenarios are on either side. Michaels used only Scenario A in his testimony.

Michael's extraction of Scenario A:[570]

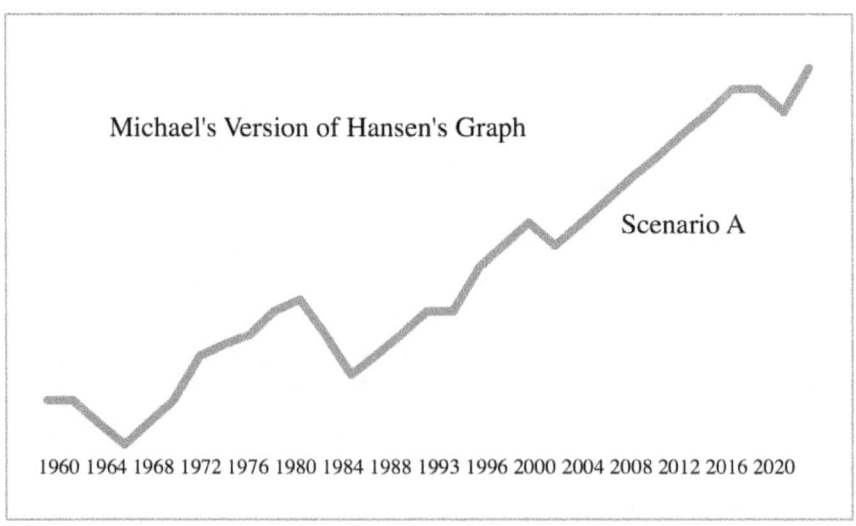

In this graph, Michaels used Hansen's Scenario A to track projected temperature changes between 1988 (when Hansen testified) and 1997 (when Michaels testified). From this scenario, it appears that Hansen predicted an increase of .45° C when the actual increase was only .11° C, one-fourth as much. Hansen had in fact predicted exactly the increase of .11° C in his Scenario B, the business as usual scenario. Hansen's response to Michaels: "One of the skeptics, Pat Michaels, has taken the graph from our 1988 paper with simulated global temperatures for scenarios A, B and C, erased the results for scenarios B and C, and shown only the curve for scenario A in public presentations, pretending that it was my prediction for climate change. Is this treading close to scientific fraud?"[571]

Although "scientific fraud" is a strong accusation, it seems to fit the mold of denial distortion of science. Scientists find this mode of thinking deleterious to the pursuit of climate science findings, and regard denial ideology as a setback to human progress. Anyone concerned about climate change must confront denial ideology as a fraud.

Hansen's activism and willingness to address climate policy have got him into trouble. After three arrests (two for demonstrating against Keystone XL and one for demonstrating against mountaintop removal) and a number of harsh criticisms leveled at him, Hansen has some bruises from the climate wars. But this has not stopped him. As Michael Mann notes: "Are Dr. Hansen and his colleagues going too far? Should we resist commenting on the implications of our science? There was a time when I would, without hesitation, have answered "yes" to this question. ...It is not an uncommon view among scientists that we potentially compromise our objectivity if we choose to wade into policy matters or the societal implications of our work. And it would be problematic if our views on policy somehow influenced the way we went about doing our science. But there is nothing inappropriate at all about drawing on our scientific knowledge to speak out about the very real implications of our research."[572]

Mann highlights one of the major issues of science's response to denial, *"potentially compromising our objectivity."*

He then adds the crucial principle of the scientific approach to climate change, speaking out about *the very real implications of our research.*" While it is difficult to judge what are "real implications," it is not difficult to state the clearly established findings about increases in temperature, sea level rise and ice cap melting. Each of these and many other aspects of climate such as extreme weather are becoming more evident with each year that passes.

Because of his activism, Michael Mann has been subjected to attacks by conservative politicians. The former Virginia attorney general and gubernatorial candidate Ken Cuccinelli, for example, attacked Mann with a lawsuit but lost.[573] Other scientists have found that their research has changed their lives: "I firmly believe that I would now be leading a different life if my research suggested that there was no human effect on climate," said climate scientist Benjamin D. Santer during a Congressional hearing in 2010. "We need to follow the research wherever it leads us, without fear of the consequences of speaking truth to power."[574]

Acknowledging the drop in knowledge about climate change among the general public, the AAAS (American Association for the Advancement of Science) published a paper to address the problem.

Surveys show that many Americans think climate change is still a topic of significant scientific disagreement. Thus, it is important and increasingly urgent for the public to know there is now a high degree of agreement among climate scientists that human-caused climate change is real. Moreover, while the public is becoming aware that climate change is increasing the likelihood of certain local disasters, many people do not yet understand that there is a small, but real chance of abrupt, unpredictable and potentially irreversible changes with highly damaging impacts on people in the United States and around the world.[575]

Citing a "*high degree of agreement*," the paper warns that if scientists do not effectively address what is termed a "disconnect" between the science and policy, people will not recognize signs of climate change. In particular, the paper mentions "Recent scientific findings indicate that climate change is likely responsible for the increase in the intensity of many of these [extreme weather] events in recent years," noting that people are concerned about these events. The paper goes on to call for action to take advantage of these concerns: "**The sooner we act, the lower the risk and cost. And there is much we can do.** Waiting to take action will inevitably increase costs, escalate risk, and foreclose options to address the risk."[576]

In their publications, scientists are sometimes cautious about interpreting data to show strong trends. AAAS attributes this caution to climate skepticism: "Over the past two decades, skeptics of the reality and significance of anthropogenic climate change have frequently accused climate scientists of "alarmism": of over-interpreting or overreacting to evidence of human impacts on the climate system. However, the available evidence suggests that scientists have in fact been conservative in their projections of the impacts of climate change."[577]

Because scientists are inherently cautious in what they conclude from their data, they may have underestimated some effects of climate change: "at least some of the key attributes of global warming from increased atmospheric greenhouse gases have been under-predicted, particularly in IPCC assessments of the physical science. We suggest, therefore, that scientists are biased not toward alarmism but rather the reverse: toward cautious estimates, where we define caution as erring on the side of less rather than more alarming predictions.[578] Scientists need to make clear to the public that they are not going beyond the data, and that indeed there may be occasions to strengthen their reports.

Some of this caution may stem from the fact that, as scientists, climate researchers tend to shy away from political issues (with exceptions such as James Hansen and Michael Mann). But they are willing to address the scientific issues that do affect how societies react to climate change. The AAAS has said:

217

"As scientists, it is not our role to tell people what they should do or must believe about the rising threat of climate change. But we consider it to be our responsibility as professionals to ensure, to the best of our ability, that people understand what we know: human-caused climate change is happening, we face risks of abrupt, unpredictable and potentially irreversible changes, and responding now will lower the risk and cost of taking action."[579]

Although they do not address specific climate policies such as cap-and-trade or a carbon tax, scientists as represented by the AAAS do make clear the way that society needs to address climate change. "Emissions of greenhouse gases today commit the planet to unavoidable warming and other impacts in the future. As we continue to increase greenhouse gas emissions, we accelerate and compound the effects and risks of climate change into the future. Conversely, the sooner we make a concerted effort to curtail the burning of fossil fuels as our primary energy source and releasing the CO2 to the air, the lower our risk and cost will be."[580]

A *"concerted effort to curtail the burning of fossil fuels"* requires strong action to change the source of energy away from gas, oil and coal. Left unsaid are the need to convert to renewable sources of energy, to increase energy efficiency, and the implications of change for current patterns of economic growth. All are controversial subjects that have to be addressed in a political arena, not a scientific paper.

One of the problems of policy advocacy is that improvements in energy efficiency and other measures to combat climate change can backfire. The Jevons Paradox, named after a 19th Century British economist, informs us that improvements can sometimes lead to increased rather than decreased use of energy. Jevons was addressing the use of coal, which increased even as its effect was to reduce the costs of energy, because many more uses were found for applying it to British industry. While we can try to increase use of renewables and decrease wasted energy, we must also be attentive to the effects of increasing overall energy use. A key concept is the priority of addressing climate change while improving energy efficiency and making it available to more

218

people. For example, if the development of the light emitting diode as a light source leads to widespread use in Africa, it must be coupled with development of solar and wind power generation at the same time.

When scientists do try to address the issues, for example in designing education in science, they are sometimes stymied.

> In March, Wyoming's legislature blocked the Next Generation Science Standards, an initiative aimed at boosting science education across the country, over its inclusion of climate change. The standards were developed over years in a process that involved the National Research Council, the National Science Teachers Association, the American Association for the Advancement of Science, and Achieve, with input from about half of the states. This month, the Wyoming State Board of Education, lobbied by the governor's staff, deferred a decision on what to do about the Next Generation Science Standards, sending the issue back to the Science Standards Revision Committee, which has already recommended adoption not once but twice. While the politicians dither, nearly one-third of the school districts in the state have already started implementing the Next Generation standards.[581]

Apparently, the scientists are ahead of the politicians on this one. While the State Board of Education delays the standards, science teachers in the schools are teaching climate science. It will take a generation of learning to have an effect on the politicians, but the seeds are planted and may flower soon enough to make an impact on climate policy.

Chapter 8:
What can We Do?

It is easier to dismiss denial ideologues as buffoons than to deal with their ideology as a serious threat to sound climate policies. With the influence of politicians such as Senator James Inhofe as chairman of a Senate committee, and Congressman Fred Upton as chairman of a House committee, however, it is not a good idea to write them off. [582] State officials such as Tom Easterly of Indiana and Doug Erickson of Washington also have an impact on climate politics.[583] These politicians try to deflect the pursuit of rigorous approaches to climate with extraneous approaches of their own, and they can stall serious work on the problem and exacerbate the difficulties of managing political and social responses.

It is better to meet them on their own turf and debunk their unscientific approaches. When arguing with non-scientists about something that they think they know but have no sound basis for arguing, it is necessary to move the argument from science to ideology. When you confront a denial ideologue on the basis of what they believe about nature, it becomes a question of whether that belief is testable or not. Once you establish that it is not testable, you have several options.

- The simplest approach is to dismiss the beliefs as nonscientific, a set of assumptions about reality that do not lend themselves to tests by hypotheses or research proposals. This is one of the more common responses to statements such as "the globe is cooling, not warming," or "climate change is natural, not manmade." The best response would be, "how do you know?" When they cite some of the denial scientists you need to be prepared to counter that these scientists are quacks. This may be gratifying but may lead nowhere.

- A more effective approach would be to ask, if you believe that there is no human-induced warming, how do you explain the recent heat records or extreme weather? This moves the argument to a more realistic level, and usually there are no effective responses other than "summers are hot, get over it" or "hurricanes are normal." Such responses can be countered by describing the abnormality of heat records or extreme weather.

- Often arguing becomes futile as the denial ideologues present moving targets. Ultimately, the only strategy for countering this type of ideology is to contain the damage, through isolation of the individual or group. At a personal level, this usually means a change of subject (if you want to continue the conversation) or breaking off the discussion. At a national level, this means adopting regulations to control carbon emissions rather than counting on a balky Congress to pass legislation. It may also mean working at the state level than the national level to address renewable energy and energy efficiency.

- With regard to the conspiracy theories and accusations, there may be no response that will dissuade some true believers, but description of how science works might help with others. The notion that scientists collude in secret would be laughable if it were not taken so seriously by some denial ideologues. Peer review is a reasonable riposte, but it is also regarded as just another form of conspiracy by some denial ideologues. Perhaps the best argument I have seen is that scientists are dedicated to proving each other wrong, as a matter of professional pride and advancement. This makes disproof of any unsound findings a matter of self-interest for scientists, possibly the best response to conspiracy theories.

- Ultimately, it is necessary to deal with the fear that underlies much of denial ideology. While there is no sure way to confront fear, it is useful to try to express the fear as a possible emotional reaction and bring it to the surface. "Are you concerned about the effect of regulations on economic growth?" can elicit a response that leads to fruitful discussion about the various forms of economic growth, e.g. sustainable vs. unsustainable.

- One major question about sustainable economic growth is, "Who pays for climate change?" Insurance companies have already priced in climate change, so we are already paying through our insurance premiums or taxes (for federal flood and crop insurance). True costs of energy have not been priced in yet, but we are paying in other ways that are at least as damaging to economic growth as any carbon tax.[584]

One author cautions that talking about climate change as an environmental issue, which is the way it has been framed, increases the difficulty of convincing people of its urgency. "This may create proximity for environmentalists, but for the wider public, these associations only make climate change more distant from their immediate concerns: as a luxury that can be kept on the edge of their pool of worry by economy, jobs, crime, and war."[585] As mentioned in the preface, people do not see it as a high priority or an immediate concern. If framed as an energy and weather issue, more people might be drawn into discussions of energy costs, disasters and other more immediate concerns. But when framed only as an environmental issue, it may lose salience to many people. Environmentalists may have inadvertently narrowed the issue: "They defined climate change as an environmental issue and therefore not a resource, an energy, an economic, a health, or a social rights issue."[586]

One of the most telling arguments about the true costs of climate change is the damage caused by extreme weather. While there are still arguments about the cause of superstorms such as Hurricane Sandy, the role of climate change in weather disasters is becoming increasingly clear. Analysis of the costs of power disruption shows that they can be considerable: "A recent report from the National Academy of Sciences about the vast 2003 blackout in the Eastern United States determined that the economic cost of that disruption was about 50 times higher than the price of the actual electricity lost, and that didn't take into account deaths or other human consequences."[587]

It may be tempting to bring up the issue of climate change every time there is an extreme weather event such as those described in Chapter 2. If you were to say, however, that this or that weather is caused by climate change, you would open yourself to criticism by those who can cite chapter and verse – that scientists do not attribute any one event to climate change. It is rather the cumulative effect of climate change that makes us more vulnerable to extreme weather. Sea level rise exacerbates storm surges. Hot weather increases the effect of droughts as soils dry out faster. Warm atmosphere absorbs more water vapor, causing more severe floods when massive precipitation occurs.

It is necessary, indeed imperative, to deal with climate change denial if sound climate policies are to be developed and implemented in time to avoid serious consequences of global warming and extreme weather. Denial has had its effects: during 2013, the number of people in the U.S. stating that they do not believe that global warming is happening rose from 16% to 23%.[588] More recently, this percentage has risen another two points to 25%.[589] This is during a period when denial ideologues have been particularly active in attacking climate science by claiming, for example, that the globe is cooling. One would think that education would reduce the percentage of "know-nothings," but the same percentages (30%) of those who deny climate change and those who accept climate science are college-educated.

Respondents to public opinion polls tend to give climate change low priority. When asked how much they worry about climate change out of a number of problems facing the nation, half said "a little" or "not at all" and ranked it second to last in a list of more than a dozen choices.[590] There are a number of possible reasons for this low prioritization: many people have immediate problems of employment, family, income and other issues that they have to deal with. Learning details about climate change and how to address it can be time-consuming and competes with other demands on time. As a result, few people, including those who consider global warming a threat and want to do something about it, understand that major efforts at the national and international level are required, and even fewer understand how their own activities may be contributing to the problem.[591] Despite all of the available information to the contrary, 41% of respondents consider global warming exclusively natural or do not believe that it is happening.[592]

Have Deniers Won?

The UK *Guardian* sounded the alarm about climate change denial with the headline "The Climate Change Deniers Have Won." While I would not go so far as to say that deniers have won, they are on the upswing, as the polls cited above indicate. The article reviewed some of the denial ideology and then said the following about its effects on politics: "Tempting though it is to blame cowardly politicians, the abuse comes too easily. The question remains: what turned them into cowards? Rightwing billionaires in the United States and the oil companies have spent fortunes on blocking action on climate change. A part of the answer may therefore be that conservative politicians in London, Washington and Canberra are doing their richest supporters' bidding."[593]

It would seem likely that some cynical fossil-fuel companies are influencing denial, but their effect is more than manipulation of public opinion. The article went on to explain why denial ideology is so persistent: "Climate change deniers are committed. Their denial fits perfectly with their support for free market economics, opposition to state intervention and hatred of all those latte-slurping, quinoa-munching liberals, with their arrogant manners and dainty hybrid cars, who presume to tell honest men and women how to live."[594] While I would take issue with the stereotype of *"latte-slurping, quinoa-munching liberals,"* the *Guardian* does have a good grasp of how denial ideology fits into a general worldview.

"Deniers have won" is a theme that is echoed by Naomi Klein in her harsh critique of modern society. "The short answer is that the deniers won, at least the first round. Not the battle over climate science – their influence in that arena is already waning. But the deniers, and the ideological movement from which they sprang, won the battle over which values would govern our societies."[595] Klein's argument is that without drastic changes in these values, we will not be able to resolve the issues posed by climate change – issues of financial controls over energy.

Alienation, discussed in Chapter 5, explains one of the moral aspects of denial ideology. One writer, Nick Cohen, puts his finger on the reason that denial ideology persists. "We are alienated from our environment when we fail to recognize it as the product of our own actions and thus fail to acknowledge our own responsibility for it, and so instead it starts to look like a natural fact about which there is nothing we can do: global warming simply part of a natural cycle, pollution an inevitable byproduct of technology, urban sprawl the inexorable consequence of market forces, and so on."[596] With this attitude, it is possible for denial advocates to claim that climate change is *"part of a natural cycle,"* that there is nothing we can do about technology and market forces. Since we do not see the changes as a consequence of our own actions, we abjure responsibility for the consequences.

Denial is not limited to arguments against climate science *per se*. It relates to a whole set of ideological arguments against social change. While caricaturing agents of change as *"latte-slurping, quinoa-munching liberals, with their arrogant manners and dainty hybrid cars,"* Cohen nevertheless points out the conflict that results from the opposition of ideology and science. It is not only liberals who understand the science. Conservatives and Republicans also understand climate science, and some are as vociferous about addressing the issues as liberals. Businesses "get it" and plan for climate problems.[597]

Some people might react to climate change by downgrading its priority even though they agree with the science. Denial can be detected in reactions against the adoption of climate policies that entail costs that would set back growth and prosperity, in the eyes of the denier. It just isn't important enough to them to make any sacrifices. They may think it is too late, or the challenges too vast, to meaningfully address climate change. It is understandable that people see climate change as a worldwide problem in which they have a miniscule role to play. Governments and international organizations must address the issue on a universal basis. Actions by an individual, or even a single country or entity like the EU, are not sufficient to address the issue if others ignore it.

It is essential to see denial ideologues as "merchants of doubt," as Oreskes and Conway describe them.[598] When doubt becomes the principal method of discourse, the deliberative method of solving problems becomes impossible:

> [Doubt is corrosive] when it comes to the politics of climate change in public space in the United States. As Oreskes and Conway (2010) point out, there is no need for climate change deniers to disseminate falsehood. Instead, all they need to do is create the impression of doubt and uncertainty, to give the impression that there are two legitimate and more or less equal sides on the question of the existence of damaging anthropogenic climate change. What has actually happened is that the hardline right wing in US politics has (without admitting it) embraced postmodernism, treating truth as a subcategory of power...[which helps] explain why the deliberative system on climate change is in such disrepair in the United States. Because it facilitates inaction, this disrepair suits the hardline organized deniers.[599]

"Treating truth as a subcategory of power" is a useful extension of the definition of ideology. When truth becomes subordinate to the exercise of congressional power, or the

adoption of rules by state governments concerning the teaching of climate science as controversial, climate change can be ignored until it is too late. By making truth conditional on where one stands on an issue, the understanding of climate changes is encumbered with negative emotional responses, not rational responses. The result is delay and denial.

Some of this avoidance is psychological, but we cannot let psychological barriers impede action. "Paradoxically, the more people seek refuge in illusions, science denial, reality avoidance, and magical thinking, the more self-fulfilling the ominous climate forecasts become."[600] It is doubly significant that we confront denial, since it not only stops necessary action but delays serious consideration of fundamental changes needed in society.

While it is distasteful for scientists and anyone with a good understanding of climate science to confront it, denial ideology is an obstacle to overcome when pursuing a response to climate change threats to economic development and welfare. Arguments against denial must include review of climate science findings as well as discussion of the economic costs of delaying or impeding implementation of climate policies.

Some of these lines of argument will seem unsatisfactory to scientists and environmentalists who want to pursue climate solutions vigorously. Nevertheless, it is necessary to confront climate change denial whenever and wherever we find it. Even if we find denial distasteful, we have to deal with it in the political arena. It is better to meet it head on rather than avoiding confrontation.

One of the more frustrating things about denial is that no matter what evidence is presented, some denial ideologues will refuse to accept it. They may not be the best targets for argument against denial. Rather, it is others whom the denial ideologues seek to persuade that should be addressed. "There is a large percentage of the population that is still wondering which side of the argument to believe in. If we just sit back and let the other side spread their nonsense without ever objecting they will win by default. By publicizing the science and showing the inability of the deniers to prove any of their claims we can persuade some of the undecided to believe in the science."[601]

Often, the arguments against climate science will have a distasteful tone, when they seem to be sneering at scientists. An example: Larry Bell's discussion of climate scientists' research: "...it later turned out that they made this all up, [and] worried their Nobel Peace Prize-awarded minds and have scared us all to death..."[602] The real problem with snide comments like this is that they erode credibility of the science by making it sound petty or picayune. Perhaps the normal response would be to disregard these statements, but it might be better to confront the arguments by responding that this is not the way a civil discussion of how science proceeds. Steering arguments away from snide mannerisms toward a more sober discussion of the implications of research is essential.

Conclusion

At its core, the issue of climate change is an issue of politics and science. Neither can be dealt with exclusively, but the combination can be confusing: "Most of us, including scientists, are largely confused about the relations between facts and values, and science and policy. Many of us are scientifically ignorant, and large sums have been spent to further confuse and misinform us."[603] Because of these "*large sums*," it is an uphill battle to counter denial ideology with science. Nevertheless, it is urgent to do so as we have little leeway in setting policies into motion to reduce emissions soon enough to avoid the worst consequences of climate change. The gulf between science and ideology is an ill-fated feature of modern culture, where the response to uncomfortable scientific findings is an overreaction. This is unfortunate, as it tends to move the argument from a scientific plane down to an ideological level.

Ultimately, the question that needs to be asked is, what kind of future do we want? Do we want a future with regrets about what we failed to do, or a future with no regrets? The "*no regrets*" approach is one pursued by some policymakers who understand the gravity of climate change and can see that there are approaches to energy that can save money as well as mitigate the worst effects of climate change. This approach should be encouraged, as it is in all of our interests to move discussion forward toward resolving climate issues.

If we are concerned about the future, we are concerned about intergenerational justice. Some of us in the current generation have more responsibility than others, as we have lived longer and used more energy throughout our lives. At age 75, I am as responsible as anyone in my generation for unknowingly contributing to the problem; that is why I take it so seriously. The following statement of responsibility best describes intergenerational ethics: "We have a fundamental and collective responsibility to act with this inescapable truth in mind. Future generations will justifiably sit in judgment on what current generations chose to do in full knowledge of the devastating consequences of continuing with our energy-profligate lifestyles."[604]

Intergenerational justice is one of the areas of human concern that resonates with everyone, regardless of their views of climate science. "Evolutionary theory suggests a reason...we care most about our genetic relatives – our great-grandparents, grandparents, parents, children, grandchildren and great-grandchildren, or an approximate span of 140 years that includes both past and future family members. Beyond that, most people do not care much about the past or future."[605] While it seems cynical to say that most people *do not care much about the past or future*," it is reasonable to base our discussion of the consequences of climate change on family relations. If people are genuinely concerned about the future of their descendants, they will encourage discussion of the threats to the well-being of those descendants.

Concern for future generations is of course one of the highest moral obligations of any current generation. It is possible that some would dismiss this obligation for eschatological reasons: "Christian eschatology can be appropriated for absolutely asinine political purposes, of course; on some accounts of a world in its death throes, it makes little sense to contemplate responsibilities to future generations."[606] Most believers do not support this view, however, and most people would regard the welfare and survival of their children and grandchildren as major commitments. It is indeed possible to appeal to believers in denial ideology to consider future generations and raise doubts about their denial when they contemplate their progeny's future. It may be possible to lead them toward rational argument about climate change through such appeals.

Because of the gravity and enormity of the issue, climate change requires immense changes in political and economic systems. There are few precedents for such changes, although one in the history of the U.S., UK and other countries is informative: abolitionism. Freeing the slaves required major sacrifices by some sectors of the population, notably slaveholders, and "the climate justice movement is demanding that an existing set of political and economic interests be forced to say goodbye to trillions of dollars of wealth." Because of the scale of the changes, "it is impossible to point to any precedent other than abolition."[607]

Abolitionism is an interesting metaphor, but there is one major difference with climate change. Slave ownership identified those who were responsible for maintaining slavery, and the abolitionists could target them along with the legal system that supported them. In the case of climate change, this assignment of responsibility is more tenuous. "Despite the fact that serious, clearly identifiable harms will have occurred because of human agency, conventional morality would have trouble finding anyone to blame. For no one intended the bad outcome or brought it about or even was able to foresee it. Today, we face the possibility that the global environment may be destroyed; yet no one will be responsible."[608] It is difficult to understand that we are all responsible because the assignment of responsibility for energy use involves so many indirect and ambiguous relationships. Just by living day-to-day, we are incurring responsibility while failing to make connections to the environment.

One might argue that fossil fuel interests are responsible – after all they (the companies and their political allies) promote continued exploration for and use of fossil fuels when there are five times as many reserves as can be safely burned. Attacks on fossil fuel interests are the tactics of many climate activists such as 350.org and the Sierra Club. Movements such as divestment and the Sierra Club's "beyond coal" campaign are directed at specific fossil fuel companies. But did the fossil fuel companies always really "intend the bad outcome?" Of course not. They now know that there will be bad outcomes (and many acknowledge this in their public statements). Yet they still act as if there will be few consequences of their own actions. After all, the customer is always right.[609]

Intention is key to understanding the morality of climate change. Since no one intends to harm the earth by using energy, why should they feel guilt or moral compulsion to do anything? "[The] problem with climate change is that that intention is lacking. Not only are we all involved in it in various ways, certainly in the rich world and the way that we live, but we have no intention to cause harm, we're just living our lives and driving our kids to school and putting food on the table. So when we try to turn it into a moral argument, which is what it needs to be in order to compel us to take action, of course, not surprisingly people get very angry and they push the thing away."[610]

While fossil fuel interests struggle with their own moral problems, the rest of us also have to face up to our own responsibilities. Anyone over the age of 50 has been using fossil fuels since before they were widely known to be dangerous. While many of us realized in our early adulthood that coal, gasoline and other fuels had the potential for causing dangerous pollutants, we thought those emissions could be controlled, and indeed some were controlled with scrubbers and catalytic mufflers. There was also a belief that *the solution to pollution is dilution*," a trite phrase that assumes unlimited capacity of nature to absorb our wastes. Both of these assumptions are now invalidated by the findings of climate science.

We have to abandon our easy logic about the control of fossil fuel pollution. We cannot solve the climate problem with technology. Stopping carbon dioxide emissions from power plants costs about 40% of the fuel just for carbon capture and storage, and the technology has not scaled up well. Electric cars and building efficiency are helpful, but they require massive turnover of existing capital investments as well as major infrastructure modifications. We should all live in high-rise apartments, use mass transit and cultivate urban farms, but when and how can that occur? All of these changes require wrenching reorientation of the mindset of older generations. Younger generations may adapt more readily as they are facing the more severe consequences in their lifetimes.

As Carl Pope, former Executive Director of the Sierra Club said, "legacy may be environmentalism's ethical bedrock."[611] Writing is my legacy. While I do not expect that my books will change many minds, I do expect that they will provide a record of how and why we failed to address climate change in a timely manner. I understand some of the implications of climate change, not as a scientist, but as an observer of human behavior and interaction. My lifelong interest is the role of ideology in influencing behavior.[612]

Ideology is the focus of this book because it impedes our ability to see the rationality of the solutions such as the "no regrets" approach, that is, energy policies that will save money even if they do not solve climate change. Because of the disparity between ideology and science, distorted discussion of climate and weather will continue to divert attention from reality into polemicized unreality. While we must pay close attention to reality at all times, we also need to give full attention to the ideology that can sidetrack the solutions required to address that reality.

Beyond the question of our future, there is a much more profound question of the future of the planet. In answering this question, the harmful role of humans is significant but not fatal. The planet will survive without us, albeit changed significantly. One commentator put it eloquently: "The recent report by the

United Nations Intergovernmental Panel on Climate Change documents the damage now being done by human-created greenhouse gases and global warming. In reacting to the report, we should not be concerned about protecting our planet. Nature can survive far more than what we can do to it and is totally oblivious to whether homo sapiens lives or dies in the next hundred years. Our concern should be about protecting ourselves – because we have only ourselves to protect us."[613]

Nature will not protect humans against human folly, only humans will. Denial ideology is paramount in our folly about climate change. Ideology does not protect us; it blinds us.

References

AAAS: American Association for the Advancement of Science. 2014. *WHAT WE KNOW: THE REALITY, RISKS AND RESPONSE TO CLIMATE CHANGE.* AAAS.org

Ackerman, Diane. 2014. *The Human Age: The World Shaped By Us.* W. W. Norton & Company. Kindle Edition.

Ambler, Harold. 2011. *Don't Sell Your Coat.* Lansing International Books

Archibald, David. 2014. *Twilight of Abundance: Why Life in the 21st Century Will Be Nasty, Brutish, and Short.* Kindle eBook

Avery, Samuel. 2014. *The Pipeline and the Paradigm: Keystone XL, Tar Sands, and the Battle to Defuse the Carbon Bond.* Ruka Press

Ball, Tim. 2014. *The Deliberate Corruption of Climate Science.* Stairway Press. Kindle Edition.

Bagley, Katherine and Maria Galluci. 2013. *Bloomberg's Hidden Legacy: Climate Change and the Future of New York City,* Inside Climate News

Berger, John J. 2014. *Climate Peril: The Intelligent Reader's Guide to Understanding the Climate Crisis.* Northbrae Books.

Bell, Larry. 2011. *Climate of Corruption.* Greanleaf

Bell, Larry. 2012, *Man The Lifeboats! Global Warming Has Oceans Rising At Alarming Rate! (Or Maybe not).* Forbes, December 25

Berners-Lee, Mike; and Clark, Duncan. 2013. *The Burning Question: We Can't Burn Half the World's Oil, Coal, and Gas. So How Do We Quit?.* Greystone Books. Kindle Edition.

Brainard, Curtis. 2012. ***Bad hippie!*** *Is it wrong to 'scold' exaggerations about climate and weather?* Columbia Journalism Review, November

Bryce, Robert. 2014. *Smaller Faster Lighter Denser Cheaper: How Innovation Keeps Proving the Catastrophists Wrong.* PublicAffairs.

Brysse, Keynyn, Naomi Oreskes, Jessica O'Reilly, Michael Oppenheimer. 2013. *Climate change prediction: Erring on the side of least drama?.* Global Environmental Change, Volume 23, February 2013, Pages 327–337

Caruso, Paul. 2013. *How to Cure a Climate Change Denier.* Kindle

Charles HRH The Prince of Wales. 2010. *Harmony.* HarperCollins.

CRS: Congressional Research Service. 2012. *Drought in the United States: Causes and Issues for Congress.* Peter Folger, Betsy A. Cody, Nicole T. Carter, August 15, www.crs.gov

Darling, Seth B.; Sisterson, Douglas L. 2014. *How to Change Minds About Our Changing Climate: Let Science Do the Talking the Next Time Someone Tries to Tell You... The Experiment.* Kindle Edition.

Darwall, Rupert. 2013. *The Age of Global Warming.* Quartet Books

Delingpole, James. 2013. *The Little Green Book of Eco-Fascism: The Left's Plan to Frighten Your Kids, Drive Up Energy Costs, and Hike Your Taxes!* Regnery Publishing.

Dessler, Andrew E. and Edward A. Parsons. 2010, *The Science and Politics of Global Climate Change.* Cambridge University Press

Diogenes, Laputa. 2012. *Global Warming Revelations (Second*

Coming). Kindle Edition.

Dryzek, John S., Richard B. Norgaard, and David Schlosberg. 2013. *Climate-Challenged Society.* Oxford University Press

Emanuel, Kerry. 2012. *Probable Cause, Are scientists too cautious to help us stop climate change?* Foreign Policy, Nov. 13

Emerson, Ralph Waldo. 2011. *Nature.* Kindle Edition.

Fasullo, John T. and Kevin E. Trenberth. *A Less Cloudy Future: The Role of Subtropical Subsidence in Climate Sensitivity.* Science, November 9, 2012, sciencemag.org

Festinger, Leon, Henry Riecken, and Stanley Schachter. 1956. *When Prophecy Fails.* Pinter & Martin

Fone, Joe. 2013. *Climate Change Natural or Manmade?* Stacy International

Freudenburg, William R., and Muselli, Violetta. 2010. *Global Warming Estimates, Media Expectations, and the Asymmetry of Scientific Challenge.* Global Environmental Change, August 2010

Funk, McKenzie. 2014. *Windfall: The Booming Business of Climate Change.* Penguin Group.

Giddens, Anthony. 2013. *The Politics of Climate Change.* Wiley. Kindle Edition.

Giles, Slade. 2013. *American Exodus: Climate Change and the Coming Flight for Survival.* Kindle Edition

Gillis, Justin. 2013. *Temperature Rising,* New York Times Books

Glover, Peter C. and Michael J. Economides. 2010. *Energy and Climate Wars.* Continuum Books

Guimaraes, Renato. 2014. *Cooling Up: The interconnected public sphere and the "science" of climate denial.* Kindle Edition.

Hamilton, Clive. 2013. *Earthmasters: The Dawn of the Age of Climate Engineering*. Yale University Press.

Hansen, James. 2005. *Michael Crichton's "Scientific Method."* Crichton_20050927.pdf

Hansen, James; Pushker Kharecha, Makiko Sato, Valerie Masson-Delmotte, Frank Ackerman, David J. Beerling, Paul J. Hearty, Ove Hoegh-Guldberg, Shi-Ling Hsu, Camille Parmesan, Johan Rockstrom, Eelco J. Rohling, Jeffrey Sachs, Pete Smith, Konrad Steffen, Lise Van Susteren, Karina von Schuckmann, James C. Zachos *"Assessing 'Dangerous Climate Change': Required Reduction of Carbon Emissions to Protect Young People, Future Generations and Nature."* PLOS ONE, December 3, 2013

Helm, Dieter. 2012. *The Carbon Crunch.* Yale University, Kindle Edition

Hillman, Mayer, Tina Fawcett and Sudhir Chella Rajan. 2008. *How We Can Save the Planet: Preventing Global Climate Catastrophe*. Kindle Edition

Hoggan, James. 2009. *Climate Cover-Up.* Greystone Books

Hulme, Mike. 2009. *Why We Disagree About Climate Change.* Cambridge University Press. Kindle Edition.

Inhofe, James. 2012. *The Greatest Hoax.* WND Books

IPCC (Intergovernmental Panel on Climate Change). 2012. *Managing The Risks Of Extreme Events And Disasters To Advance Climate Change Adaptation.* IPCC.int.

IPCC, Intergovernmental Panel on Climate Change. 2001. *Climate Change 2001: Synthesis Report.* ipcc.ch

IPCC: Intergovernmental Panel on Climate Change. 2007. *Fourth Assessment Report.* ipcc.int

IPCC: Intergovernmental Panel on Climate Change. 2013-14. *Fifth Assessment Report.* ipcc.int NOTE: the report has two publication dates because the science section was published in 2013 and the impacts and policies sections were published in 2014.

Isaac, Rael Jean. 2013. *Roosters of the Apocalypse: How the Junk Science of Global Warming is Bankrupting the Western World* (new, revised and expanded edition). Kindle Edition.

Ismail, Nae. 2010. *A hot Tea by the Giza: The real Global Warming, Not CO2 Hoax.* iUniverse

Jackson, Tim. 2009. *Prosperity without Growth: Economics for a Finite Planet.* Routledge.

Jamieson, Dale. 2014. *Reason in a Dark Time: Why the Struggle Against Climate Change Failed -- and What It Means for Our Future.* Oxford University Press.

Johnson, Warren. 2014. *End of an Era, Not the End of the World: Creating Good Work as the Economy Slows.* Kindle Edition.

Keating, Christopher. 2014. *Undeniable: Dialogues on Global Warming.* Kindle Edition.

Kehr, John. 2011. *The Inconvenient Skeptic: The Comprehensive Guide to the Earth's Climate.* Kindle Edition

Kingsolver, Barbara. 2012. *Flight Behavior: A Novel.* HarperCollins.

Klein, Naomi. 2014. *This Changes Everything: Capitalism vs. The Climate.* Simon & Schuster.

Kolbert, Elizabeth. 2010. *Field Notes from a Catastrophe: Man, Nature, and Climate Change.* Bloomsbury Publishing Plc.

Kolbert, Elizabeth. 2014. *Rethinking How We Think About Climate Change.* climate.audubon.org Sept. 9, 2014

Koomey, Jonathan. 2012. *Cold Cash, Cool Climate: Science-Based Advice for Ecological Entrepreneurs.* Analytics Press.

Kunreuther, Howard C. and Erwann O. Michel-Kerjan. 2009. *At War with the Weather: Managing Large-Scale Risks in a New Era of Catastrophes.* Kindle Edition

Laframboise, Donna. 2013. *Into the Dustbin: Rajendra Pachauri, the Climate Report & the Nobel Peace Prize.* Ivy Avenue Press.

Leggett, Jeremy. 2013. *The Energy of Nations.* Routledge.

Leiserowitz, A., Maibach, E., Roser-Renouf, C., Feinberg, G., & Howe, P. 2012. *Public support for climate and energy policies in September, 2012.* Yale University and George Mason University. Yale Project on Climate Change Communication

Leiserowitz, A., Maibach, E., Roser-Renouf, C., Feinberg, G., Rosenthal, S., & Marlon, J. 2014. *Climate change in the American mind: Americans' global warming beliefs and attitudes in November, 2013.* Yale University and George Mason University. New Haven, CT: Yale Project on Climate Change

Lewandowsky, Stephan, Klaus Oberauer and Gilles Gignac. 2013. *MOTIVATED REJECTION OF SCIENCE: NASA faked the moon landing. Therefore (Climate) Science is a Hoax: An Anatomy of the Motivated Rejection of Science.* Psychological Science

Mann, Michael. 2012. *The Hockey Stick and the Climate Wars: Dispatches from the Front Lines.* Perseus Books Group.

Marsa, Linda. 2013. *Fevered: Why a Hotter Planet Will Hurt Our Health—and How We Can Save Ourselves.* Rodale Books.

Marshall, George. 2014. *Don't Even Think About It: Why Our Brains Are Wired to Ignore Climate Change.* Bloomsbury Publishing.

Mayer, Jane. 2010. *Covert Operations.* New Yorker, August 31

McKibben, Bill. 2012. *Global Warming's Terrifying New Math.* Rolling Stone, July 19

McNall, Scott G. 2012. *Understanding Rapid Climate Change: Causes, Consequences, and Solutions (Framing 21st Century Social Issues).* Taylor and Francis.

McPherson, William. 1973. *Ideology and Change.* National Press Books

McPherson, William. 2012. *Tales of a Hot Planet.* Kindle Edition

McPherson, William. 2014. *Ideology versus Science: Climate Change Denial.* Kindle Edition

Melton. P.E., Bruce. 2013. *Climate Discovery Chronicles: Recent, Relatively Unknown Discoveries About Our Rapidly Changing World.* Kindle Edition.

Michaels, Patrick. 1998. *Testimony, House Committee on Small Business.* Cato.org

Montford, A.W. 2010. *Hockey Stick Illusion.* Stacey International

Moore, Kathleen Dean; Nelson, Michael P. 2011. *Moral Ground: Ethical Action for a Planet in Peril.* Trinity University Press.

NAS: National Academy of Sciences. 2012. *Climate and Social Stress: Implications for Security Analysis.* John D. Steinbruner, Paul C. Stern, and Jo L. Husbands, Editors; Committee on Assessing the Impact of Climate Change on Social and Political Stresses; Board on Environmental Change and Society.

NASA: National Aeronautic and Atmospheric Administration. 2012, *Climate Likely to Be on Hotter Side of Projections.* nasa.gov, November 8, 2012

NCA. 2014. Melillo, Jerry M., Terese (T.C.) Richmond, and Gary W. Yohe, Eds. *Climate Change Impacts in the United States: The Third National Climate Assessment. U.S. Global Change*

Research Program. U.S. Government Printing Office

NOAA. 2012a. *State of the Climate Drought. October 2012,* National Oceanic and Atmospheric Administration, National Climatic Data Center, noaa.gov/sotc/drought

NOAA. 2012b. *August 2012 National Overview.* ncdc.noaa.gov

Nordhaus, William D. 2013. *The Climate Casino.* Yale University Press.

Oreskes, Naomi, and Conway, Erik. 2011. *Merchants of Doubt: How a Handful of Scientists Obscured the Truth on Issues from Tobacco Smoke to Global Warming.* Bloomsbury Press.

Oreskes, Naomi; Conway, Erik M. 2014. *The Collapse of Western Civilization: A View from the Future* Columbia University Press.

Peters, Kirsten, 2012. *The Whole Story of Climate,* Kindle Edition.

Prugh, Tom and Renner, Michael (Project Directors). 2014. *State of the World, 2014: Governing for Sustainability.* Island Press.

Ricoveri, Giovanna. 2013. *Nature for Sale: The Commons versus Commodities.* Pluto Press. Kindle Edition.

Robert, Dr. 2010. *The Climate Conspiracy.* Kindle Edition.

Robinson, John. 2013. *A Plague of People.* Smashwords Edition.

Sadar, Anthony J. 2012. *In Global Warming We Trust, A Heretic's Guide to Climate Science.* Telescope Books.

Schulman, Daniel. 2014. *Sons of Wichita: How the Koch Brothers Became America's Most Powerful and Private Dynasty.* Grand Central Publishing.

Shapiro, Ben. 2014. *How to Debate Leftists and Destroy Them: 11 Rules for Winning the Argument*. David Horowitz Freedom Center.

Shrader-Frechett, Kristin. 2011. *What Will Work: Fighting Climate Change with Renewable Energy, Not Nuclear Power*. Oxford University Press.

Stern, Nicholas. 2006. *Stern Review on the economics of climate change*. hm-treasury.gov.uk

Stevenson, Hayley and Dryzek, John S. 2014. *Democratizing Global Climate Governance*. Cambridge University Press.

Sullivan, Peter. 2013. *Punch-Drunk on CO2...Dizzy from Spin: Catastrophic Man-Made Global Warming Sustainable Hypothesis or Unsustainable Hoax?* Xlibris.

Sussman, Brian. 2010. *Climategate*. WorldNetDaily Books.

Sussman, Brian. 2012. *Eco-Tyranny: How the Left's Green Agenda will Dismantle America*. Midpoint Trade Books.

Thompson, Allen; Bendik-Keymer, Jeremy. 2012. *Ethical Adaptation to Climate Change: Human Virtues of the Future*. The MIT Press. Kindle Edition.

Tisdale, Bob. 2013. *Climate Models Fail*. Kindle Edition.

Tokar, Brian. 2014. *Toward Climate Justice: Perspectives on the Climate Crisis and Social Change*. New Compass Press.

USDA. 2012, *US Drought 2012 Farm and Food Impacts*. ers.usda.gov/topics/in-the-news/us-drought-2012-farm-and-food-impacts.aspx

Weisman, Alan. 2013. *Countdown: Our Last, Best Hope for a Future on Earth?* Little, Brown and Company.

Winston, Andrew S. 2014. *The Big Pivot: Radically Practical*

Strategies for a Hotter, Scarcer, and More Open World. Harvard Business Review Press

Wishart, Ian. 2013. *Totalitaria: What If The Enemy Is The State?*. Howling At The Moon Publishing Ltd.

Notes

---

1 *New York Times*, January 11, 2013

2 Ibid.

3 Ibid.

4 *Climate Change and the American People*, draft report of the National Climate Assessment (NCA) and Development Advisory Committee, January 11, 2013, ncadac.globalchange.gov/

5 Dr. Roy Spencer went so far as to use the Holocaust denial analogy (i.e., denial of the extermination of Jews by the Nazi regime in Germany) as a basis for calling climate scientists "global warming Nazis," apparently as a means of positing "denial" and "Nazism" as mirror images of an invective spectrum. He considers denial of climate science the reasonable alternative, and climate science itself a kind of Nazism. Drroyspencer.com, February 20, 2014

6 Kert Davies of the Climate Investigations Center

7 Tisdale, 2013

8 McPherson, 2014.

9 Lieserowitz et.al, 2012

10 McPherson, 2014

11 http://www.inhofe.senate.gov/newsroom/press-releases/inhofes-opening-statement-at-epw-clean-air-and-nuclear-safety-subcommittee-hearing-entitled-climate-change-the-need-to-act-now-

12 *The Hill*, July 8, 2014

13 *Providence Journal*, May 27, 2014. Just to prove how crazy they are, the Republican Party of Texas put the following statement in their platform: "While we all strive to be good stewards of the earth, *'climate change' is a political agenda* which attempts to control every aspect of our lives. We urge government at all levels to ignore any plea for money to fund global climate change or 'climate justice' initiatives." It would be weird to call natural forces, even natural climate change unrelated to any human activity, "a political agenda." Of course, the Texas Republicans are probably conflating climate science with climate policies as "global climate change."

14 Jon Krosnick of the Stanford Woods Institute for the Environment, news.stanford.edu, November 13, 2013

15 *Seattle Times*, September 12, 2014. Washington State has developed one of the more advanced plans for responding to climate change, and one of its tenets is to overcome obstacles such as "Outdated assumptions that future conditions will vary within historic bounds." This Washington State senate candidate is clearly using outdated assumptions. *Preparing for a Changing Climate, Washington State's Integrated Climate Response Strategy,* Washington State Department of Ecology, April 2012

16 McPherson, 2014

17 Stevenson and Dryzek, 2014

18 democracynow.org/2014/4/8/ science_does_not_exist_on_capitol_hill

19 *The Hill*, April 5, 2014

20 IPCC, 2007

21 IPCC, 2013

22 *Nature*, May 25, 2012

23 Ibid.

24 Fasullor and Trenberth, 2012

25 E.g. Bell, 2011, Sussman, 2012

26 *Guardian*, May 27, 2014 Interestingly, some Republicans also recognize this difference. In a memo, Frank Luntz, consultant to Republicans, said "It's time for us to start talking about 'climate change' instead of global warming ... 'climate change' is less frightening than 'global warming'." Luntz wanted to change the terms of the dialogue to reduce public concern about climate change, but facts keep interfering as temperatures rise. This is not just a semantic issue. Many denial ideologues use "global warming alarmism" to describe climate science and accuse scientists of falsely predicting temperature increases.

27 *Science* magazine, August 22, 2014. Scientists attribute this slowdown in the rate to shifting patterns of ocean warming, in which the deeper ocean layers warmed more than the surface layers and thus the rise in atmospheric temperatures slowed.

28 Source: www.ncdc.noaa.gov/sotc/global/2012/13

29 Robert, 2010

30 For example, Brian Sussman

31 Kehr, 2011. John Kehr uses paleoclimatology to map out periods of glaciation and warmer periods, and contends that we are nearing the end of one of those warm periods, the Holocene. He expects that we will enter another "ice age" regardless of human emissions of greenhouse gases. Another view of paleoclimatology is offered by Peters, 2012, who says "Climate may become a lot warmer in response to the spike in greenhouse gases we have created."

32 The issue of carbon dioxide as a pollutant vexes many denial ideologues. Some will declare it is not a pollutant at all (McPherson, 2014) but others will admit there may be some effect on climate but that it is not significant. An example is the following statement from the Cornwall Alliance Declaration titled *Protect the Poor: Ten Reasons to Oppose Harmful Climate Change Policies*: "While human addition of greenhouse gases, particularly carbon dioxide (CO_2), to the atmosphere may slightly raise atmospheric temperatures, observational studies indicate that the climate system responds more in ways that suppress than in ways that amplify CO_2's effect on temperature, implying a relatively small and benign rather than large and dangerous warming effect."

33 Kehr, 2011

34 Peters, 2012

35 Ibid.

36 Ibid.

37 Robert, 2010

38 McPherson, 2014

39 Cornwall Alliance Newsletter, August 17, 2014

40 Archibald, 2014

41 *www.ncdc.noaa.gov/sotc/global/2012/13* I used the period 1980 to 2010 as an example of the hottest period on record because many climatologists consider thirty years to be a minimum for describing the climate. Another consideration in the history of climate as a basis for forecasting the future is the fact that there was some cooling between 1940 and 1980, due mainly to aerosols from industrial activities that were reduced by pollution controls after 1980.

42 A cycle of earth movements involving revolution around the sun, tilting of the north and south poles, and other astronomical phenomena that was named after Serbian geophysicist and astronomer Milutin Milanković (Anglicized as Milankovitch). These movements are sometimes identified as the sole source of climate change because they affect the amount of sunshine falling on the Earth.

43 Darling and Sisterson, 2014

44 Ibid.

45 Kehr, 2011

46 A summary of studies is provided by the World Glacier Monitoring Service: 10% are growing, 90% are shrinking.

47 Marshall, 2014

48 *New York Times*, September 22, 2014

49 Weisman, 2013

50 *New York Times*, August 12, 2014

51 Ibid.

52 World Meteorological Organization (WMO) Press Release, March 24, 2014. The statement quoted the WMO Secretary-General, Michel Jarraud, as saying "There is no standstill in global warming. The warming of our oceans has accelerated, and at lower depths. More than 90 percent of the excess energy trapped by greenhouse gases is stored in the oceans. Levels of these greenhouse gases are at record levels, meaning that our atmosphere and oceans will continue to warm for centuries to come. The laws of physics are non-negotiable."

53 huffingtonpost.com, June 30, 2014

54 Kehr, 2011

55 Weisman, 2013

56 *Spectator,* October 17, 2013

57 thinkprogress.org, July 22, 2014

58 Hansen et al., 2013

59 Kansas House Resolution 6043

60 Archibald, 2014

61 Sullivan, 2013

62 *Science,* October 15, 2010

63 Delingpole, 2013

64 Robert, 2010

65 Kehr, 2009
66 Keating, 2014
67 *breitbart.com,* October 29, 2014
68 http://www.esrl.noaa.gov/gmd/ccgg/trends/
69 Kehr, 2011
70 Darling and Sisterson, 2014
71 *Washington Times,* October 23, 2012
72 Archibald, 2014
73 Adapted from Archibald, 2014. Since Archibald provides only two data points, the intermediate levels were interpolated.
74 Congressman Bill Posey (R-FL), December 19, 2011, interview with Tea Party activist Victoria Jackson. hillheat.com, March 25, 2014
75 "The Frustrating Climate Change Memes That Just Won't Die", *New Republic*, August 11, 2014
76 *Washington Times,* August 31, 2014
77 *National Review,* September 23, 2014
78 IPCC, 2012
79 Cfact.org, April 21, 2014
80 NAS, 2012
81 Kunreuther and Michel-Kerjan, 2009
82 Ibid.
83 IPCC, 2013-14. Emphasis in original
84 NOAA, 2012a
85 USDA, 2012
86 CRS 2012
87 Ibid.
88 *New York Times*, November 28, 2012
89 CRS 2012
90 Ibid.
91 Ibid.
92 Ibid.
93 *Los Angeles Times*, November 20, 2012
94 *New York Times*, November 27, 2012
95 New York Times, January 6, 2014
96 Ibid.
97 McPherson, 2014
98 *New York Times*, January 31, 2014

99 Ibid.
100 *New York Times*, January 31, 2014
101 *New York Times*, February 2, 2014
102 *New York Times*, May 15, 2014
103 *San Luis Obispo Tribune*, February 2, 2014
104 *New York Times*, February 14, 2014
105 Ibid.
106 *Sacramento Bee*, May 17, 2014
107 CNN, March 5, 2014
108 The Declaration signed by these companies and more than 100 others reads, in part: "The very foundation of our country is based on fighting for our freedoms and ensuring the health and prosperity of our state, our community, and our families. Today those things are threatened by a changing climate that most scientists agree is being caused by air pollution. We cannot risk our kids' futures on the false hope that the vast majority of scientists are wrong. But just as America rose to the great challenges of the past and came out stronger than ever, we have to confront this challenge, and we have to win. And in doing this right, by saving money when we use less electricity, by driving a more efficient car, by choosing clean energy, by inventing new technologies that other countries buy, and creating jobs here at home, we will maintain our way of life and remain a true superpower in a competitive world."
109 McPherson, 2014
110 Giles, 2013
111 Ibid.
112 Funk, 2014
113 *Mother Jones*, March-April 2013
114 *New York Times*, February 16, 2014
115 Ibid.
116 Marsa, 2013
117 AAAS, 2014
118 Ibid.
119 NCA, 2014
120 Bagley and Gallucci, 2013
121 Ackerman, 2014
122 *Bloomberg* Winston *week*, November 1, 2012

123 Tisdale, 2013

124 *New York Times*, November 19, 2012

125 Keating, 2014. Charles Keating, a physicist, offered $10,000 to any climate denier who could prove that anthropogenic global warming did not or could not occur. Denial ideologues predictably dismissed the offer as meaningless. "Keating's [offer] is nothing but a publicity stunt." Cornwall Alliance Newsletter, June 25, 2014

126 Kehr, 2011

127 Tisdale, 2013

128 Emanuel, 2012

129 Ibid.

130 Ibid.

131 *Washington Post,* May 19, 2013

132 Guimaraes, 2014

133 Naomi Oreskes, interviewed by the *Guardian*, July 24, 2014

134 Koomey, 2012

135 Dryzek, Noorgard and Schlosberg, 2013

136 thinkprogress.org, April 28, 2014

137 Ibid.

138 *New York Times,* June 17, 2013

139 NCA, 2014

140 *Louisville Courier-Journal*, May 9, 2014

141 *Huffington Post*, June 27, 2014

142 Cory Gardner, R-CO, made this statement in an October 2014 debate with Senator Mark Udall.

143 Rep. Shelley Moore Capito (R-WV), who is running for U.S. Senate in West Virginia, on October 6, 2014 said that the climate was indeed changing because it was "raining" outside. Capito's Democratic challenger, Natalie Tennant, said she does not doubt climate science.

144 Beneshik's comments were reported in thinkprogress.org, October 9, 2014. For further discussion of Heartland Institute, see Chapter 5.

145 *National Geographic*, May 6, 2014

146 *New York Times*, May 12, 2014

147 ABC News, June 14, 2014

148 Berger, 2014

149 *New York Times*, November 12, 2013
150 Funk, 2014
151 Reuters, March 20, 2014
152 McPherson, 2014
153 Sadar, 2012
154 Most notably, this line has been promoted by Bjorn Lomborg and the Copenhagen Consensus Center, a think tank founded by the noted climate skeptic (McPherson, 2014).
155 *National Review,* September 23, 2014
156 Cornwall Alliance *Newsletter,* September 18, 2014
157 Ibid.
158 Klein, 2014
159 *The Hill*, March 7, 2014
160 U.S. Chamber of Commerce, *"Energy Institute Report Finds That Potential New EPA Carbon Regulations Will Damage U.S. Economy,"* May 28, 2014, uschamber.com
161 *New York Times*, May 30, 2014
162 *Delaware News-Journal*, June 28, 2014
163 *New York Times,* September 23, 2014
164 Ibid.
165 Ibid.
166 Hillman, Fawcett and Rajan, 2008
167 thinkprogress.org, June 10, 2014
168 Jamieson, 2014
169 Stern, 2006
170 *New York Times*, November 12, 2013
171 John Stossel, Washington Examiner, Jan. 21, 2014. Emphasis in Original
172 This is a "Tweet" from Pat Sajak, host of TV's game show "Wheel of Fortune." Twitter, May 20, 2014. Emphasis in Original
173 NPR, May 22, 2014. The text of the bill: *"SEC. 318. PROHIBITION ON USE OF FUNDS TO IMPLEMENT CERTAIN CLIMATE CHANGE ASSESSMENTS AND REPORTS.* None of the funds authorized to be appropriated or otherwise made available by this Act may be used to implement the U.S. Global Change Research Program National Climate Assessment, the Intergovernmental Panel on Climate Change's Fifth Assessment Report, the United Nation's Agenda 21 sustainable

development plan, or the May 2013 Technical Update of the Social Cost of Carbon for Regulatory Impact Analysis Under Executive Order 12 12866."

174 IPCC 2013-14. Emphasis in original

175 Leggett, 2013

176 *New York Times*, August 23, 2014

177 Berners-Lee and Clark, 2013

178 Hillman, Fawcett, and Rajan, 2008

179 Thompson and Bendik-Keymer, 2012

180 Ibid.

181 Geoengineering is application of technology to reduce effects of climate change, including technology to reduce warming (such as aerosols to reduce sunlight) or reduce carbon concentrations (such as iron filings in the ocean to take up CO2). Some authors have pointed out the hazards in geoengineering: "The difficulty with technological, control-oriented approaches to addressing climate change and its ecological effects, such as seeding the oceans with iron and releasing aerosols into the atmosphere, is that they depend for their success on our capacity to predict and control the effects of the intervention. We have not done this well in the past, and doing it well in the future is likely to be made more difficult by global warming." Thompson and Bendik-Keymer, 2012.

182 http://www.carbontracker.org/site/wastedcapital The limit of 2 degrees is one that has been debated since it was incorporated in the Copenhagen Accord in 2009, and some observers, notably James Hansen, think even that limit is too high. Nevertheless, governments have not made much progress toward limiting emissions sufficiently to hold warming to 2 degrees. "In interviews with former negotiators and longtime observers of the U.N. climate negotiations, not one person expressed confidence that the sum of countries' targets will be enough to keep rising global temperatures below the internationally agreed 2-degree-Celsius "guardrail" between dangerous and extremely dangerous warming." *Scientific American*, August 21, 2014

183 Prugh and Renner, 2014

184 *Cincinnati Enquirer*, March 7, 2014

185 *New York Times,* September 27, 2014

186 Avery, 2014. Emphasis in original.

187 *Wall Street Journal,* September 22, 2014

188 I put "reserves" into quotes because as we have learned about companies such as Shell Oil, they will often exaggerate the amount of recoverable oil (or coal or gas) to deceive markets. Nevertheless, the reserves are probably four to five times more than can be burned without severe effects on the climate.

189 Cfact.org, April 21, 2014

190 *The Nation*, April 22, 2014

191 Ibid.

192 Ricoveri, 2013

193 Ibid.

194 Ibid.

101 As can be seen in the section on extreme denial, there is a tendency among denial ideologues to blame climate science for undermining capitalism. This was best expressed in a sarcastic manner in the fictional treatment of an environmental movement, putting the following words in the mouth of its leader: "You must move the nation toward the era beyond fossil fuels. The only way to achieve this is a steep carbon tax on oil, gas, and coal at the well-head or port of entry. A rising carbon price is essential to bring the capitalist system to its knees." Diogenes, 2012

196 Pittsburgh Post-Gazette, September 28, 2014

197 Delingpole, 2013

198 McPherson, 2014

199 Smith, 2014

200 Ibid.

201 Giddens, 2013

202 McPherson, 2014

203 Adapted from Berners-Lee and Clark, 2013

204 *New York Times*, March 26, 2014

205 KC Golden, "Live on Stage in the Great Northwest: King Coal's Tragic Puppet Show, Part 1," Getting a GRIP on Climate Solutions, March 4, 2013.

206 Koomey, 2012

207 *The Hill*, September 10, 2014

208 McPherson, 2014

209 *Vancouver Columbian*, September 11, 2014

210 Michael Mann, climatologist at Pennsylvania State University, quoted in *Ecowatch,* October 2, 2014
211 Shrader-Frechette, 2011
212 Climateprogress.org, January 20, 2012
213 *Daily Express (UK),* October 22, 2014
214 Darling and Sisterson, 2014
215 McPherson, 2014
216 Jamieson, 2014
217 Ibid.
218 *Billings Gazette*, July 20, 2014
219 Darling and Sisterson, 2014
220 : http://www.dailymail.co.uk/news/article-2780587/Scientists-fast-track-evidence-linking-extreme-weather-climate-change-sign-panic-losing-propaganda-battle-sceptics.html#ixzz3FJ0DFb1E
221 For example, Kevin Trenberth, a senior scientist at the NOAA's National Center for Atmospheric Research in Boulder, Colorado
222 *Wall Street Journal*, July 1, 2014
223 This does not mean that such areas are valueless, however. It has been estimated that ecological services such as water filtration, carbon sequestration and biological diversity are worth $120 trillion worldwide, compared to $70 trillion total world product (sum of all national GDP values). Perhaps that would give readers of the *Wall Street Journal* pause about dismissing extreme weather events.
224 Biologist Chis Thomas of the University of York, quoted in Kolbert, 2010
225 Avery, 2014
226 Quoted in Melton, 2013
227 Oreskes and Conway, 2014
228 Marshall, 2014
229 Robinson, 2013
230 Tokar, 2014
231 *Wall Street Journal*, July 25, 2014
232 Winston, 2014
233 *New Republic*, August 5, 2014
234 *American Spectator*, August 21, 2014

235 Quoted by Melton, 2013
236 NCA, 2014
237 Nordhaus and Shellenberger, New York Times, April 8, 2014
238 McPherson, 2014
239 http://www.theepochtimes.com/n3/948666-climate-change-protesters-rally-against-future-typhoons/
240 sciencedaily.com, February 5, 2013
241 Marshall, 2014
242 Sullivan, 2013
243 Bryce, 2014
244 Tisdale, 2013
245 Ibid. The research paper, by Kevin Trenberth and John Fasullo, did not link any one storm to climate change but characterized extreme weather events as part of a trend, a "clustering of extremes." *Journal of Geophysical Research,* September 5, 2012
246 National Association of Scholars, July 19, 2010
247 Committee on Science, Space and Technology Press Release, March 26, 2014
248 *New York Times,* June 21, 2014
249 *Wall Street Journal,* July 2, 2014
250 Klein, 2014
251 *New York Times,* April 14, 2014
252 *New York Times,* May 6, 2014
253 NCA, 2014
254 Ibid.
255 *Washington Post,* March 14, 2014
256 *New York Times,* April 17, 2012
257 *New York Times,* March 16, 2014
258 *Bloomberg News,* September 22, 2014
259 Berger, 2014
260 Conservative Society of America ad, January 2011
261 Jackson, 2009
262 Prince Charles, 2010
263 Thompson and Bendik-Keymer, 2012
264 Winston, 2014
265 Weisman, 2013
266 Johnson, 2014

267 Weisman, 2013
268 Moore and Nelson, 2011
269 CNN, February 19, 2014
270 *Indianapolis Star*, April 4, 2014
271 *New York Times*, February 21, 2014
272 *Washington Post*, February 28, 2014
273 AAAS, 2014
274 Diogenes, 2012
275 Of course, there is also plenty of fiction about climate change that does not convey misinformation. One of the better novels is by Barbara Kingsolver, *Flight Behavior,* in which her main character says, "You've explained to me how big this is. The climate thing. That it's taking out stuff we're counting on. But other people say just forget it. My husband, guys on the radio. They say it's not proven." In a few words, Kingsolver conveys both the significance of climate science and the gist of denial ideology.
276 Inhofe, 2012
277 Bell, 2011
278 Fone, 2013
279 Ibid.
280 Both British and American science academies reviewed the e-mails and authors (purloined from the servers at the University of East Anglia in the UK), and absolved them of any crimes other than indiscreet and injudicious language. McPherson, 2014
281 Fone, 2013
282 Delingpole, 2013
283 Fone, 2013
284 Ibid.
285 Ibid.
286 Guimaraes, 2014
287 *Washington Post,* December 15, 2010
288 Ibid.
289 Avery, 2014
290 Ibid.
291 Ibid.
292 The 97% data has been confirmed in several studies, including by Naomi Oreskes in a 2004 article in *Science* titled

"Beyond the Ivory Tower: The Scientific Consensus on Climate Change", and by the American Association for the Advancement of Science (AAAS) in a 2014 paper titled *"What We Know."* In Oreskes' study, the 97% refers to peer-reviewed published papers that described human-caused climate change or its effects. The remaining 3% were *not* papers that denied human-caused climate change; they did not refer to it.

Nevertheless, denial advocates such as Joseph Bast, president of Heartland Institute, and Roy Spencer of the University of Alabama, continue to attack the figure as a "myth." *Wall Street Journal*, May 26, 2014. Some op-ed articles deny the 97% figure outright: "Despite claims to the contrary, 97 percent of scientists do not agree that human beings are causing climate change." *Washington Times*, September 4, 2014. A good review of this issue can be found at *Salon.com*, May 29, 2014 and *outsideonline.com*, May 30, 2014.

293 planetsave.com, December 5, 2013

294 Lieserowitz et.al. 2014

295 Montana Congressional Candidate Ryan Zinke, *Billings Gazette*, October 2, 2014

296 Hulme, 2009

297 Klein, 2014

298 House Subcommittee on Environment, December 11, 2013

299 McPherson, 2014

300 truth-out.org, April 5, 2014

301 The Audubon Society President David Arnhold described this public-private ying-yang as follows: "Most Republicans say the same thing behind closed doors: 'Of course, I get that the climate is changing, of course I get that we need to do something – but I need to get reelected.' Somehow they're going to have to find a safe place on this." *National Journal*, May 9, 2013

302 Ball, 2014

303 Ambler, 2011

304 Sussman, 2012

305 Darwall, 2013

306 Archibald, 2014

307 Klein, 2014

308 Johnson, 2014

309 McPherson, 2014
310 Hillman, Fawcett and Rajan, 2008
311 Ibid.
312 Crichton, 2009
313 McPherson, 2014
314 Delingpole, 2013. Emphasis Added.
315 Bell, 2011
316 Ibid.
317 Laframboise, 2013
318 Johnson, 2014
319 Nordhaus, 2013
320 McPherson, 2014
321 Ibid.
322 Berners-Lee and Clark, 2013
323 Fox News, Cavuto on Business, June 22, 2013
324 Wishart, 2013
325 Cornwall Alliance Newsletter, January 16, 2014
326 *Washington Post*, February 20, 2014
327 climateprogess.org, January 20, 2012
328 Delingpole, 2013
329 Slate.com, July 9, 2014
330 http://blog.heartland.org/2013/11/faith-based-ipcc-turns-science-into-sin/
331 Archibald, 2014
332 Delingple, 2013
333 Cornwall Alliance *Newsletter*, June 2, 2014
334 Cornwall Alliance, *Newsletter.* February 16, 2011
335 Kingsolver, 2012
336 *Telegraph,* October 17, 2014
337 Hartford Courant, September 2, 2014
338 *Wall Street Journal,* October 3, 2014
339 The term "theory" is also a problem for many denial ideologues. They regard anything labeled "theory" as simply a set of ideas, not practical concepts with real-world applications. Instead, scientific theories are systems of proven facts that explain phenomena. Perhaps the best statement of how theory relates to nature is from Ralph Waldo Emerson's essay *Nature*: "All science has one aim, namely, to find a theory of nature...We

are now so far from the road to truth, that religious teachers dispute and hate each other, and speculative men are esteemed unsound and frivolous. But to a sound judgment, the most abstract truth is the most practical. Whenever a true theory appears, it will be its own evidence. Its test is, that it will explain [natural phenomena]." Emerson's mention of "religious teachers" and "speculative men" fits denial ideology well.

340 Sullivan, 2013

341 In a candidates' debate in September 2011, Perry compared climate skeptics to Galileo, who was attacked by the established religion of his time. Ironically, the scientists whom Perry is defending, for example, Roy Spencer and Fred Singer, are affiliated with religious conservatives. Spencer is affiliated with the Cornwall Alliance, and Singer is affiliated with the Moonies, the Unification Church, founded by Rev. Sun Myung Moon. McPherson, 2014

342 Hulme, 2009

343 Rep. Jeff Miller (R-FL), quoted by MSNBC, June 8, 2014. Emphasis in original.

344 IPCC, 2013-14

345 Realclearpolitics.com, April 28, 2014

346 *UK Telegraph*, April 6, 2014

347 Smith, 2014

348 Bryce, 2014

349 businessweek.com, May 22, 2014

350 Ibid.

351 Koomey, 2012

352 CNBC, February 28, 2014

353 Ibid.

354 Wishart, 2013

355 Richard Cizik, Vice President for Governmental Affairs of the National Association of Evangelicals, is one of the leading advocates of emissions reductions. He has been the object of attack by some other evangelicals, such as Cornwall Alliance, who consider him apostate on climate science. Evangelical Christians can be supporters or deniers of climate change since Christian theology does not dictate a position on the science. It

would be misleading to equate evangelical religion with denial ideology.

356 Moore and Nelson, 2011
357 Ibid.
358 McNall, 2012
359 Tisdale, 2013
360 Quoted in Marshall, 2014
361 McPherson, 2014
362 Hulme, 2009
363 Ibid.
364 Laframboise, 2013
365 Ibid.
366 *Wall Street Journal*, April 5, 2014
367 I was the U.S. representative to the IPCC secretariat in Geneva from 1996 to 2000. I knew the one professional "bureaucrat" who actually "ran" the IPCC. He was the sole employee, hardly a professional power-hungry bureaucrat. He was a scientist, formerly with the U.S. National Weather Service, with no ambitions to take over the world economy. All the other officers were part-time volunteers, whose principal careers were in climate science. They also had no political ambitions.
368 Cfact.org, April 21, 2014
369 Dryzek, Norgaard and Schlosberg, 2013
370 Description of the DVD on amazon.com
371 Inhofe, 2012
372 Stevenson and Dryzek, 2014
373 IPCC, 2013-14
374 Salon, March 31, 2014
375 Shrader-Frechette, 2011
376 climategatebook.com, November 1, 2012
377 Tisdale, 2013
378 "Long-Term Sea Surface Temperature Variability along the U.S. East Coast," *Journal of Physical Oceanography,* 2009
379 Climaterealist.com, August 21, 2012
380 Ibid.
381 Energy and Power Subcommittee, House Committee on Energy and Commerce, testimony by John R. Christy, 20 September 2012

382 *NPR,* November 6, 2014
383 McPherson, 2014
384 McPherson, 1973
385 Glover and Economides, 2010
386 Moore and Nelson, 2011
387 Glover and Economides, 2010
388 Fox News, April 9, 2014
389 Ball, 2014
390 Isaac, 2013
391 Hamilton, 2013
392 tbo.com, February 20, 2014
393 Jamieson, 2014
394 New York Times, June 4, 2014
395 Hoggan, 2009
396 Inhofe, 2012
397 politicususa.com, April 7, 2014
398 McPherson, 2014
399 Glover and Economides, 2010
400 Bryce, 2014
401 Ball, 2014
402 This concept of alienation raises the question, "Is it possible that a symptom of our alienation is that we think of our environment as nature – which is to say, as something that we did not build, and for which we are thus not responsible?" One might be able to build an ethical case that denial ideology is based on alienation from nature and thus abjures responsibility for climate change. (Thompson and Bendik-Keymer, 2012) This certainly explains quotes such as "man cannot destroy the earth, only God can," attributed to Representative John Shimkus (R-IL), and "My point is, God's still up there. The arrogance of people to think that we human beings would be able to change what he is doing in the climate is to me outrageous," attributed to Senator James Inhofe (R-OK). McPherson, 2014
403 Bryce, 2014
404 Ball, 2014
405 Ibid.

406
epw.senate.gov/public/index.cfm?FuseAction=Minority.Press,
October 18, 2012
407 www.epw.senate.gov/inhofe
408 Marc Lee, *Enbridge Pipe Dreams and Nightmares: The Economic Costs and Benefits of the Proposed Northern Gateway Pipeline,* Vancouver, BC: Canadian Centre for Policy Alternatives, March 2012
409 Scienceblog.com, May 18, 2012
410 Sullivan, 2013
411 Ibid.
412 Kunreuther and Michel-Kerjan, 2009
413 *New York Times*, November 29, 2012
414 Robert Shiller, "Buying Insurance Against Climate Change," *New York Times*, May 22, 2014
415 mintpressnews.com, May 27, 2014
416 Heartland Institute is also offering $10,000 to any scientist who can "prove" climate science is wrong. In conjunction with its 2014 conference, Heartland invited organizations and scientists to submit entries for a chance to be featured in a Washington Times special section as part of its 9th International Conference on Climate Change in Las Vegas in early July. At the same time, a scientist named Christopher Keating has also offered $10,000 to any scientist who can conclusively prove climate science is wrong. He is confident that no one will win the $10,000: "I am certain my money is safe. They are in the business of denial and deception, not science. But, if someone could give me a scientific proof global warming isn't real, it would be worth the money." Thinkprogress.org, June 23, 2014
417 Schulman, 2014
418 *New York Times*, May 22, 2014
419 For a fuller discussion of AFP, see McPherson, 2014
420 *New York Times,* October 30, 2014
421 New York Times, July 29, 2014
422 Ibid.
423 McPherson, 2014
424 *Washington Post*, November 25, 2012
425 More details can be found in McPherson, 2014

426 Ibid.

427 Delingpole, 2013

428 Gleick is a respected scientist who has won a MacArthur fellowship and directs the Pacific Institute.

429 *Washington Post*, November 25, 2012

430 ALEC Position Paper On Climate Change, 2014

431 Nongovernmental International Panel on Climate Change (NIPCC) PowerPoint presentation, July 31, 2014. NIPCC collaborates closely with ALEC. NOTE: the NIPCC is a joint effort of the Center for the Study of Carbon Dioxide and Global Change, the Science and Environment Policy Project of Fred Singer, and the Heartland Institute. It has produced a number of "reports" that parallel the reports of the IPCC, each attempting to refute findings of the IPCC. Further details can be found in McPherson, 2014

432 "Climate Change: The Need to Act Now," Senate Committee on Environment and Public Works, Subcommittee on Clean Air and Nuclear Safety, June 18, 2014

433 Ibid.

434 Isaac, 2013

435 *Washington Post*, April 28, 2014

436 ALEC Position Paper On Climate Change, 2014

437 *Washington Post,* September 22, 2014. Schmidt's full statement was "Everyone understands climate change is occurring and the people who oppose it are really hurting our children and our grandchildren and making the world a much worse place. And so we should not be aligned with such people – they're just, they're just literally lying." Almost on cue, the *Wall Street Journal* lashed back on September 30, 2014 with an op-ed that accused Schmidt of name-calling. The quibbling about ALEC is likely to continue as long as the organization continues to promote denial ideology.

438 Lisa Nelson, ALEC's chief executive officer, reported by *Bloomberg News,* September 22, 2014

439 *Guardian*, December 4, 2013

440 Huffingtonpost.com, November 22, 2012

441 Kunreuther and Michel-Kerjan, 2009

442 IPCC, 2013-14 Emphasis in original

443 Weisman, 2013
444 *Wall Street Journal*, September 2, 2014
445 Shapiro, 2014
446 Stern, 2006
447 Jackson, 2009
448 McPherson, 2014
449 Guimaeres, 2014
450 Jamieson, 2014
451 *New York Times*, May 22, 2014
452 *Guardian*, February 20, 2014
453 *Houston Chronicle*, February 29, 2012
454 A number of states have considered and/or passed resolutions and laws mandating that schools "teach the controversy" in the past few years: South Dakota, Oklahoma, Louisiana, and Tennessee. (McPherson, 2014) An example is Wyoming, which in May 2014 passed a resolution that rejected the National Science Standards for schools. Ron Micheli, a former Regional Vice President of the Wyoming Stock Growers and chairman of the State Education Board, told the Casper Star-Tribune that he does not believe in climate science and that the new standards are "very prejudiced in my opinion against fossil-fuel development." Another example: Texas, whose Board of Education Member David Bradley will propose a textbook standard that requires teaching the controversy: "In November, Bradley and the rest of the state's 15-member board will vote to adopt new social-studies textbooks for public schools from kindergarten to 12th grade. When he does, he says that part of his mission will be to shield Lone Star schoolchildren from green propaganda. Instead, Bradley plans to push for textbooks that teach climate-science doubt – presenting the link between greenhouse gas emissions caused by human activity and global warming as an unsubstantiated and controversial theory." *National Journal,* September 14, 2014
455 *Washington Post*, December 3, 2012
456 Ibid.; emphasis in original
457 Mann, 2012
458 *Washington Post*, December 3, 2012
459 *The Nation*, April 22, 2014

460 Mann, 2012
461 Sadar, 2012
462 Melton, 2013
463 Marshall, 2014
464 McPherson, 2014
465 *Sydney Morning Herald*, June 17, 2014
466 *Rolling Stone*, December 5, 2012
467 Huffingtonpost.com, January 30, 2012
468 Ibid.
469 McPherson, 2014
470 Mann, 2012
471 Judith Curry, quoted in oilprice.com August 21, 2014
472 Cited in Hulme, 2009
473 IPCC, 2013-14
474 Adapted from: skepticalscience.com/solar-activity-sunspots-global-warming.htm
475 Tisdale, 2013
476 Lockwood, M., and C. Fröhlich, *Recent oppositely directed trends in solar climate forcings and the global mean surface air temperature. II. Different reconstructions of the total solar irradiance variation and dependence on response time scale*, Proc. R. Soc. A 464, 1367-1385, doi: 10.1098/ rspa. 2007.0347, 2008.
477
http://blogs.telegraph.co.uk/news/jamesdelingpole/100194166/man-made-global-warming-even-the-ipcc-admits-the-jig-is-up/
478 Michael Oppenheimer, Princeton, email message to Huffingtonpost.com, December 14, 2012
479 Michael Mann, Penn State, email message to Huffingtonpost.com, December 14, 2012
480 Melton, 2013
481 The 97% figure was explained earlier, see footnote 264. Interestingly, there is a similar figure, 95%, for economists who agree on the need for climate policies such as carbon taxes. Source: *Economists and Climate Change: Consensus and Open Questions,* 2009, Institute for Policy Integrity at the New York University School of Law.
482 Hulme, 2009

483 "http://www.boozman.senate.gov/public/index.cfm/2014/6/ questioning-administration-s-climate-change-statistics

484 *Guardian*, May 28, 2014

485 http://www.realclimate.org/index.php/archives/2008/05/how- to-cook-a-graph-in-three-easy-lessons/#sthash.VM5Mhodc.dpuf

486 Robert, 2010

487 *Salon,* October 1, 2014

488 Smith, 2014

489 *New York Times,* October 27, 2014

490 Naomi Oreskes, *"Beyond the Ivory Tower: The Scientific Consensus on Climate Change",* Science, December 3, 2004. Oreskes and Conway (2011) also studied the phenomenon of denial of health effects of smoking. In that research, there was also a consensus of scientists that was under attack by tobacco companies, who used pseudo-science to try to deny the health effects of smoking and secondhand smoke. Many of the same ideologists who deny climate change also denied this scientific consensus.

491 *Cornwall Alliance Newsletter*, July 16, 2014

492 *New York Post*, September 14, 2014

493 *Guardian*, April 18, 2014

494 *Nature*, July 28, 2011

495 Smith, 2014

496 Stephen Pacala and Robert H. Socolow, "Stabilization Wedges," http://cmi.princeton.edu/wedges/

497 Jamieson, 2014

498 Oreskes and Conway, 2014

499 Ibid.

500 Marshall, 2014

501 Calvin Beisner of Cornwall Alliance, quoted in Marshall, 2014

502 Mann, 2012

503 Klein, 2014. IPCC findings are actually rather conservative in terms of projecting some of the more drastic consequences of climate change.

504 Ibid.

505 McPherson, 2014

506 Sussman, 2010

507 Lendanowsky, Oberaur and Gignac, 2013
508 Thenewamerican.com, December 4, 2012
509 Cornwall Alliance Newsletter, May 2, 2014
510 Gillis, 2013
511 Howard Hayden, *The Energy Advocate*, March 2011.
512 Ismail, 2010
513 Fox News, April 9, 2014
514 Ibid.
515 IPCC, 2007
516 IPCC, 2013
517 Isaac, 2013
518 Cornwall Alliance Newsletter, September 9, 2014
519 Sullivan, 2013
520 Ibid.
521 McPherson, 1973
522 Climate Depot, October 20, 2011
523 Isaac, 2013
524 McPherson, 2014
525 IPCC, 2013-14
526 Climate Depot, April 14, 2014. Emphasis in original
527 Emanuel, 2012
528 Ibid.
529 Dessler and Parsons, 2010
530 Jamieson, 2014
531 Kolbert, 2014
532 *New York Post*, December 27, 2012
533 Ibid.
534 Cited in Hulme, 2009
535 Giddens, 2013
536 Sadar, 2012
537 Stern, 2006. Since the first Stern Report came out, climate science has increased its estimate of costs of climate change, and Stern himself has estimated that those costs will outrun his earlier estimates.
538 Tisdale, 2013
539 Smith, 2014
540 telegraph.co.uk, December 19, 2012
541 Caruso, 2013

542 Washington Post, May 28, 2014

543 Bryce, 2014

544 Ibid.

545 Ball, 2014

546 McPherson, 2014

547 Leggett, 2013

548 Troy Campbell, lead author of "Denying Problems When We Don't Like the Solutions" and a doctoral candidate at Duke University's Fuqua School of Business. *Duke Today,* November 6, 2014

549 berkeleyearth.org/pdf/muller-testimony-31-march-2011.pdf

550 Ibid.

551 During one of its sessions, the House committee defeated an amendment offered by Democrats that said "Congress accepts the scientific finding of the Environmental Protection Agency (contained in the proposed rule referred to in section 4(2)) that '[g]reenhouse gas (GHG) pollution threatens the American public's health and welfare by contributing to long-lasting changes in our climate that can have a range of negative effects on human health and the environment." Apparently members of the committee did not know that GHG pollution threatens health and the environment.

552 guardian.co.uk, August 3, 2012

553 Festinger et.al., 1956

554 Scienceprogress.org, March 16, 2011

555 Representative Peter Welch of Vermont, quoted in democracynow.org/2014/4/8/

556 *National Journal*, July 8, 2014

557 Thinkprogress.org, September 29, 2014

558 Quoted in *Huffington Post,* October 27, 2014

559 Associated Press, October 14, 2014

560 *Seattlepi.com,* November 3, 2014

561 Quoted in MSNBC, November 3, 2014

562 *Grist,* October 10, 2014

563 *New York Times,* October 30, 2014

564 *Hill Heat,* December 3, 2013

565 *The Hill,* October 15, 2014

566 Source: adapted from mediamatters.org, December 5, 2012

567 In.gov/idem

568 Polluterwatch.com, December 31, 2012

569 Adapted from Hansen, 2005

570 Adapted from Michaels, 1998

571 Hansen, 2005

572 *New York Times*, January 17, 2014

573 Details are available in McPherson, 2014

574 *Think Progress,* November 10, 2014

575 AAAS, 2014

576 Ibid., Emphasis in original

577 Ibid.

578 Brysse et.al, 2013

579 Ibid.

580 Ibid.

581 Washington Post, April 20, 2014

582 Inhofe, 2012

583 Easterly, Indiana's Commissioner of the Department of Environmental Management, is trying to stop EPA regulation of coal plants. Erickson, a state senator who is chairman of the Washington State Senate Committee on Energy, Environment and Telecommunications, has invited denial ideologues to testify at his committee hearings. In his role as a member of the Washington State Climate Legislative and Executive Workgroup, Erickson emphasized the costs of emission reduction policies: "We do note that much of the information on costs that the Workgroup did receive indicates that the costs of policies that other members of the Workgroup would recommend would be extremely costly to the citizens and families of Washington. This would be an unacceptable burden to place on the families of Washington, and to the businesses that employ Washingtonians." He did not emphasize the costs of climate change such as the wildfires that have plagued Washington recently. Owners of over 300 homes burned in those wildfires find climate change "extremely costly." State governments find it difficult to deal with climate change. When Pennsylvania's Department of Conservation and Natural Resources tried to put climate change on the agenda in September 2014, Governor Tom Corbett's administration ordered any references on the website removed. The offending language read "Our changing climate is perhaps the most significant environment issue facing the world

today. The overwhelming scientific consensus is that the earth's climate is warming rapidly due to the atmospheric buildup of heat-trapping emissions, primarily carbon dioxide pollution from power plants and automobiles." North Carolina's Department of Environment and Natural Resources (DENR) also removed links and documents containing information about climate change from its website.

584 Helm, 2012
585 Marshall, 2014
586 Ibid.
587 *New York Times*, December 29, 2012
588 Lieserowitz et al 2014
589 *Time*, April 22, 2014
590 *Washington Post*, March 14, 2014
591 Hillman, Fawcett and Rajan, 2008
592 *New York Times,* September 22, 2014
593 *Guardian*, March 22, 2014
594 Ibid.
595 Klein, 2014
596 Thompson and Bendik-Keymer, 2012
597 McPherson, 2014
598 Oreskes and Conway, 2011.
599 Stevenson and Dryzek, 2014
600 Berger, 2014
601 Keating, 2014
602 *Forbes*, December 25, 2012
603 Jamieson, 2014
604 Hillman, Fawcett and Rajan, 2008
605 Prugh and Renner, 2014
606 Moore and Nelson, 2011
607 Christopher Hayes, "The New Abolitionism," *The Nation,* April 22, 2014
608 Thompson and Bendik-Keymer, 2012
609 This trite phrase epitomizes the "biggest market failure in history," according to Stern, Stiglitz and others. If the customer (and producer) are always right in their increasing use of energy, in a "free market" that is free of externalized costs, they are likely to destroy the very market that they are operating in. Eventually

this market will fall of its own weight as all of the external costs press down in the form of extreme weather that destroys its physical base.

610 George Marshall, author of *Don't Even Think About It,* interview with CBC, September 26, 2014
611 Ibid.
612 McPherson, 1973
613 *New York Times*, May 3, 2014